Understanding the Artificial:
On the Future Shape of Artificial Intelligence

ARTIFICIAL INTELLIGENCE AND SOCIETY

Series Editor: KARAMJIT S. GILL

Massimo Negrotti (Ed.)

Understanding the Artificial: On the Future Shape of Artificial Intelligence

With 13 Figures

Springer-Verlag
London Berlin Heidelberg New York
Paris Tokyo Hong Kong

Massimo Negrotti
Universita 'Degli Studi di Urbino,
Istituto Metodologico Economico Statistico (IMES),
Via Saffi 15,
61029 Urbino (PS), Italy

ISBN 3-540-19612-9 Springer-Verlag Berlin Heidelberg New York
ISBN 0-387-19612-9 Springer-Verlag New York Berlin Heidelberg

British Library Cataloguing in Publication Data
Understanding the artificial: on the future shape of artificial intelligence. – (Artificial
intelligence and society).
1. Artificial intelligence
1. Negrotti, Massimo 1944–   Series
006.3
ISBN 3-540-19612-9

Library of Congress Cataloging-in-Publication Data
Negrotti, Massimo, 1944–
Understanding the artificial: on the future shape of artificial intelligence/Massimo
Negrotti.
p. cm. – (Artificial intelligence and society)
Includes index.
ISBN 0-387-19612-9
1. Artificial intelligence.   I. Title.   II. Series.   III. Series: Artificial intelligence and
society.
Q335.N435 1991   90-21519
006.3–dc20   CIP

© Springer-Verlag Berlin Heidelberg 1991
Printed in Germany

Typeset by Saxon Printing Ltd., Saxon House, Derby
34/3830–543210 (printed on acid-free paper)

To Professor Angelo Scivoletto

Preface

In recent years a vast literature has been produced on the feasibility of Artificial Intelligence (AI). The topic most frequently discussed is the concept of *intelligence*, with efforts to demonstrate that it is or is not transferable to the computer. Only rarely has attention been focused on the concept of the *artificial per se* in order to clarify what kind, depth and scope of performance (including intelligence) it could support. Apart from the classic book by H.A. Simon, *The Sciences of the Artificial*, published in 1969, no serious attempt has been made to define a conceptual frame for understanding the intimate nature of intelligent machines independently of its claimed or denied human-like features.

The general aim of this book is to discuss, from different points of view, what we are losing and what we are gaining from the artificial, particularly from AI, when we abandon the original anthropomorphic pretension. There is necessarily a need for analysis of the history of AI and the limits of its plausibility in reproducing the human mind. In addition, the papers presented here aim at redefining the epistemology and the possible targets of the AI discipline, raising problems, and proposing solutions, which should be understood as typical of the *artificial* rather than of an information-based conception of man.

The result, I hope, could be initiation of a new wave of debate which, assuming that the critiques generated by the first one were fundamentally right, might help human culture to adapt itself to the artificial rather than to assimilate it according to a pure and dangerous user-oriented philosophy.

Urbino   *Massimo Negrotti*
August 1990

Acknowledgement

The editor is grateful to David Smith for his help in editing the material in this book into its final form.

Contents

Contributors

Mario Borillo
Dr, Research Director, CNRS, Institut de Recherche au Informatique de Toulouse, Laboratoire Langages et Systemes Informatiques, Université Paul Sabatier, 118 Route de Narbonne, 31062 Toulouse Cedex, France

Hubert L. Dreyfus
Professor, Department of Philosophy, Univeristy of California, Berkeley, CA 94720, USA

Stuart E. Dreyfus
Professor, Department of Electrical Engineering, University of California, Berkeley, CA 94720, USA

Massimo Negrotti
Professor, Director, Istituto Metodologico Economico Statistico (IMES), University of Urbino, Via Saffi 15, I-61029 Urbino (PS), Italy

Ephraim Nissan
Professor, Department of Mathematics and Computer Science, Ben-Gurion University of the Negev, PO Box 653, 84105 Beer-Sheva, Israel

Alberto Oliverio
Professor, CNR Institute of Psychobiology and Psychopharmacology, University of Rome, Via Reno 1, 00198 Rome, Italy

Henrik Sinding-Larsen
Department of Social Anthropology, University of Oslo, PO Box 1091 Blindern, N-0317 Oslo 3, Norway

John R. Searle
Professor, Department of Philosophy, University of California, Berkeley, CA 94720, USA

Luigi Stringa
Professor, Director of the Institute of Scientific and Technological Research (IRST), University of Trento, Loc. Pantè, 38050 Povo, Trento, Italy

Chapter 1

Introduction: Artificial Intelligence: Its Future and its Cultural Roots

Massimo Negrotti

The Need to Understand the Artificial

The history of the human species has involved a continual process of adaptation to the physical dimensions and fluctuations of the natural environment. Their success in this respect has been achieved not only through an ancient biological and non-intentional evolutionary process but also through intentional efforts aimed at building devices able to provide useful tools for survival. Science and technology are, simultaneously, the main causes and effects of these efforts, and the concrete result of their advances is summed up in the concept of "The Technological Environment". In other words, in order to adapt themselves to the external environment, humans have built up a new one and now they have to deal with two distinct, though interrelated, spaces of fluctuating dimensions, each with its own problems of adaptation, namely the natural and artificial environments.

In addition, we have begun very recently, due to natural and unpredictable adjustments or abnormal events, to investigate the relations between the technological environment and the natural one. But while we know enough to be able to build particular classes (or "species", in Butler's terms) of technological devices very effectively indeed, we lack a body of organised knowledge about the whole technological system we have built up around us (and in some cases even within us). On the one hand we know almost all the rules (for instance the physical rules) for designing and building different machines but we lack any systematic knowledge on the relations among them and, furthermore, between them and humans. Whatever we call it: "Technological Environment" (Negrotti 1975) or "Cybernetic Society" (Arbib 1984), the new environment seems to be largely unknown in concrete terms.

Generally speaking, we lack well-founded knowledge of the sorts of general interfaces we have built between ourselves and the natural environment. Specialist doctrines, such as the so-called "general systems theory", "systems dynamics", "organisation theory" or even ecology itself, are only initial attempts in particular fields to understand the whole system of interrelations. But in order to give the right balance to the system constituted by humans, machines and the natural world, it is imperative that we should also understand the intimate nature of whatever constitutes the artificiality of the technological environment, both in scientific or philosophical terms (Simondon 1969; Simon 1973), and, ultimately, in terms of what it requires in order to be and remain compatible with the other two sub-systems.

In other words, since artificiality resides and flows both in the technological environment as a whole as well as in man–machine sub-systems, we need at a collective level a sort of "ecology of the technological environment", linked to natural ecology. Similarly, we need, at the individual or species level, accurate knowledge, such as can come from cognitive ergonomics, about the limits of our compatibility with machines.

Artificial Intelligence (AI) is ideally suited to be considered a good case study in the latter area. In fact, the progress of AI, not only in the scientific field but even in everyday life, well illustrates our difficulty in accepting the idea that machines are something radically different from human or natural things. As a consequence of our historically rooted inclinations to dominate nature on the one hand and to mimic ourselves in an anthropomorphic way on the other hand, AI is trying not only to build machines, but also to re-create humans. At least, that is the way it is actually perceived by people, and that is the path our cultures have followed in accepting AI as the ultimate pinnacle of the last two centuries of technological advance.

Current approaches to doing AI research do not provide us with an adequate basis on which we can draw conclusions about the scientific status of such a viewpoint. All we can do is set up a debate on its plausibility (as exemplified in this volume, particularly in the chapters by Dreyfus and Dreyfus, Searle, and Negrotti). But we are particularly emphasising the need, which is completely avoided by definition in the AI field, to go deep into the concept and the phenomenology of "the artificial", conceived as a field of things and facts different from the natural, but rationally understandable and adaptable to human needs and interests.

A basic concept, to this end, should be that of heterogeneity, i.e. the most fundamental dimension of the integration process in which the human–computer (or, more generally, human–machine) interactions could be conceived in discrete terms, with well-defined lines of demarcation involving specific attitudes and mutually compatible boundaries. In other words, we should avoid the illusion of continuity between the natural and the artificial, replacing it with that of complementarity.

We are sure that, in doing so, that is, in conceiving the artificial as a field of research *in se*, we can get useful and perhaps strategic insights into the right way to integrate harmonically (or at least with minimal waste and danger), humans, technology and that part of the external world on which our survival depends.

AI and the Renewed Interest in Cybernetics

Though the "symbol manipulation" approach to AI is very far from having explored all its own possibilities, a great many AI people are now convinced that we are approaching the limits of this kind of research tradition in emulating human mental faculties.

Even in the expert systems field, where AI techniques have demonstrated their greatest power, promises seem to have run far ahead of reality (Ostberg 1986). From many points of view, the future of AI, both in terms of pure abstract scientific research and the practical development of real-life products (a distinction which is not always clearly made, either in the public perception or among the specialist community; see the paper by Nissan in this volume) is seen as linked to a deeper understanding of the relationship between what we could call "non-perturbed intelligence", i.e. the ability to follow formal rules and algorithms, and the external environment with its variety and fluctuations which "perturb" our clarity of reasoning.

This problem may be seen at two levels, namely a dualistic and monistic one. From the dualistic point of view (which is represented by the symbol manipulation tradition) the complex and variable nature of the external world is implicitly conceived as a constraint on and radically separated from the true nature of mind. As an implicit premise, the external world is the counterpart of rationality. Consequently, AI should find ways to reduce the external world to something manageable by means of well-reasoned models (Sojat 1987; see also Stringa's paper in this volume). Furthermore, the ability of the human mind to deal with uncertainty should be reproduced through *ad hoc* logics (such as the fuzzy types) in order to assign to programs the same plasticity achieved by humans but without renouncing the power of formal reasoning.

In this view, the "discovery" of the external world has introduced or reinforced in the AI field the rationalistic persuasion that human intelligence is due to the ability to cope with the noise and disturbances of the environment by means of the clarity of formal reasoning and its aptitude for building models and theories.

On the other hand, the monistic point of view (which is represented to some extent by neo-cybernetic studies and the "connectionist" or neural networks tradition) seems to point out the constitutive nature of the external world in a sort of empiricist way of looking at man. Far from being a constraint on thought, the external world induces our mental states and activates the self-organisational dynamics of our brains. Without this process, we could have no intelligent ability.

For the supporters of this view, the ancient debate about "thinking machines" is overridden by the demonstrated adaptiveness of a suitable network to an example or by the convergence of a plurality of sets of inputs to a final "right" state (but see the incisive criticism of these expectations made by Dreyfus and Dreyfus, this volume). Significantly, an advertising "blurb" for a primer in this field asserts that "neural networks think in the same ways as people do".

Both dualistic and monistic positions agree about the relevance of the external world but diverge strongly in the ways in which they conceive of its role in defining the characteristics of intelligence. While the former inclines to conceive the external world as a source of perturbations which reason should reduce, or at least understand and control, the latter tends to point out that the system of interactions with the external world is the necessary environment in which intelligence develops, according to a self-organising view of living systems in general and of the human brain in particular (Andrew 1987).

Perhaps the coming era of parallel processing could be a bridge, in technical terms, between these two ways of doing AI (though there are again many problems to solve in this direction; see for instance Bibel 1987). Furthermore:

architectures can significantly influence the way we program them, and perhaps if we had the right kind of [parallel] architecture, programming it for perception and knowledge representation would be easy and natural. (Kumar 1985)

But for now the distance is very great and refers not only to very different philosophical premises, but even to a different use of cybernetic theory.

The contraposition is even linked to different neurobiological doctrines, namely the holistic and the localistic, as clearly indicated by Oliverio, this volume. But, despite these rather general references, the real work in AI follows ways in which the strength of the artificiality of the matter prevails anyway. So it is not surprising that, for example:

The power of non-serial (but parallel) computational algorithms has been strongly emphasised but we are far from finding the eventual underlying neural implementations. (Erdi 1988)

The only common point seems to be that of conceiving AI, by tacit assumption, as that science whose principal aim is to reproduce human intelligent faculties as they are in everyday life and not as they could be if we were to isolate them from the external world: in a truly artificial way.

For the symbol manipulation tradition, both human and artificial minds are machines that have or, rather, should have, *in se* the power of surviving among fluctuations, randomness, variety and so on, and that power is provided by the right program. Therefore, despite the possible presence of local sub-decision rules, intelligent behaviour is a process cybernetically controlled by a central decision maker.

For the neural networks tradition (including connectionism and pattern-matching studies) a mind develops exactly because of the external fluctuations and noise, through an adaptive process of self-organisation. Therefore, despite some kind of overall supervisor, intelligent behaviour is cybernetically the result of co-operative processes in distributed control.

While the main problem of the former doctrine is that of formalising the right way to deal with external entropy, the latter refers to randomness as a source of order (Atlan 1973).

And while the former doctrine seems to accept the idea of secondary regulation, which implies well defined roles of observation, action and control interacting with a separated memory, the latter gives supremacy to what has been called "primary regulation": according to von Bertalanffy (1971), that kind of regulation which is due to dynamic interactions within the system. Of course, secondary regulation is much more powerful in dealing with problems which require great amounts of analysis or, in the case of humans, evaluation, abstraction and formalisation. On the other hand, primary regulation is much more powerful in rapidly processing large amounts of data (or signals) according to rather simple models or examples and tasks.

It is apparent that in principle there should be enough room for an integration of the two perspectives: for some groups of applications, the "limited inference" capability of neural networks (Shastri 1986) could be compensated by the high inferential power of symbolic manipulation programs, while the more rigid and slow capabilities of these programs in handling tasks such as pattern recognition could be counterbalanced by the speed and adaptiveness of networks. But in reality these two different approaches seem just as strongly opposed to each other today as they were at the time of the Rosenblatt–Minsky polemics, as recalled in this volume by Dreyfus and Dreyfus.

The reason is cultural: dualism and monism have deep roots and can only be harmonised superficially. In other words, and remaining in the field of computer science:

Traditions are important in both culture and science. Tradition controls what we can believe, what we can do, and the thoughts we can have. In science it controls the kind of work we can do. In computing it controls the kinds of computers, the kinds of operating systems and the kinds of programming languages we can have. (Gabriel 1989)

A fortiori, it controls, just like a cybernetic loop, our image of the human mind and what should be done in order to get an accurate reproduction of it. If there is a real possibility of integrating the two mainstreams cited above, this will be verified through the work of new generations of AI people.

In any case, what remains clear is that the current traditions, both dualist and monist, appear to be all too closely linked to the tacit assumption that we can only get anything interesting or useful by emulating the human mind as it is (which means, in fact, what we think it is). In fact, both traditions incline to the belief that the only intelligence which deserves to be emulated is human intelligence and that higher power in the field of the artificial can be attained only by means of more and more human-like behaviour on the part of machines.

Thus, for instance, if we agree that intuition is a fundamental attitude of our mind, then we should make efforts to give machines the same ability. But even if it is plausible that intuition is not a rule-based activity (Partridge 1987), we can have little hope in the power of neural networks, due to their very low level of performance: in the end they are primary regulation devices that can statistically recognise patterns or classify signals, and do not bypass long chains of inference within complex reasoning areas as intuition does.

In any case, intuition is presumably more complex than a process of recognition, especially when we have to deal with concepts or when its result is something new. Though we can admit that intuition does not appear to follow explicit rules, we can also admit that it often seems to follow at least some kind of personal mental style, whose dynamics are unknown but which surely cannot be reduced to the matching of pre-ordered or purely stored patterns.

The situation would be different if we could persuade ourselves that the artificial is something which may amplify some of our capacities after separating them from the rest of our nature.

Far from being a problem of widening the spectrum of human faculties which are transferable to the machine, the science of the artificial should be conceived as the effort to know more deeply what quality and quantity of performance we could get from a non-perturbed intelligent machine. This is, in part, the *de facto* aim of the symbol manipulation tradition, though it does not correspond exactly to its explicit programme. On the other hand, it should be clear that every real system exists in an external world and, therefore, the exchange of information/energy with the external world is surely an important issue in other sub-areas of AI devices, such as robotics.

It does not matter at this point whether we are or are not proceeding towards a more accurate representation of the human mind: what is important is to recognise that the artificial one we have built is an actual and new source of knowledge (from a scientific point of view) and of devices (from a technological viewpoint) which should be effectively interfaced with humans.

AI and Culture: New Directions for Research

It is quite possible that in the near future, there could be fields in which computers will be capable of much more human-like performance than is the case today. All the same, I am convinced that they will achieve this in ways which will remain distinct from human intelligence. Despite the often-emphasised analogies or suggestive research findings arising from time to time from the field of neuroscience, the deep heterogeneity between human and artificial minds will become an accepted fact of our culture.

The real problem is, therefore, to put forward new ideas about what we should do in order to facilitate the development of a conception of the artificial which could be useful to establish a clear discrimination between itself and the natural faculties of man.

We could see this enterprise in terms of a new debate (a propositive debate, this time) following on the heels of the first round of debate (exemplified in this volume by the chapters by Searle, Dreyfus and Dreyfus, and Sinding-Larsen), which had the effect of disabusing the AI community of the illusion that they had found the key to the human mind in terms of digital computation.

The new debate should start from the premise that in both its symbol manipulation and self-organisation versions, AI has little chance of emulating the complexity of the human mind, while it has every possibility of developing intelligent devices whose complexity could be synergetically integrated with humans.

Though the reproduction of human mental faculties is a very fascinating target, we should admit that at the level of real applications, AI is interesting independently of both its human-like and non-human-like performance. In other words, when dealing with something artificial, people are more interested in its input/output relations than its capacity to reproduce such relations in an accurate human-like way.

The process of persuading people to adopt and to trust the artificial is, however, a very sensitive matter, since it involves introducing our perceptions of the machine directly into our culture and producing feedbacks into the sub-culture of researchers and designers. One of the motives behind this book is simply to emphasise the need for accurate monitoring of this kind of reality construction process.

The roots of the artificial need to be carefully analysed both in their nature and aims. For instance, there are already limits beyond which we have no technological interest in pursuing further similarity with biological structures. For instance, if we have to design an artificial heart, the biological example, both in its complexity and its interrelations with the rest of the biological system, has no more relevance when we have reached the reproduction of those performances which are strategic in order to allow an extra-biological blood circulation compatible with the human body. Further advances are useful only in so far as they can improve the selected performance, and we add nothing of value by the reproduction of additional human-like features as such. We have no interest in reproducing in an artificial heart the pain associated with the real heart: its possible significance in terms of alerting the system might be taken over by other artificial devices which could be both easier to build and in fact more reliable.

This is, in the end, the essence of artificiality. Its proper aim is not that of reproducing the whole natural system. Its aim is always that of replicating by means of non-natural procedures, some natural dimensions of a system after having conceptually captured them through a process of isolation or extraction from the whole set of performances of that system. In doing so, sometimes we get an impoverished feature (though often less expensive) as compared to the one we had observed in the natural system, but in other cases we discover a more powerful performance in the isolated dimension rather than its natural context within the real organism. This is the case, I think, with the faculty named intelligence, at least in so far as it is defined in terms of the ability to solve problems by recognising and following the most suitable rule-based strategies (sometimes recombined or bypassed by heuristics).

Our ability to carry out well reasoned problem-solving strategies does not depend only on the self-organising tendency of our mind and its capacity for adapting itself to the uncertainty of the external world, but also on our success in reducing or controlling perturbations and isolating ourselves from them. The process of intelligent behaviour is due to the continual shifting between the level of the real world and that of the mind, and the complete dominance of one or the other is fatal. In philosophical terms it would mean a complete reduction of man to empirical dimensions or his complete dependency on innate reasoning. A functional dualism is thus quite acceptable.

Nevertheless, everyday evidence shows that we are rather better at survival (adapting ourselves to the fluctuations and the uncertainty of the external world) than at isolating our mind for pure reasoning. Reflection, creativity, critical thinking and just pure reasoning are much rarer, more expensive and more difficult than biologically determined behaviour.

Human intelligence is by its very nature always to some degree constituted or perturbed (according to the monist or dualist points of view) by the external world, even when we are forcing ourselves to concentrate and to isolate ourselves from it in order to perform complex reasoning tasks. Therefore, AI should be able to give machines a kind of non-perturbed intelligence which could amplify our own, rather than emulating it as a whole.

The great task facing AI should be that of compensating humans where they are lacking. In natural language processing, for instance, we should extract those dimensions which are compatible with the nature of computers from the human way of performing and go deeply in that direction without making any anthropomorphic claims (see Borillo, this volume). Accepting the thesis that computers will never be language users (Winograd and Flores 1986) does not mean that they cannot be useful for a better understanding of our linguistic behaviour, or very important in helping us in many communication processes.

The Reliability of the Artificial

One major problem is, in my opinion, that of clarifying the changes in the concept of reliability which arise from AI applications. The concept of reliability traditionally refers to the degree of confidence we can have in the fine working of a device, i.e. its constancy in producing the right outputs. In the AI field, this concept should be carefully redefined, since AI devices carry out direct reasoning processes, whose reliability cannot be treated in trivial input/output terms.

In conventional technological fields, reliability measurement is often based on large scale test procedures carried out before and after the introduction of a device into routine use. In AI these tests may often be complicated and eventually impossible due to the complexity and the polyvalence of the performed tasks and also, as in the case of the Strategic Defense Initiative (SDI), due to the impossibility of setting up accurate simulations or real-world experiments. In this situation, designers are satisfied when it appears that performance targets are attained and there are no more obvious bugs. Designers are thus forced to neglect a deep search for side-effects or possible degeneration over time.

Solutions to problems of reliability in software and hardware have traditionally been based on the redundancy principle. More recently, systems modularity or distributed architectures have been used, but:

Modular systems are not magic. They don't of themselves solve problems. They merely provide a framework in which human designers and programmers have a better opportunity to see and understand interactions between the pieces of a system.... Subtle and unsuspected interactions continue to plague the designers of even the most carefully partitioned systems. (Ornstein 1986)

It is still not possible to make self-organising machines which show meaningful fault-tolerant behaviour. The reason is quite simple, and derives from the fact that the biological complexity of living systems is intrinsically teleological, and we are very far from being able to give such a characteristic to non-biological machines beyond limited and design-specific thresholds such as occur in many self-regulating cybernetic devices.

Furthermore, apart from systems failure or problems with side-effects, it should be clear that in AI machines, "reliability" refers implicitly to another aspect, namely the match between the user's methodology of reasoning and that of the designers.

If we take this to include the actual ways humans follow in inferring, hypothesising, connecting facts or concepts, and even the mental styles adopted in selecting a point of view and therefore in looking at reality, then we should conclude that the concept of reliability should be enlarged due to the great variety of cultures and of individuals within each culture.

In fact, we should take into account not only the quality of the final output and the consequent degree of satisfaction on the part of the user, but also his objective or subjective needs in terms of critical thinking and self-perception as a member of a particular culture. The concept of reliability should relate to the integration between the user and new kinds of tools, and to the issue of responsibility in designing and using them, particularly in the educational field.

The role of the user should obviously not be conceived as passive. There is evidence that human malperceptions about machines tend to lead to their rejection (as happened in the case of the space shuttle; Michie 1987). This can perhaps be related to inadequate depth and clarity of the definition of "artificiality". Human users of machines clearly need to be able to gain a more discriminating awareness of the heterogeneity between machines (in terms of, for example, their artificial nature and characteristics) and the methodology of reasoning adopted by their human designers.

The issue is the same faced in a wider sense by human–computer interaction (HCI) studies where the problem is more that of reaching "improvement of people's working conditions and the humanisation of working life" rather than making "systems more perfect and simpler to handle by means of 'cosmetics at the interface'" (Maas and Oberquelle 1988).

But it is not only a matter of respecting human values and cultures: it could also be a strategic way of improving the benefits of working with the artificial. In fact, if we could easily become aware of the methodology adopted by the machine (and of course if we had been trained by the educational process to understand what is a methodology at all in the first place) then we could select the best one, i.e. the one we most prefer or which best matches our own predispositions. Having done this, we could then hand over the task to the machine, which would then perform it more rigorously than we could, that is, with a "non-perturbed intelligence".

In the end, this is the true nature of the simulation tradition which, in fact, tends to be more and more revalued and even integrated with some of the most promising fields of AI such as expert systems technology. This growing area is a crucial example with regard to the above considerations.

Today's expert systems, at least in principle, can substitute for human experts but they do not improve the intrinsic quality of the work to be done. They can enhance the economic and the technologically established and predefined "efficiency" of an industrial process, but they cannot help find new roads to follow. They are reliable in the sense that they perform like trustworthy humans. But they do not amplify human intelligence in general, simply transmitting the one which they emulate. Nevertheless, expert systems work well, even in a socially perturbed environment, during an earthquake or in a hurricane (the only problem there being sustaining the power supply to the computer!). In other words, they represent a good partial example of what we mean by the concept of non-perturbed intelligence, even though they only mimic the reasoning of actual human experts, fixed, as it were, in space and time.

Thus, expert systems are reliable in the sense that they are typically able to develop their reasoning performance without being perturbed by the same dimensions of the external world which act on humans. The fact that they cannot yet totally compete with human experts is surely due to an aspect of human intelligence which is strongly linked to its own ability to deal with the external world (uncertainty, ambiguity etc.) or to take advantage of the internal world (tacit knowledge, intuition etc.). But I think that the reproduction in a human-like way of that "residual" kind of intelligence is intrinsically incompatible with the machine and will in any case require ever higher intellectual and economic investments simply to produce increasingly marginal improvements, even in terms of reliability. The right way to follow in AI would be, on the contrary, that of integrating the human-like strategies with other techniques oriented to the open acceptance of the nature of the artificial, of its original power and of its limits in performing useful tasks.

This could be our only opportunity to introduce clearly the concept of the artificial in our culture and finally in the user's perception of the machine and of the technological environment in which he lives.

References

Andrew AM (1987) Self-organizing systems and artificial intelligence. Systems Research and Information Science 2:212– 226

Arbib MA (1984) Computers and the cybernetic society. Academic Press, Orlando

Atlan H (1973) Le principe d'ordre a partir de bruit, l'apprentissage non dirige' e le reve. In: Morin E, Piattelli Palmarini M (eds) Le cerveau humain. PUF, Paris

Bibel W (1987) Introduction for the Panel on parallel inference machines. In: McDermott J (ed) Proceedings IJCAI–87. Morgan Kaufmann, Los Altos, CA

Erdi P (1988) From brain theory to future generation computer systems. In: Carvallo ME (ed) Nature, cognition and system. Kluwer, Dordrecht

Gabriel RP (1989) Introduction. LISP and Symbolic Computation 1(3/4)

Kumar V (1985) Parallel processing for artificial intelligence. AITR–85–10, The University of Texas

Maas S, Oberquelle H (1988) Human–computer interaction from the perspective of software development and reality construction. In: Proceedings software development and reality construction. Preprints, Schloss Eringerfeld

Michie D (1987) Six points concerning knowledge-based systems. In: Taylor G (ed) Expert systems for decision making

Negrotti M (1975) Sociologia dell'ambiente tecnico. Saggio sull'equilibrio futuro del sistema cultura-tecnica. Angeli, Milano

Negrotti M (1980) La degenerazione dei sistemi autoregolati. Il simulatore SYSDE. Sociologia e Ricerca Sociale I(1):117– 134

Ornstein SM (1986) Loose coupling: does it make the SDI software trustworthy? CPSR, WS–100–1, Palo Alto

Ostberg O (1986) Expert systems in a social environment – human factor concerns. Proceedings of the human factor society, 30th annual meeting

Partridge D (1987) Is intuitive expertise rule based? Proceedings of the 3rd international expert systems conference. Learned Information, London

Shastri L (1986) Massive parallelism in artificial intelligence. Working paper of the department of computer and information science, University of Pennsylvania

Simon HA (1973) Le scienze dell'artificiale. Mondadori, Milano

Simondon G (1969) Du objet technique. PUF, Paris

Sojat Z (1987) Cybernetics and systems: present and future. In: Proceedings of the 7th international congress of cybernetics and systems. Thales, London

von Bertalanffy L (1971) Teoria generale dei sistemi. ILI, Milano
Winograd T, Flores F (1986) Understanding computers and cognition: a new
   foundation for design. Ablex, Norwood

Chapter 2

The Cognitive Dimension in the Processing of Natural Language

Mario Borillo

Towards a Broadening of Formal Knowledge

One of the clearest examples of the new type of knowledge inferred from research into the extension of machine reasoning is the expression of time and spatial relationships in language. Whereas for twenty-five centuries mathematics and physics, when dealing with the perception and expression of time and space, have tried to purge any traces of subjectivity related to individual experience, approximation and instability due both to the limits of our sensory organs and to those of ordinary language, work on the formalisation of natural language (NL) semantics, evolving today at the confluence of computer science, linguistics and logic, is trying, in a way which at first seems rather astonishing, to introduce scientific game rules into the analysis of something which seemed to oppose the application of these same rules for describing the objective world.

It is noteworthy that scientific endeavour is now trying to integrate elements from which it formerly tried to detach itself. Not that the formal theories of NL have the same aims as geometry, topology and mechanical models (their field is the time and space of the external world and the objective phenomena which take place in it: the properties of straight lines and planes, the movement of bodies, the composition of forces etc.) but an attempt is now being made to master the instruments which NL uses to refer to and describe this world. In the first instance, theories refer to idealisations which are sometimes quite distant from the field of sensory perception, whereas NL instruments most often refer to the world in a direct way, in particular through the use of what we may conveniently call "common sense".[1] There is therefore no reason for these formal instruments to be the same.

In spite of this, in both cases it is a matter of gradually constructing intersubjective conceptualisations, symbolic descriptions which are regular with respect to empirical observation, consistent format systems with worth-while mathematical properties, and explanatory/predictive capacities which may be validated in the framework of experimental protocols. The parallelism is however limited: this latter point is problematic for NL. The procedures for validating its models may be far removed from those handed on by the "physicist" tradition. We need only remember the thought experiments of language philosophers.

Even though linguistics, logic and philosophy did not wait for computer science before tackling the problems mentioned above, these latter have today taken on a particular intensity. The reasons are surely economic and strategic, as computer systems offer potential processing not only of the language message media – as in the framework of Shannon's theory – but also of their informative content, their semantic dimension. In fact this functional perspective is not the only and perhaps not the primary stimulus for the extensive current of cognitive research which includes the automatising of spatio-temporal reasoning.

Computer Science and the Cognitive Project

From the material organisation of the brain and the development of its biophysical processes to language comprehension and production which demonstrate mental activity, the cognitive project stands out because of the priority it gives to studying the interdependence of the components whose functional interaction determines the human cognitive system. The cognitive question deals simultaneously with the nature of knowledge, its different states and modalities, its processes of acquisition, transformation and communication, the organic devices which materialise it in the body, its manifestation in human behaviour, the formal theories which account for it, and the hardware and software systems which are used to inscribe such and such a meaningful segment outside of the human being and which in doing so open the way to a computer simulation of reasoning processes.

Now, both in its foundations and in its most recent evolution, computer science gives expression to a project which is by its very nature cognitive:[2] at the same time, the theory of computation has been extended to ever wider forms of reasoning, to the dynamic execution of algorithms and the physical realisation (electronic implementation) of those theories; and as well as becoming an empirical device which enables syntactic generation through simple rewriting of an open set of formal expressions, some of them being interpreted as thought processes (Artificial Intelligence, AI).

Because of its dual nature, *physical* in terms of calculating and reasoning artefacts (objects constructed by human genius) and *mathematical* in terms of materialised calculation and reason (calculation subjected to physical constraints), computer science constitutes in the present state of the research – because of this very fusion of the material and immaterial dimension of the knowledge in a unified scientific construction – the abstract heart of the cognitive project.

The inscription of logic in matter, the existence of machines, also results in reasoning in its widest meaning becoming an activity which may be subjected to experimental study in all of its different states. On the empirical level, it is generally admitted that its natural production is done in the brain even though our ability to associate meaning with neurophysiological phenomena is still restricted to relatively elementary units. It is therefore natural that co-operation between computer science and neurophysiology has little to do with the reproduction by machines of real cerebral processes. Biochemistry and neurophysiology contribute their ideas on the material level, whether these concern the elementary organic components (organic transistors) of highly parallel networks or abstract neurons in the lineage of models of the 1950s. For its part, neurophysiology provides hypotheses concerning the modular architecture of information processing.

Thought processes as such are more easily identified empirically from behaviour, attitudes, speech – in short from a set of observable exteriorisations. The task of neuropsychology and neurolinguistics is to deal with the transition by studying the relations between the internal and external physical states of the processes (brain damage and speech impairments, for example) and by associating all of them with elements of the signification system. The external layer of this successive transformation arrangement is that of behaviour and especially language which are the sensory systems for expressing thought and which are therefore responsible for its socialisation.

In limiting themselves to language, which is, after all, the clearest example of the transition from a system of physical phenomena to a system of meanings – from the acoustic signal or its written encoding to semantics and pragmatics – it is remarkable that all of the main contemporary lines of research have selected, despite the diversity of their particular methodological and theoretical choices, a shared perspective which is more or less that of the calculation of meaning from the representation of observable entities, whether they start at the phonetic level, as with generative grammars or at the syntactic level, as with, for example, Montague's semantics. This research therefore appears as so many bridges arching out from the empirical material of which language is constructed, towards the formal theories of reasoning discussed above.

With its restrictions and its stumbling blocks, the venture of speech understanding illustrates an extreme case of this integration in a unique formal and functional device. The linking between "calculating the meaning" and "automating reasoning" is here obvious because in an intelligent system, the meaning of the linguistic message is only calculated from an acoustic level in order to trigger, in the (formalised) knowledge universe of the system the execution of other stages of calculation – corresponding to the reasoning induced by the message – whose task is to produce in one or other exterior form the pertinent answers in the system's universe. If we accept that the behaviour of the system translates the logical–semantic theories which structure it, we may conceive that its systematic observation opens the possibility of real experimental testing of the reasoning models embedded in it.

A more precise examination of the functional architecture of an NL understanding system (Fig. 2.1) will enable us to better define the nature of this understanding, especially by getting rid of its anthropomorphic analogies.

What Does it Mean to "Understand" NL?

First of all, let us use $S_i(NL_i, U_i)$ to designate the meaning of a (written) message expressed in a chosen fragment of natural language NL_i and related to universe of discourse U_i. The first module, here called "translation" should do the main part of the linguistic work. It necessarily includes a set of devices for dealing with the processing of the morpho-lexical, morpho-syntactic, semantic and even pragmatic layers of the message. Each device brings into play one or several formal models of the linguistic layer in question, as well as linguistic knowledge bases (lexicons, dictionaries) containing the description of elementary material relating to the $<NL_i, U_i>$ couple, and finally a set of algorithms applying the formal models mentioned above to the symbol string input, with the following twofold objective: first, to recognise the underlying structure at each level through a set of hypothesis tests which are in some way related to the technique of problem solving in the framework of logic programming; then to calculate recursively the meaning of the message by composition of the elementary meanings of its words according to rules defined from the above structures (lexical and syntactical).

The complexity of linguistic structures, and especially the interdependence of different levels of description is reflected in the translation structure. Its different layers, far from being sealed off, interact with continual exchanges of information. Moreover, we now know that the complexity of the necessary calculations, and therefore their run-time, is extremely great: hence the apparently more and more indispensable use of parallel computing (Miller and Torris 1990).

The complexity of the problem increases when not only sentence structures but also discourse structures are taken into account. With respect to this latter, from the perspective of the logical semantics of NL, it may be assumed that theoretical research has only just begun with the seminal work of Hans Kamp (Kamp 1981).

The task of the translator is to produce a set $S'_i(FL_i, FU_i)$ of expressions, i.e. a set of formulae in the formal language FL_i interpretable in the reference universe (context) which has itself been formalised FU_i. In the designer's view, FL_i would, for example, be a formalism of knowledge representation. Considering that the central role of logic is more and more widely recognised, this language might be PROLOG or one of its extensions.

If we wish to stay as close as possible to the metaphor of "understanding", then translation into FL_i is only just a beginning. It is in fact only after processing and after the modifications thus induced in the internal state of the computer system and the observable behaviour associated with it that we can evaluate the appropriateness of $S'_i(FL_i, FU_i)$ with respect to $S_i(NL_i, U_i)$.

It would take too much time to enter into the details of all the other system modules. The compiler appears in Fig. 2.1 to remind us of the evidence, too often forgotten, that the ultimate reality for the machine consists of the dynamic configuration of its physical states. The compiler transduces FL_i into executable code. It is therefore the compiler which connects the formalisms S'_i and FU_i with particular internal states of the system. The connection of the software dimension and the material dimension of the processing is a crucial function which has up to now only been considered in its technical aspect. It

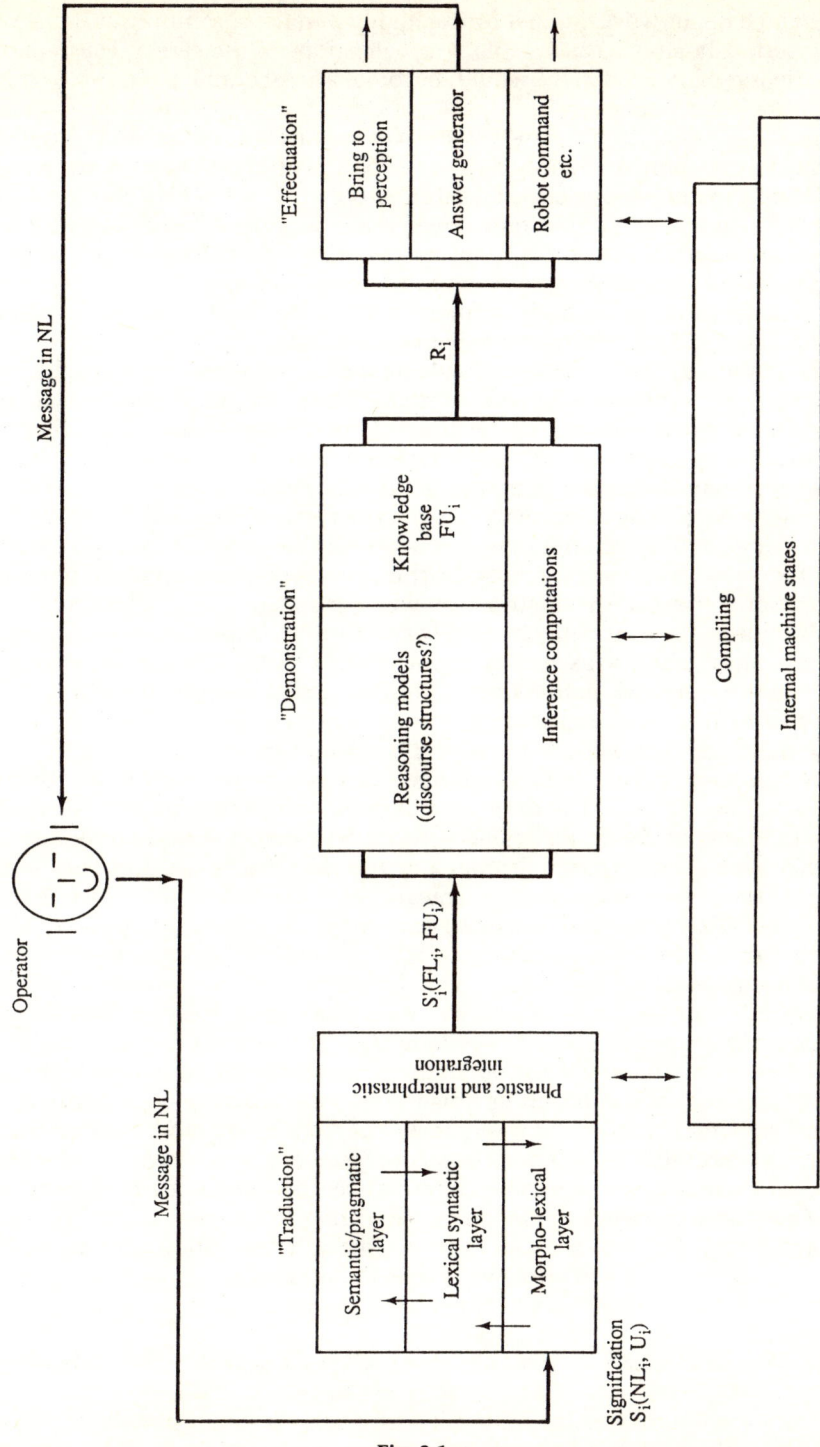

Fig. 2.1.

might well be, however, that if future highly parallel computing systems were to be seriously studied as acceptable idealisations of the cerebral system, that the theory of compilation would become an essential pillar of cognitive research.

The "demonstration" handles the computing of the instructions commanded by S'_i in the knowledge universe FU_i. It could just as easily concern the updating of a knowledge base (S'_i acts to modify the set of FU_i), as it could be a real deduction (S'_i is a question, interpreted as a set of formulae which are either validated or not in FU_i). Let us remember that the perspective of the automatisation of reasoning rests on the definition of formal models representing the inferential mechanisms implemented in the NL and that in this respect, linguistics, logic and philosophy are involved.[3]

The results R_i of the preceding calculations are themselves translated into internal representations in the system. They are therefore not directly accessible to the operator. Given the exceptions, they will have to be displayed externally in one way or another. This is the role assigned to the "effectuation". This term may designate both a generator of answers in NL, which would inform the human operator in the loop of the results produced by the message S_i, or a device for commanding external physical organs, for example, a robot. In either case, success or failure of the processing, the appropriateness or inappropriateness of the answers, may be evaluated. This diagnosis tests the <translation– demonstration> couple as a formal coupled theory of language and reasoning but also as an algorithmic interpretation of these theories in the restrictive framework defined by $<NL_i,U_i>$ and the hardware and software architecture of a computer system.

Greatly increased knowledge of the brain and decisive progress in neuropsycholinguistics will no doubt be necessary before we can tell whether NL processing as described here or as glimpsed on the horizon of forthcoming developments in computer science and AI has anything to do with our own mechanisms of understanding language. It is clear, however, that if we needed a formula to sum up the underlying meaning of current research, it would be: *to program in NL*. We would, however, have to give it very restricted acceptance. This would involve choosing fragments NL_i from an NL in such a way that NL_i could be considered as a very high level programming language, which supposes therefore that its lexicon, its syntax and its semantics are procedurally interpreted in a compiled language.

However impatient we may be, in the current state of our knowledge of the brain, language and computing, this framework seems to be the only one in which the relationships between language, reasoning and computing can today be expressed in true scientific terms. But we may reassure ourselves that, far from leading to questions of no importance, this approach sets very difficult problems on the nature of language! Returning to our first argument and to illustrate what has just been said, what follows is an outline of a method for formalising part of the expression of time in French.

Elements for a Formal Semantics of Time in Language

The construction of feasible models of temporal reasoning requires first of all that the nature of the time concerned be specified. Without evoking the extraordinary range of scientific conceptions and descriptions of time, computer science is already a very good example of this diversity within a single discipline: linear or branching temporal models for specifying, synthesising or proving parallel programs, models for planning, chronologies and updating in information systems etc.

Cognitive study of reasoning introduces a new idea, that of time in language. Without going into philosophical speculations, we see immediately that the notion of time will here have a subjective dimension (the time of the speaker's mental representations) which does not appear in the notion of time associated with the objective universes mentioned above. The first task will therefore be to focus the analysis on empirical ground (observable) where the use of language is objectively expressed: this is by definition the role of linguistics.

Our intention is to illustrate with a simple example the methodology which we propose for associating linguistic analysis with the project of representing knowledge and automatising reasoning. In this case, the methodology is applied to temporal reasoning, but it is clear that it has a more general range as demonstrated by work which we are pursuing elsewhere on concepts of localisation and movement, this latter combining time and space (Laur 1989).

After giving a glimpse of the means used in French for expressing time and describing the problems we have worked on up to now, we show how lexical–syntactical analysis enables rigorous defining of formal semantics for certain limited classes of temporal constructions in NL. The compositionality and truth conditionality of this semantics, implemented in PROLOG, have enabled us to prepare the way for another approach to the automatising of temporal reasoning.

Some Elements of Expressing Time in Language

Time may be grasped at the level of the word, the sentence or of discourse (Borillo 1983). We will deal here only with the first two, even though we are doing research elsewhere into the processing of the temporal reference in the framework of the Discursive Representations Theory (DRT) (Kamp 1981). In outline, the temporal notions expressed may be divided into two large categories:

(a) *Localisation* in time:
   precedence/succession
   simultaneity
   situation with respect to the utterance

(b) *The temporal structure* of events and situations, which linguists call "aspect" (A. Borillo 1986a):
   duration (durative/limited)
   perfectivity (finished/unfinished)
   iteration, habit
   progressiveness
   etc.

Fig. 2.2 summarises the role in these two dimensions of the main temporal markers, arranged in grammatical categories.

The substantives – missing from this list – are obviously another very important class of temporal markers. According to their lexical structure or their syntactical combination, the syntagma that they form also belong to one or other of the following categories (A. Borillo 1986b):

	Verbs	Adverbs		Temporal conjunction
Localisation in time	Present	Temporal Reference		Simultaneousness, anteriority successivity
	Past/ Pluperfect	deictiques *(speaker)*	anaphoric *(marker)*	
	Future/ Future perfect	*hier* *demain* *dernièrement* *autrefois*	*plus tard* *après* *alors* *avant*	*(quand, dès que, avant que...)*
Structure of events in time	1. Durative/limited 2. Perfective/ imperfective 3. Progressive 4. Iterative 5. Inchoative etc. with aspect auxiliary	Temporal structure *(soudain, longtemps, périodiquement, souvent....)*		Aspectuality
	1. passer, mettre 3 jours à ... *2. finir de ..., cesser de ...* *3. être en train de* *4. recommencer à* *5. se mettre à ...*			

Fig. 2.2. Temporal markers in language.

(a) *Localisation* in time
    deictics:

la semaine prochaine	(next week)
dans les jours à venir	(in the days to come)
il y a trois mois	(three months ago)

    anaphorics:

le jour suivant	(the following day)
un mois après	(one month later)
trois semaines avant	(three weeks before)

(b) *The temporal structure*
    duration:

pendant trois heures	(for three hours)
toute la semaine	(the whole week)
depuis quelques mois	(for a few months now)

    frequency:

chaque semaine	(each week)

un mois sur deux   (every other month)
tous les lundis   (every Monday)

Considering the central role played by the verb in the sentence, the description of the propositional structure of all elementary utterances is constructed around the representation of the verb and its arguments. In French, as in most natural languages, each utterance is doubly "temporalised" through its verb: by the morphology of the verb, which expresses a conjugation tense, i.e. a relative localising of the proposition in time:

Max vient/Max viendra
Max is coming/Max will come

by the verb's own semantics, which express the intrinsic characteristics of the temporal meaning of the utterance (lexical semantics):
rencontre (A,B)/*adhere* (A,B)
meet (A,B)/join (A,B)

These different semantic components will be discussed in turn.

Lexical Semantics of Verbs

The categorisation of verbs according to the nature of the temporal implications which may be associated with them is an undertaking which goes back at least to Aristotle's *Metaphysics*. Linguists and philosophers (Nef 1986) agree that the credit for renewing this question goes to Zeno Vendler (Vendler 1967), to the extent that his categorisation has paved the way for formal lexical semantics.

On the basis of syntactic tests (objective), four categories of situations may be distinguished: thus, in French, application of the duration component in the form *during x time* or *in x time* enables us to separate *terminative* and *non-terminative* situations, with each one of them then subdividing according to Fig. 2.3.

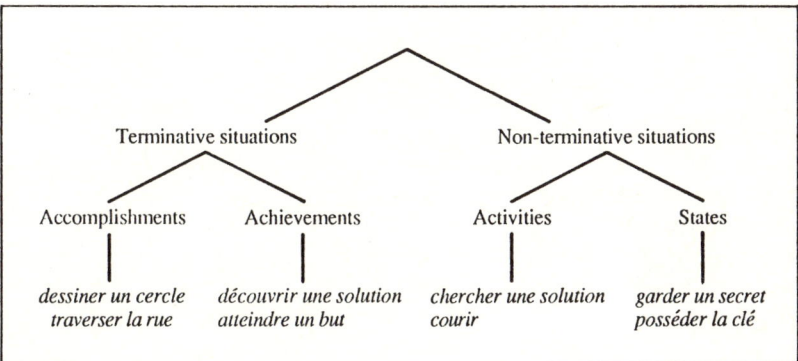

Fig. 2.3.

The accomplishments and achievements accept a duration complement with *en* and not so easily with *pendant*, whereas the activities and states show the opposite property:

Il a dessiné un cercle en cinq minutes
(He drew a circle in five minutes)
Il a découvert une solution en cinq minutes
(He found a solution in five minutes)
Il a cherché une solution pendant des heures
(He looked for a solution for hours)
Il a gardé le secret pendant des années
(He kept the secret for years)

The difference is due to the fact that the *states* and *activities* are homogeneous situations which do not have a natural end – the situation is true at any moment of its duration and can be prolonged indefinitely – whereas the *accomplishments* and *achievements* have a structure which includes its own end; the situation is only true when this end is reached. The difference between these latter is due to the fact that with the non-durative achievements, the adverb complement *in x time* does not give the time of happening between the beginning and the end of the situation, but the time that was necessary before the situation was achieved. The use of *avant* (before) or *presque* (almost) shows the difference clearly. In order to separate the activities and the states we might suggest a second test, marking their active/stative difference, tied to the use of aspectual auxiliaries: *se mettre a* (begin to), *s'arreter de* (stop doing something):

Terminative situations: accomplishments/achievements

For ≠ before:
Il a pris trois minutes (pour/avant de) traverser la rue
(He took three minutes (for/before) crossing the street)

For = before:
Il a pris trois minutes (pour/avant de) decouvrir la solution
(He took three minutes (for/before) discovering the solution)

Non-terminative situations: activities/states

Il s'est mis à chercher la solution
(He started to look for the solution)
Il s'est mis à posseder la clef
(He began to have the key)

This syntactic analysis provides an objective basis for the speaker's intuitive semantics. The classification established by these tests becomes a lexical semantics which formally defines each of the classes. Different structurings have been suggested. Thus, Taylor (1977) distinguishes between *state verbs* S (know the solution) and *activity verbs* E (look for the solution) and he groups in the same class *event verbs* K, *accomplishment verbs* (draw a circle) and *achievement verbs* (discover the key).

The semantics of these classes are defined by a certain number of axioms in a first order language, where:

Per(t) is a time interval
Mom(t) is a temporal point
$V_n t$ is a predicate with n places (with the nth reserved for time)

Research is focusing both on more refined categorising, so that each lexical entry may be associated with its specific temporal "signification", and on the definition of more expressive formal languages, possibly easier to implement.

Semantics of Verb Tense: The Formal and Linguistic Framework

The study of temporalised propositions has laid the foundation for a temporal logic, propositional or predicative, modal or not modal (e.g. Prior 1967). We have however chosen for the basis of our semantics a language which is much less commonly used: the representation system proposed by Reichenbach (1947) and revived later by other researchers (Hornstein 1977). Unlike "classical" temporal logics, this system in fact offers a specific description of verb tense which expresses the particular structure of the natural utterances.

The significant axioms for each class are:
For the state verbs S:

$$(1)\ \text{Per}(t) \rightarrow (V_n t \leftrightarrow \forall t'\, (\text{Mom}(t') \wedge t' \subset t \rightarrow V_n t'))$$
example:

$$\text{Per}(t) \rightarrow (\textit{connaître}\ (x_1, x_2, t) \leftrightarrow \forall t'(\text{Mom}(t') \wedge t' \subset t \rightarrow \textit{connaître}\ (x_1, x_2, t')))$$

For the activity verbs E and event verbs K:

$$(2)\ V_n t \rightarrow \text{Per}(t)$$

We distinguish between each of these two classes by two new predicates indicating the opening of intervals:

OF(t) for open-fronted (t),
OE(t) for open-ended (t),
where t is an interval.

$$\text{OF}(t) \leftrightarrow \text{Per}(t) \wedge \forall t'\, (\text{Mom}(t') \wedge t' \subset t \rightarrow \exists t''\, (t'' \subset t \wedge t'' < t'))$$
$$\text{OE}(t) \leftrightarrow \text{Per}(t) \wedge \forall t'\, (\text{Mom}(t') \wedge t' \subset t \rightarrow \exists t''\, (t'' \subset t \wedge t'' < t'))$$

For activity verbs E:

$$(3)\ V_n t \rightarrow \text{Per}(t) \wedge \exists t'\, (\text{OF}(t') \wedge t \subseteq t' \wedge V_n t') \wedge \exists t''\, (t'' \subseteq t \wedge \text{Per}(t'') \rightarrow V_n t'')$$
example:

$$\textit{chercher}\ (x_1, \ldots x_{n-1}, t) \rightarrow \text{Per}(t) \wedge \exists t'\, (\text{OF}(t') \wedge t \subseteq t' \wedge \textit{chercher}\ (x_1, \ldots x_{n-1}, t'))$$
$$\wedge\ \exists t''\, (t'' \subset t \wedge \text{Per}(t'') \rightarrow \textit{chercher}\ (x_1, \ldots x_{n-1}, t''))$$

For event verbs K:

$$(4)\ V_n t \rightarrow \text{Per}(t) \wedge \forall t'\, (t' \subseteq t \rightarrow \neg\, V_n t')$$
example:

$$\textit{découvre}\ (x_1, x_2, t) \rightarrow \text{Per}(t) \wedge \forall t'\, (t' \subseteq t \rightarrow \neg\, \textit{découvre}\ (x_1, x_2 t'))\ (1)\ \text{Per}(t)$$

Fig. 2.4.

To do this, he distinguishes the three following markers for each utterance: S, the discourse time (the speaker's time); E, the time of the event expressed by the sentence; and R, the time of the temporal reference used by the speaker to place himself and to place the event.

The necessity of R becomes clear if we compare the following pairs of utterances:

	Je vis Max			
	(I saw Max)	E,R	S	t
Past	J'avais vu Max			
	(I had seen Max)	E	R	S	t
	Je verrai Max			
	(I shall see Max)	S	E,R	t
Future	J'aurai vu Max			
	(I shall have seen Max)	S	E	R	t

Our approach consists of linking the following three stages in a coherent manner:

1. Defining a pertinent formal language
2. Delimiting precisely the extension of the linguistic field
3. Proposing a representation only after filtering the linguistic forms with acceptance algorithms

The temporal language chosen is based on the linear intervals logic proposed by Allen (1984). Let us simply note that it is a first order logic, with types admitting predefined predicates as terms (it is "reified"). These types of predicates, moreover, correspond to Vendler's lexical classes. The language was revised by Shoham (1987) who proposed a "normalised" and extended version.

One of the main advantages of Allen's language is its coding in the form of interval graphs, where its deductive component is expressed by a transitive closure rule. The complex algebraic structure of this representation was studied by Granier (1987), who with Divin (1988) also improved the algorithms proposed by Allen for exploiting the inferential properties of the temporal knowledge bases. Granier and Divin also extend the language to point structures.

The conjugation of a verb tense in a sentence places the three intervals E, R, S with respect to each other, thus defining the temporal component of its propositional structure. Of course, even inside the carefully limited domain with which we are working, grammatical tenses may be polysemic: there will then be several corresponding representations for one verb tense. But just as in NL the addition of modifiers (adverbs) and connectors helps to resolve these ambiguities by specifying the meaning of the utterance, and the recursive rules of our models will select the resulting representation.

A complete graph with three nodes corresponding to the intervals E, R, S is associated with a verb tense. Each directed node is labelled with the relationship(s) existing between its two nodes, noted in Allen's code.

The relationships are two-place predicates and a graph is no more than the visualisation of a logical formula. Several relationships between two nodes are expressed by the disjunction of the corresponding predicates. The complete graph is taken into account by the conjunction of its disjunctions.

The circumscription of the linguistic area, whose importance we have emphasised, is defined as follows:

for the verb tenses:
    by Vendler's *achievement* and *activity* lexical categories
    by tenses in the indicative mood

for adverbs of time (propositional modifiers):
> by deictics (marking the relationship of the speaker to the utterance situation): *hier* (yesterday), *aujourd'hui* (today), *demain* (tomorrow)

for the interpropositional temporal conjunctions:
> study of *quand* (then) which is one of the most complex, for the forms p1 (t1) *quand* p2 (tj).

Semantics of Verb Tenses, Adverbs and Connectors

The Verb Tenses

Through linguistic analysis we have constructed a representation for each of the indicative tenses of the verbs belonging to the two Vendler classes mentioned above. For the purpose of illustrating the method, we will describe here only the representation of the simple present tense:

$$((S<R)\lor(S=R)\lor(S\ s\ R)\lor(S\ d\ R)\lor(S\ f\ R))\land((S<E)\lor(S=E)\lor(S\ s\ E)\lor(S\ d\ R)\lor(S\ f\ R))\land((R=E)\lor(R\ s_i\ E)\lor(R\ d_i\ E)\lor(R\ f_i\ E))$$

$<$, $>$, s, d, f, ..., s_i, d_i, f_i represent the relationships between the temporal intervals E, R, and S in the language. An extended description may be found in Bras (1987). It constitutes part of the linguistic knowledge base necessary for interpretation (associated with the lexical semantics).

The Temporal Adverbs

The deictic adverbs *hier* (yesterday), *aujourd'hui* (today), *demain* (tomorrow) position the reference interval with respect to the discourse interval (S–>–R) in an "absolute" manner: they enable the establishment of fixed relationships with the reference, whereas the anaphoric adverbs (*la veille, ce jour-la, le lendemain*) position the reference interval in a relative way with respect to the event interval; thus binding R and E throughout their use. They prevent the use of R for finalising the representations.

The Representation of Deictic Adverbs

The role of the deictic adverb is to establish a reference in relation to discourse. In general, the deictic adverb describes the reference interval. The result of this property is that introducing this type of adverb into a proposition specifies the relationship between the discourse interval and the reference interval. The restriction given by the adverb is therefore materialised in the S–>–R relationship.

The event interval E is not necessary for defining the adverb: it is not involved and may be linked with S and R in different ways.

The three adverbs chosen are represented as follows:

Hier (yesterday): $S>R$
Aujourd'hui (today): $(S=R)\vee(S\ s\ R)\vee(S\ d\ R)\vee(S\ f\ R)$
Demain (tomorrow): $S<R$

Rule for Introducing Deictic Adverbs

The role of this procedure is to check the compatibility between the relationships associated with the S–>–R verb tenses edge and those represented with the S–>–R adverb edge.

Let SR_t be the set of relationships appearing on the edge S–>–R of the verb tense t. Then SR_a, the set of relationships appearing on the edge S–>–R of the adverb a, is acceptable in a sentence p if it positions the reference with respect to the discourse time without infringing on the relationships authorised by this time.

The test is written as follows:

$$SR_t \cap SR_a \neq 0$$

Compositional Rule

If the introduction of the adverb a is permitted in the sentence p(t), then the representation of the temporal structure of the sentence (p(t)+a) is constructed. The introduction of the adverb selects the possibilities for relationships between S and R: a temporal structure of the sentence is then obtained by "filtering" the relationships associated with the edge S–>–R of the verb tense with the relationship associated with the edge S–>–R of the adverb.

If SR_n, SE_n, RE_n represent the temporal relationships associated with the resulting sentence (p(t)+a), the composition rule is then:

$$SR_n = SR_t \cap SR_a; SE_n = SE_t; RE_n = RE_t$$

The Temporal Connectors

The introduction of temporal connectors is used to form complex sentences from elementary sentences, but their semantics are completely different from those of the usual logic connectors. As for the previous examples, the semantics will be established through linguistic analysis. We know the temporal structure of a simple sentence: it is the temporal structure of the verb tense within which it is conjugated, or else it is modified by the introduction of an adverb. It is also modified when we connect a second sentence by means of a temporal conjunction. In this case, we have a grammatical structure with the main-subordinate form and it is the subordinate clause which establishes the reference.

In general, given $p(t_1)$ and $q(t_2)$, two propositions to be connected with the temporal conjunction ct, we will obtain the proposition $p(t_1)$ ct $q(t_2)$ where (ct $q(t_2)$) is used to establish the reference of $p(t_1)$.

The subordinate proposition may be introduced by different temporal conjunctions: *quand* (when), *pendant* (while), *apres que* (after), *avant que* (before), *alors que* (whereas), *depuis que* (since).

Each of these conjunctions induces its own final temporal structure and we notice that:

1. The compatibility of the times t_1 and t_2 depends on the conjunction itself: *Je travaillerai quand tu reposeras* (literally translated as "I shall work when you will rest", but rendered in English as "I shall work when you are resting")

but

Je travaillerai depuis que tu reposeras (literally "I shall work as soon as you will be resting", but in English this would be "I shall work as soon as you are resting")

2. The semantics of the temporal conjunction indicate the way in which the reference may be established: If $p(t_1)$ is represented by a structure $<S_1, R_1, E_1>$, $q(t_2)$ by a structure $<S_2, R_2, E_2>$, the temporal structure is used to establish a relationship between E_1 and E_2, for example:

avant (before) induces $E_1 < E_2$
apres (after) induces $E_1 > E_2$
pedant que (while) induces $(E_1 = E_2) \lor (E_1 \text{ s } E_2) \lor (E_1 \text{ d } E_2) \lor (E_1 \text{ f } E_2)$

The Temporal Connector "Quand"

The diversity of its use shows that its semantics construct different types of temporal links (A. Borillo 1988):

1. Expression of "coincidence-anteriority": *quand* has the meaning *une fois que* (as soon as)
2. Expression of "coincidence": *quand* has the meaning of *au moment où* (just as, at the moment that)
3. Expression of "partial covering": *quand* has the meaning of *dès que* (whereas) and *alors que* (while)
4. Expression of "total covering": *quand* has the meaning of *tout temps où* (always when), *au temps où* (at the time when)

The first decision to be made is whether it is possible to link two given sentences $p(t_1)$ and $q(t_2)$ with the temporal conjunction *quand*. This means testing whether the combination $p(t_1)$ *quand* $q(t_2)$ is acceptable.

If the first stage gives a positive result, then the temporal structure of the new complex sentence $p(t_1)$ *quand* $q(t_2)$ must be constructed.

The semantics of *quand* will be represented by a set of programs including:

(a) a set of preliminary acceptance rules
(b) a set of rules for constructing the temporal structure

Acceptance Rules

These rules take the form of a three-stage filter: we apply successively rule 1, rule 2, then rule 3:

let $p(t_1)$ be a sentence conjugated in tense t_1, represented by $<S_1,R_1,E_1>$
let $q(t_2)$ be a sentence conjugated in tense t_2, represented by $<S_2,R_2,E_2>$

Rule 1

Given SR_1 the set of relationships appearing on the edge $S_1 -> -R_1$
Given SR_2 the set of relationships appearing on the edge $S_2 -> -E_2$

If $SR_1 \cap SR_2 = 0$ then the sentence ($p(t_1)$ *quand* $q(t_2)$) is rejected
    if not continue filtering

Rule 2

Given SE_1 the set of relationships appearing on the edge $S_1 -> -E_1$
Given SE_2 the set of relationships appearing on the edge $S_2 -> -E_2$

If $SE_1 \neq SE_2$ then the sentence ($p(t_1)$ *quand* $q(t_2)$) is rejected
    if not continue filtering

Rule 3

Given c_1, the category of the verb in $p(t_1)$
Given c_1, the category of the verb in $q(t_2)$

If (t_1 = "simple past" and t_2 = "past continuous 2")
or (t_1 = "past continuous 2" and t_2 = "simple past") then the sentence ($p(t_1)$
quand $q(t_2)$) is rejected
    if not
if (c_1 = "activity" and c_2 = "activity") and ((t_1 = "simple past" or t_1 = "past
continuous 2") then the sentence ($p(t_1)$ *quand* $q(t_2)$) is rejected
    if not
if (c_1 = "activity" and c_2 = "activity") and ((t_1 = "simple past" and t_2 = "simple
past") or (t_1 = "past continuous 2" and t_2 = "past continuous 2")
or (t_1 = "imperfect" and t_2 = "simple past") or (t_1 = "imperfect" and t_2 = "past
continuous 2")) then the sentence ($p(t_1)$ *quand* $q(t_2)$) is rejected
    if not
the sentence ($p(t_1)$ *quand* $q(t_2)$) is accepted

Rules for Constructing the Temporal Structure

In applying the acceptance rules, we get the sentences ($p(t_1)$ *quand* $q(t_2)$) which
belong to the French. We may then try to represent the temporal structure. This
structure will be represented in the form of a directed graph whose nodes are
the intervals and whose edges are labelled by the set of the relationships.

Given the temporal structure $<S_1,R_1,E_1>$ whose main proposition is the
basis for the representation, the construction is done from the following
factors:

1. The discourse interval S of the sentence ($p(t_1)$ *quand* $q(t_2)$) is the same as that
   of $p(t_1)$ and of $q(t_2)$: $S = S_1 = S_2$.
2. The reference of the main proposition is established by the subordinate
   (*quand* $q(t_2)$), and we therefore define a relationship between R_1 and E_2. This

relationship $R_1 -> -E_2$ is established as a function of the connector *quand* and of the tenses t_1 and t_2 of the propositions p and q.
3. The intervals E_1 and E_2 still have to be related. For this we use the relationships $R_1 -> -E_2$ and $R_1 -> -E_1$ already known.

A rather complex algorithm implements this method of representation using the results of linguistic analysis in the form of tests. A complete description of the method can be found in Borillo et al. (1989).

Perspectives of the Cognitive Approach

Starting with temporal logic (Allen's language), we see how its use for the precise description of temporal structures of NL modifies its semantics and modifies its use. First of all, and perhaps the most important, the rule of transitive closure which forms Allen's basic inferential device (from relations associated with two adjacent edges are deduced the values associated with the third) is here replaced with the assignment of linguistically observed values to the third edge of the graph. The difference from a computing point of view is essential, as the complexity of the "reasoning" algorithms associated with Allen's model are prohibitive ($0(n2.n!)$ for a graph with n nodes).

In general, the introduction of restrictions coming from analysis of acceptable linguistic reasoning is promising if only in that it reduces the combinatory expansion of formal deduction. It will definitely be necessary to return to these differences in order to measure the technical consequences on computing and also on the conception of automatised reasoning, closer, in our approach, to the natural reasoning structures (Bernard et al. 1990).

My intention here was more modest: to show how the construction of a compositional semantics of time, based on linguistic analysis, may be progressively extended to more complex fragments of temporal expression, as well as to other conceptual fields, especially spatio-temporal (M. Borillo and Vieu 1989), thus providing an instrument for formalising and implementing knowledge and inferences which may be expressed in the NL source fragment. The necessity of having a lexical semantics is not the least of the problems encountered with this approach, even more so in that the electronic dictionaries should also include the detailed syntactic information necessary for the tests used in the programs (Gross 1968).

In addition, articulation of sentences (elementary or complex) in discourse structures raises considerable difficulties (co-references, conditional clauses etc.) for linguistic analysis. The theoretical framework set up by the works of Kamp (1981) (DRT) is one of the rare satisfactory perspectives in this area. We therefore intend to explore its possibilities, both from the point of view of the precise definition of suitable linguistic conditions and in terms of the appropriateness of formal systems and their implementation (Bras 1990).

The analysis of NL, the definition of semantic theories, for instance of the expression of time and space, are laying the foundations for the construction of dynamic reasoning models which will establish a coherent link, in the present state of knowledge, between certain cognitive processes used in language (and indirectly in the brain) and the computing capacities of machines, their physical structure and the theoretical knowledge which they materialise. Tentative as it may be, this approach has the advantage of giving a precise meaning – and without any anthropomorphic illusion – to the expression "understanding NL" when referring to a machine.

Notes

1 NL also allows discussion of theoretical entities in "spatio-temporal" terms: "in the expression XY, X is to the left of Y", "the Big Bang preceded the expansion of the Universe" etc. NL is the meta-language of the object-language of the theory.
2 For a systematic description of the relations between computer science and cognitive research see M. Borillo, Une machine speculative. Revue Internationale de Philosophie 44(172):47–61.
3 For concrete examples of this cognitive impact on human sciences, see M. Borillo (1984) Informatique pour les sciences de l'Homme. Bruxelles.

References

Allen JA (1984) Towards a general theory of action and time. AI Journal 23(2):123–154
Bernard D, Borillo M, Gaume B (1990) From event calculus to the scheduling problem: Semantics of action and temporal reasoning in aircraft maintenance. Applied Intelligence (submitted)
Borillo A (1983) Les adverbes de référence temporelle dans la phrase et dans le texte. Revue du DRLAV, Université Paris VIII(29):109–131
Borillo A (1986a) La quantification temporelle: durée et itérativité en français. Cahiers du Grammaire, Université de Toulouse le Mirail, 11:32–57
Borillo A (1986b) Les emplois adverbiaux des noms de temps. Lexique et Traitement Automatique des Langages. UPS, Toulouse
Borillo A (1988) Quelques remarques sur quand connecteur temporel. Langue française 77, Larousse, Paris, pp 71–91
Borillo A, Borillo M, Bras M (1989) A temporal reasoning cognitive approach. Semistica 77(1/3):173–194
Borillo M, Vieu L (1989) Eléments pour la formalisation du raisonnement spatio-temporel naturel. Actes di Congrés RFIA 89, AFCET, Paris, pp 181–196
Bras M (1987) Sémantique des temps de l'indicatif des adverbes temporels déictiques et du connecteur quand. Rapport LSI 283, Toulouse
Bras M (1990) Calcul des structures temporelles du discours. Thése de l'Université Paul-Sabatier, Toulouse
Divin A (1988) Automatisation du raisonnement temporel. Complexite des algorithmes. Rapport LSI 305, Toulouse
Granier T (1987) Etude symbolique des chronologies entre intervalles de temps. Rapport LIFIA, Grenoble
Gross M (1968) Méthodes en syntaxe. Hermann, Paris
Hornstein N (1977) Towards a theory of tense. Linguistic Inquiry 8(3):521–557
Kamp H (1981) Evénements, representations discursives et référence temporelle. Langages 64, Larousse, Paris, pp 39–64

Laur D (1989) Sémantique du déplacement. Cahiers de Grammaire, Université de Toulouse le Mirail, 14:67–84

Nef F (1986) Sémantique de la référence temporelle en français moderne. Peter Lang, Berbe

Miller Ph, Torris Th (1990) Formalismes syntaxiques pour le traitement du language naturel. Editions Hermés, Paris

Prior A (1967) Past, present and future. Oxford University Press, Oxford

Reichenbach H (1947) Elements of symbolic logic. McMilland, New York

Shoham Y (1987) Temporal logics in AI: semantical and ontological considerations. AI Journal 33:89–104

Taylor B (1977) Tense and continuity. Linguistics and Philosophy 1(2):199–220

Vendler Z (1967) Linguistics in philosophy. Cornell University Press, Ithaca

*Chapter 3**

Making a Mind Versus Modelling the Brain: Artificial Intelligence Back at the Branchpoint

Hubert L. Dreyfus and Stuart E. Dreyfus

Nothing seems more possible to me than that people some day will come to the definite opinion that there is no copy in the ... nervous system which corresponds to a particular thought, or a particular idea or memory. (Wittgenstein 1948)[1]

Information is not stored anywhere in particular. Rather, it is stored everywhere. Information is better thought of as "evoked" rather than "found". (Rumelhart and Norman 1981)[2]

In the early 1950s, as calculating machines were coming into their own, a few pioneer thinkers began to realise that digital computers could be more than number-crunchers. At that point two opposed visions of what computers could be, each with its correlated research programme, emerged and struggled for recognition. One faction saw computers as a system for manipulating mental symbols; the other, as a medium for modelling the brain. One sought to use computers to instantiate a formal representation of the world; the other, to simulate the interactions of neurons. One took problem solving as its paradigm of intelligence; the other, learning. One utilised logic; the other, statistics. One school was the heir to the rationalist, reductionist tradition in philosophy; the other viewed itself as idealised, holistic neuroscience.

The rallying cry of the first group was that both minds and digital computers are physical symbol systems. By 1955, Allen Newell and Herbert Simon, working at the Rand Corporation, had concluded that strings of bits manipulated by a digital computer could stand for anything – numbers, of course, but also features of the real world. Moreover, programs could be used as rules to represent relations between these symbols, so that the system could infer further facts about the represented objects and their relations. As Newell put it recently in his account of the history of issues in Artificial Intelligence (AI):

The digital computer field defined computers as machines that manipulated numbers. The great thing was, adherents said, that everything could be encoded into numbers, even instructions. In contrast, the scientists in AI saw computers as machines that manipulated symbols. The great thing was, they said, that everything could be encoded into symbols, even numbers.[3]

Reprinted by permission of *Dædalus*, Journal of the American Academy of Arts and Sciences, 117(1):15–43 (winter 1988).

This way of looking at computers became the basis of a way of looking at minds. Newell and Simon hypothesised that the human brain and the digital computer, while totally different in structure and mechanism, had at a certain level of abstraction, a common functional description. At this level both the human brain and the appropriately programmed digital computer could be seen as two different instantiations of a single species of device – a device that generated intelligent behaviour by manipulating symbols by means of formal rules. Newell and Simon stated their view as a hypothesis:

The Physical Symbol System Hypothesis. *A physical symbol system has the necessary and sufficient means for general intelligent action.*
By "necessary" we mean that any system that exhibits general intelligence will prove upon analysis to be a physical symbol system. By "sufficient" we mean that any physical symbol system of sufficient size can be organised to exhibit general intelligence.[4]

Newell and Simon trace the roots of their hypothesis back to Gottlob Frege, Bertrand Russell and Alfred North Whitehead,[5] but Frege and company were of course themselves heirs to a long tradition stretching down from Plato through Descartes, who thought that all understanding consisted of forming and manipulating appropriate representations, that these representations could be analysed into primitive elements (*naturas simplices*) and that all phenomena could be understood as complex combinations of these simple elements. Moreover, at the same time, Hobbes had implicitly assumed that the elements were formal components related by purely syntactic operations, so that reasoning could be reduced to calculation. "When a man reasons, he does nothing else but conceive a sum total from addition of parcels", Hobbes wrote, "for REASON … is nothing but reckoning …"[6] Finally, Leibniz, working out the classical idea of mathesis – the formalisation of everything – sought support to develop a universal symbol system so that "we can assign to every object its determined characteristic number."[7] According to Leibniz, in understanding, we analyse concepts into simpler elements. In order to avoid a regress into ever more simple elements, there must be ultimate simples in terms of which all complex concepts can be understood. Moreover, if concepts are to apply to the world, there must be simple features that these elements represent. Leibniz envisaged "a kind of alphabet of human thoughts"[8] whose "characters must show, when they are used in demonstrations, some kinds of connection, grouping and order which are also found in the objects."[9]

    Ludwig Wittgenstein, drawing on Frege and Russell, stated in his *Tractatus Logico-Philosophicus* the pure form of this syntactic, representational view of the relation of the mind to reality. He defined the world as the totality of logically independent atomic facts:

1.1 The world is the totality of facts, not of things.

Facts in turn, he held, could be exhaustively analysed into primitive objects:

2.01 An atomic fact is a combination of objects …
2.0124 If all objects are given, then thereby all atomic facts are given.

These facts, their constituents and their logical relations, Wittgenstein claimed, were represented in the mind:

2.1 We make to ourselves pictures of facts.
2.15 That the elements of the picture are combined with one another in a definite way, represents that the things are so combined with each other.[10]

AI can be thought of as the attempt to find the primitive elements and logical relations in the subject (man or computer) that mirror the primitive objects and their relations that make up the world. Newell and Simon's physical symbol system hypothesis in effect turns the Wittgensteinian vision (which is itself the culmination of the classical rationalist philosophical tradition) into an empirical claim and bases a research programme on it.

The opposed intuition, that we should set about creating AI by modelling the brain rather than the mind's symbolic representation of the world, drew its inspiration not from philosophy but from what was soon to be called "neuroscience". It was directly inspired by the work of Hebb, who in 1949 suggested that a mass of neurons could learn, if when neuron A and neuron B were simultaneously excited, that excitation increased the strength of the connection between them.[11]

This lead was followed by Frank Rosenblatt, who reasoned that since intelligent behaviour based on our representation of the world was likely to be hard to formalise, AI should instead attempt to automate the procedures by which a network of neurons learns to discriminate patterns and respond appropriately. As Rosenblatt put it:

The implicit assumption [of the symbol manipulating research programme] is that it is relatively easy to specify the behaviour that we want the system to perform, and that the challenge is then to design a device or mechanism which will effectively carry out this behaviour ... [I]t is both easier and more profitable to axiomatise the physical system and then investigate this system analytically to determine its behaviour than to axiomatise the behaviour and then design a physical system by techniques of logical synthesis.[12]

Another way to put the difference between the two research programmes is that those seeking symbolic representations were looking for a formal structure that would give the computer the ability to solve a certain class of problems or discriminate certain types of patterns. Rosenblatt, on the other hand, wanted to build a physical device, or to simulate such a device on a digital computer, that could then generate its own abilities:

Many of the models which we have heard discussed are concerned with the question of what logical structure a system must have if it is to exhibit some property X. This is essentially a question about a static system ... An alternative way of looking at the question is: what kind of system can evolve property X? I think we can show a number of interesting cases that the second question can be solved without having an answer to the first.[13]

Both approaches met with immediate and startling success. By 1956, Newell and Simon had succeeded in programming a computer using symbolic representations to solve simple puzzles and prove theorems in the propositional calculus. On the basis of these early impressive results it looked as if the physical symbol system hypothesis was about to be confirmed, and Newell and Simon were understandably euphoric. Simon announced:

It is not my aim to surprise or shock you ... but the simplest way I can summarise is to say that there are now in the world machines that think, that learn and that create. Moreover, their ability to do these things is going to increase rapidly until – in a distant future – the range of problems they can handle will be coextensive with the range to which the human mind has been applied.[14]

He and Newell explained:

We now have the elements of a theory of heuristic (as contrasted with algorithmic) problem solving; and we can use this theory both to understand human heuristic processes and to simulate such processes with digital computers. Intuition, insight and learning are no longer exclusive possessions of humans: any large high-speed computer can be programmed to exhibit them also.[15]

Rosenblatt put his ideas to work in a type of device that he called a "perceptron".[16] By 1956, Rosenblatt was able to "train" a perceptron to classify certain types of patterns as similar and to separate these from other patterns that were dissimilar. By 1959 he too was jubilant and felt his approach had been vindicated:

It seems clear that the ... perceptron introduces a new kind of information processing automaton: for the first time we have a machine which is capable of having original ideas. As an analogue of the biological brain, the perceptron, more precisely, the theory of statistical separability, seems to come closer to meeting the requirements of a functional explanation of the nervous system than any system previously proposed ... As concept, it would seem that the perceptron has established beyond doubt the feasibility and principle of non- human systems which may embody human cognitive functions ... The future of information processing devices which operate on statistical rather than logical principles seems to be clearly indicated.[17]

In the early sixties, both approaches looked equally promising and both made themselves equally vulnerable by making exaggerated claims. Yet the results of the internal war between the two research programmes were surprisingly asymmetrical. By 1970, the brain simulation research, which had its paradigm in the perceptron, was reduced to a few lonely, underfunded efforts, while those who proposed using digital computers as symbol manipulators had undisputed control of the resources, graduate programmes, journals and symposia that constitute a flourishing research programme.

Reconstructing how this came about is complicated by the myth of manifest destiny that any ongoing research programme generates. Thus, it looks to the victors as if symbolic information processing won out because it was on the right track, while the neural network or connectionist approach lost because it simply didn't work. But this account of the history of the field is a retrospective illusion. Both research programmes had ideas worth exploring, and both had deep unrecognised problems.

Each position had its detractors, and what they said was essentially the same: each approach had shown that it could solve certain easy problems, but that there was no reason to think either group could extrapolate its methods to real-world complexity. Indeed, there was evidence that as problems got more complex, the computation required by both approaches would grow exponentially and so would soon become intractable. In 1969, Marvin Minsky and Seymour Papert said of Rosenblatt's perceptron:

Rosenblatt's schemes quickly took root, and soon there were perhaps as many as a hundred groups, large and small, experimenting with the model ... The results of these hundreds of projects and experiments were generally disappointing, and the explanations inconclusive. The machines usually work quite well on very simple problems but deteriorate very rapidly as the tasks assigned to them get harder.[18]

Three years later, Sir James Lighthill, after reviewing work using heuristic programs such as Simon's and Minsky's reached a strikingly similar negative conclusion:

Most workers in AI research and in related fields confess to a pronounced feeling of disappointment in what has been achieved in the past 25 years. Workers entered the field around 1950, and even around 1960, with high hopes that are very far from having been realised in 1972. In no part of the field have the discoveries made so far produced the major impact that was then promised ... One rather general cause for the disappointments that have been experienced: failure to recognise the implications of the "combinatorial explosion". This is a general obstacle to the construction of a ... system on a large knowledge base which results from the explosive growth of any combinatorial expression, representing numbers of possible ways of grouping elements of the knowledge base according to particular rules, as the base's size increases.[19]

As David Rumelhart and David Zipser have succinctly summed it up "Combinatorial explosion catches you sooner or later, though sometimes in different ways in parallel than in serial."[20] Both sides had, as Jerry Fodor once put it, walked into a game of three-dimensional chess, thinking it was tic-tac-toe. Why, then, so early in the game, with so little known and so much to learn, did one team of researchers triumph at the total expense of the other? Why, at this crucial branchpoint, did the symbolic representation project become the only game in town?

Everyone who knows the history of the field will be able to point to the proximal cause. About 1965, Minsky and Papert, who were running a laboratory at MIT dedicated to the symbol- manipulation approach and therefore competing for support with the perceptron projects, began circulating drafts of a book attacking the idea of the perceptron. In the book they made clear their scientific position:

Perceptrons have been widely publicised as "pattern recognition" or "learning" machines and as such have been discussed in a large number of books, journal articles and voluminous "reports". Most of this writing ... is without scientific value.[21]

But their attack was also a philosophical crusade. They rightly saw that traditional reliance on reduction to logical primitives was being challenged by a new holism:

Both of the present authors (first independently and later together) became involved with a somewhat therapeutic compulsion: to dispel what we feared to be the first shadows of a "holistic" or *Gestalt* misconception that would threaten to haunt the fields of engineering and artificial intelligence as it had earlier haunted biology and psychology.[22]

They were quite right. Artificial neural nets may, but need not, allow an interpretation of their hidden nodes* in terms of features a human being could recognise and use to solve the problem. While neural network modelling itself is committed to neither view, it can be demonstrated that association does not require that the hidden nodes be interpretable. Holists like Rosenblatt happily assumed that individual nodes or patterns of nodes were not picking out fixed features of the domain.

Minsky and Papert were so intent on eliminating all competition and so secure in the atomistic tradition that runs from Descartes to early Wittgenstein, that their book suggests much more than it actually demonstrates. They set out to analyse the capacity of a one-layer perceptron† while completely ignoring in the mathematical portion of their book Rosenblatt's chapters on multilayer machines and his proof of the convergence of a probabilistic learning algorithm based on back-propagation‡ of errors.[23] According to Rumelhart and McClelland:

Minsky and Papert set out to show which functions can and cannot be computed by [one-layer] machines. They demonstrated, in particular, that such perceptrons are unable to calculate such

---

*Hidden nodes are nodes that neither directly detect the input to the net nor constitute its output. They are, however, either directly or indirectly linked by connections with adjustable strengths to the nodes detecting the input and those constituting the output.

†A one-layer network has no hidden nodes, while multilayer networks do contain hidden nodes.

‡Back-propagation of errors requires recursively computing, starting with the output nodes, the effects of changing strengths of connections on the difference between the desired output and the output produced by an input. The weights are then adjusted during learning to reduce the difference.

mathematical functions as parity (whether an odd or even number of points are on the retina) or the topological function of correctness (whether all points that are on are connected to all other points that are on either directly or via other points that are also on) without making use of absurdly large numbers of predicates. The analysis is extremely elegant and demonstrates the importance of a mathematical approach to analysing computational systems.[24]

But the implications of the analysis are quite limited. Rumelhart and McClelland continue:

Essentially ... although Minsky and Papert were exactly correct in their analysis of the one-layer perceptron, the theorems don't apply to systems which are even a little more complex. In particular, it doesn't apply to multilayer systems nor to systems that allow feedback loops.[25]

Yet in the conclusion to *Perceptrons*, when Minsky and Papert ask themselves the question, "Have you considered perceptrons with many layers?", they give the impression, while leaving the question rhetorically open, of having settled it:

Well we have considered Gamba machines, which could be described as "two layers of perceptron". We have not found (by thinking or by studying the literature) any other really interesting class of multilayered machine, at least none whose principles seem to have a significant relation to those of the perceptron ... We consider it to be an important research problem to elucidate (or reject) our intuitive judgement that the extension is sterile.[26]

Their attack on *Gestalt* thinking in AI succeeded beyond their wildest dreams. Only an unappreciated few, among them Stephen Grossberg, James A. Anderson and Teuvo Kohonen, took up the "important research problem". Indeed, almost everybody else in AI assumed that neural nets had been laid to rest forever. Rumelhart and McClelland note:

Minsky and Papert's analysis of the limitations of the one- layer perceptron, coupled with some of the early successes of the symbolic processing approach in artificial intelligence, was enough to suggest to a large number of workers in the field that there was no future in perceptron-like computational devices for artificial intelligence and cognitive psychology.[27]

But why was it enough? Both approaches had produced some promising work and some unfounded promises.[28] It was too early to close accounts on either approach. Yet something in Minsky and Papert's book struck a responsive chord. It seemed AI workers shared the quasi-religious philosophical prejudice against holism that motivated the attack. One can see the power of the tradition, for example, in Newell and Simon's article on physical symbol systems. The article begins with the scientific hypothesis that the mind and the computer are intelligent by virtue of manipulating discrete symbols, but it ends with a revelation: "The study of logic and computers has revealed to us that intelligence resides in physical symbol systems".[29]

Holism could not compete with such intense philosophical convictions. Rosenblatt was discredited along with the hundreds of less responsible neural network research groups that his work had encouraged. His research money dried up and he had trouble getting his work published. By 1970, as far as AI was concerned, neural nets were dead. In his history of AI, Newell says that the issue of symbols versus numbers "is certainly not alive now and has not been for a long time."[30] Rosenblatt is not even mentioned in John Haugeland's or Margaret Boden's histories of the AI field.[31]

But blaming the rout of the connectionists on an anti-holistic prejudice is too simple. There was a deeper way philosophical assumptions influenced intuition and led to an overestimation of the importance of the early symbol-processing results. The way it looked at the time was that the perceptron people had to do an immense amount of mathematical analysis and calculating to solve even the most simple problems of pattern recognition, such as discriminating horizontal from vertical lines in different parts of the receptive field, while the symbol-manipulating approach had relatively effortlessly solved hard problems in cognition, such as proving theorems in logic and solving combinatorial puzzles. Even more important, it seemed that given the computing power available at the time, the neural net researchers could do only speculative neuroscience and psychology, while the simple programs of symbolic representationists were on their way to being useful. Behind this way of sizing up the situation was the assumption that thinking and pattern recognition are two distinct domains and that thinking is the more important of the two. As we shall see later in our discussion of the common-sense knowledge problem, to look at things this way is to ignore both the pre-eminent role of pattern discrimination in human expertise and also the background of common-sense understanding that is presupposed in everyday real-world thinking. Taking account of this background may well require pattern recognition.

This thought takes us back to the philosophical tradition. It was not just Descartes and his descendants who stood behind symbolic information processing, but all of Western philosophy. According to Heidegger, traditional philosophy is defined from the start by its focusing on facts in the world, while "passing over" the world as such.[32] This means that philosophy has from the start systematically ignored or distorted the everyday context of human activity.[33] The branch of the philosophical tradition that descends from Socrates through Plato, Descartes, Leibniz and Kant to conventional AI takes it for granted, in addition, that understanding a domain consists in having a theory of that domain. A theory formulates the relationships among objective, context-free elements (simples, primitives, features, attributes, factors, data points, cues etc.) in terms of abstract principles (covering laws, rules, programs etc.).

Plato held that in theoretical domains such as mathematics and perhaps ethics, thinkers apply explicit context-free rules or theories they have learned in another life, outside the everyday world. Once learned, such theories function in this world by controlling the thinker's mind, whether he or she is conscious of them or not. Plato's account did not apply to everyday skills but only to domains in which there is a priori knowledge. The success of theory in the natural sciences, however, reinforced the idea that in any orderly domain there must be some set of context-free elements and some abstract relations among those elements that account for the order of the domain and for man's ability to act intelligently in it. Thus, Leibniz boldly generalised the rationalist account to all forms of intelligent activity, even everyday practice:

The most important observations and turns of skill in all sorts of trades and professions are as yet unwritten. This fact is proved by experience when passing from theory to practice we desire to accomplish something. *Of course, we can also write up this practice, since it is at bottom just another theory more complex and particular.*[34] (emphasis added)

The symbolic information processing approach gains its assurance from this transfer to all domains of methods that have been developed by philosophers and that are successful in the natural sciences. Since, in this view, any domain must be formalisable, the way to do AI in any area is obviously to find the context-free elements and principles and to base a formal symbolic representation on this theoretical analysis. In this vein, Terry Winograd describes his AI work in terms borrowed from physical science:

We are concerned with developing a formalism, or "representation," with which to describe ... knowledge. We seek the "atoms" and "particles" of which it is built and the "forces" that act on it.[35]

No doubt theories about the universe are often built up gradually by modelling relatively simple and isolated systems and then making the model gradually more complex and integrating it with models of other domains. This is possible because all the phenomena are presumably the result of the lawlike relations between what Papert and Minsky call "structural primitives". Since no one argues for atomistic reduction in AI, it seems that AI workers just implicitly assume that the abstraction of elements from their everyday context, which defines philosophy and works in natural science, must also work in AI. This assumption may well account for the way the physical symbol system hypothesis so quickly turned into a revelation and for the ease with which Papert and Minsky's book triumphed over the holism of the perceptron.

Teaching philosophy at MIT in the mid-sixties, one of us – Hubert – was soon drawn into the debate over the possibility of AI. It was obvious that researchers such as Newell, Simon and Minsky were the heirs to the philosophical tradition. But given the conclusions of the later Wittgenstein and the early Heidegger, that did not seem to be a good omen for the reductionist research programme. Both these thinkers had called into question the very tradition on which symbolic information processing was based. Both were holists, both were struck by the importance of everyday practices, and both held that one could not have a theory of the everyday world.

It is one of the ironies of intellectual history that Wittgenstein's devastating attack on his own *Tractatus*, his *Philosophical Investigations*,[36] was published in 1953, just as AI took over the abstract, atomistic tradition he was attacking. After writing the *Tractatus*, Wittgenstein spent years doing what he called phenomenology[37] – looking in vain for the atomic facts and basic objects his theory required. He ended by abandoning his *Tractatus* and all rationalistic philosophy. He argued that the analysis of everyday situations into facts and rules (which is where most traditional philosophers and AI researchers think theory must begin) is itself only meaningful in some context and for some purpose. Thus, the elements chosen already reflect the goals and purposes for which they are carved out. When we try to find the ultimate context-free purpose-free elements, as we must if we are going to find the primitive symbols to feed a computer, we are in effect trying to free aspects of our experience of just that pragmatic organisation which makes it possible to use them intelligently in coping with everyday problems.

In the *Philosophical Investigations*, Wittgenstein directly criticised the logical atomism of the *Tractatus*:

"What lies behind the idea that names really signify simples?" Socrates says in the *Thaetetus*: "If I make no mistake, I have heard some people say this: there is no definition of the primary elements – so to speak – out of which we and everything else are composed ... But just as what consists of those primary elements is itself complex, so the names of the elements become descriptive language by being compounded together." Both Russell's "individuals" and my "objects" (*Tractatus Logico-Philosophicus*) were such primary elements. But what are the simple constituent parts of which reality is composed? ... It makes no sense at all to speak absolutely of the "simple parts of a chair."[38]

Already, in the 1920s, Martin Heidegger had reacted in a similar way against his mentor Edmund Husserl, who regarded himself as the culmination of the Cartesian tradition, and was therefore the grandfather of AI.[39] Husserl argued that an act of consciousness, or noesis, does not on its own grasp an object; rather, the act has intentionality (directedness) only by virtue of an "abstract form", or meaning in the noema correlated with the act.[40]

This meaning, or symbolic representation, as conceived by Husserl, is a complex entity that has a difficult job to perform. In *Ideas Pertaining to a Pure Phenomenology*,[41] Husserl bravely tried to explain how the noema gets the job done. Reference is provided by "predicate-senses" which, like Fregean Sinne, just have the remarkable property of picking out objects' atomic properties. These predicates are combined into complex "descriptions" of complex objects, as in Russell's theory of descriptions. For Husserl, who was close to Kant on this point, the noema contains a hierarchy of strict rules. Since Husserl thought of intelligence as a context-determined, goal-directed activity, the mental representation of any type of object had to provide a context, or a "horizon" of expectations or "predelineations" for structuring the incoming data: "a rule governing possible other consciousness of [the object] as identical-possible, as exemplifying essentially predelineated types."[42] The noema must contain a rule describing all the features that can be expected with certainty in exploring a certain type of object – features that remain "inviolably the same: as long as the objectivity remains intended as this one and of this kind."[43] The rule must also prescribe predelineations of properties that are possible, but not necessary, features of this type of object: "Instead of a completely determined sense, there is always, therefore, *A frame of empty sense*"[44]

In 1973, Marvin Minsky proposed a new data structure, remarkably similar to Husserl's, for representing everyday knowledge:

A *frame* is a data-structure for representing a stereotyped situation, like being in a certain kind of living room, or going to a child's birthday party ... We can think of a frame as a network of nodes and relations. The top levels of a frame are fixed, and represent things that are always true about the supposed situation. The lower levels have many terminals – slots that must be filled by specific instances or data. Each terminal can specify conditions its assignment must meet ... Much of the phenomenological power of the theory hinges on the inclusion of expectations and other kinds of presumptions. *A frame's terminals are normally already filled with "default" assignments.*[45]

In Minsky's model of a frame, the "top level" is a developed version of what, in Husserl's terminology, remains "inviolably the same" in the representation, and Husserl's predelineations have become "default assignments" – additional features that can normally be expected. The result is a step forward in AI techniques from a passive model of information processing to one that tries to take account of the interactions between a knower and the world.

The task of AI thus converges with the task of transcendental phenomenology. Both must try in everyday domains to find frames constructed from a set of primitive predicates and their formal relations.

Heidegger, before Wittgenstein, carried out, in response to Husserl, a phenomenological description of the everyday world and everyday objects like chairs and hammers. Like Wittgenstein, he found that the everyday world could not be represented as a set of context-free elements. It was Heidegger who forced Husserl to face precisely this problem by pointing out that there are other ways of "encountering" things than relating to them as objects defined by a set of predicates. When we use a piece of equipment as a hammer,

Heidegger said, we actualise a skill (which need not be represented in the mind) in the context of a socially organised nexus of equipment, purposes and human roles (which need not be represented as a set of facts). This context, or world, and our everyday ways of skilful coping in it, which Heidegger called "circumspection", are not something we think but part of our socialisation, which forms the way we are. Heidegger concluded:

The context ... can be taken formally in the sense of a system of relations. But ... the phenomenal content of these "relations" and "relata" ... is such that they resist any sort of mathematical functionalisation; nor are they merely something thought, first posited in an "act of thinking". They are rather relationships in which concernful circumspection as such already dwells.[46]

This defines the splitting of the ways between Husserl and AI on the one hand and Heidegger and later Wittgenstein on the other. The crucial question becomes: "Can there be a theory of the everyday world, as rationalist philosophers have always held? Or is the common-sense background rather a combination of skills, practices, discriminations and so on which are not intentional states and so *a fortiori* do not have any representational content to be explicated in terms of elements and rules?"

By making a move that was soon to become familiar in AI circles, Husserl tried to avoid the problem Heidegger posed. Husserl claimed that the world, the background of significance, the everyday context, was merely a very complex system of facts correlated with a complex system of beliefs, which, since they have truth conditions, he called validities. One could, in principle, he held, suspend one's own dwelling in the world and achieve a detached description of the human belief system. One could thus complete the task that had been implicit in philosophy since Socrates: one could make explicit the beliefs and principles underlying all intelligent behaviour. As Husserl put it:

Even the background ... of which we are always concurrently conscious but which is momentarily irrelevant and remains completely unnoticed, still functions according to its implicit validities.[47]

Since he firmly believed that the shared background could be made explicit as a belief system, Husserl was ahead of his time in raising the question of the possibility of AI. After discussing the possibility that a formal axiomatic system might describe experience and pointing out that such a system of axioms and primitives – at least as we know it in geometry – could not describe everyday shapes such as "scalloped" and "lens-shaped", Husserl left open the question whether these everyday concepts could nevertheless be formalised. (This was like raising and leaving open the AI question whether one can axiomatise common-sense physics.) Taking up Leibniz's dream of a mathesis of all experience, Husserl added:

The pressing question is ... whether there could not be ... an idealising procedure that substitutes pure and strict ideals for intuited data and that would ... serve ... as the basic medium for a mathesis of experience.[48]

But, as Heidegger predicted, the task of writing out a complete theoretical account of everyday life turned out to be much harder than initially expected. Husserl's project ran into serious trouble, and there are signs that Minsky's has too. During twenty-five years of trying to spell out the components of the subject's representation of everyday objects, Husserl found that he had to include more and more of the subject's common-sense understanding of the everyday world:

To be sure, even the tasks that present themselves when we take single types of objects as restricted clues prove to be extremely complicated and always lead to extensive disciplines when we penetrate more deeply. That is the case, for example, with ... spatial objects (to say nothing of a Nature) as such, of psycho-physical being and humanity as such, culture as such.[49]

He spoke of the noema's "huge concreteness"[50] and of its "tremendous complication"[51] and he sadly concluded at the age of seventy-five that he was a perpetual beginner and that phenomenology was an "infinite task".[52]

There are hints in his paper "A framework for representing knowledge" that Minsky has embarked on the same "infinite task" that eventually overwhelmed Husserl:

Just constructing a knowledge base is a major intellectual research problem ... We still know far too little about the contents and structure of commonsense knowledge. A "minimal" commonsense system must "know" something about cause–effect, time, purpose, locality, process and types of knowledge ... We need a serious epistemological research effort in this area.[53]

To a student of contemporary philosophy, Minsky's naivete and faith are astonishing. Husserl's phenomenology was just such a research effort. Indeed, philosophers from Socrates through Leibniz to early Wittgenstein carried on serious epistemological research in this area for two thousand years without notable success.

In the light of Wittgenstein's reversal and Heidegger's devastating critique of Husserl, one of us – Hubert – predicted trouble for symbolic information processing. As Newell notes in his history of AI, this warning was ignored:

Dreyfus's central intellectual objection ... is that the analysis of the context of human action into discrete elements is doomed to failure. This objection is grounded in phenomenological philosophy. Unfortunately this appears to be a nonissue as far as AI is concerned. The answers, refutations and analyses that have been forthcoming to Dreyfus's writings have simply not engaged this issue – which indeed would be a novel issue if it were to come to the fore.[54]

The trouble was, indeed, not long in coming to the fore, as the everyday world took its revenge on AI as it had on traditional philosophy. As we see it, the research programme launched by Newell and Simon has gone through three ten-year stages. From 1955 to 1965, two research themes, representation and search, dominated the field then called "cognitive simulation". Newell and Simon showed, for example, how a computer could solve a class of problems with the general heuristic search principle known as means–ends analysis – namely to use any available operation that reduces the distance between the description of the current situation and the description of the goal. They then abstracted this heuristic technique and incorporated it into their General Problem Solver (GPS).

The second stage (1965–1975), led by Marvin Minsky and Seymour Papert at MIT, was concerned with what facts and rules to represent. The idea was to develop methods for dealing systematically with knowledge in isolated domains called "microworlds". Famous programs written around 1970 at MIT include Terry Winograd's SHRDLU, which could obey commands given in a subset of natural language about a simplified "blocks-world"; Thomas Evan's analogy problem program; David Waltz's scene analysis program and Patrick Winston's program which could learn concepts from examples.

The hope was that the restricted and isolated microworlds could be gradually made more realistic and combined so as to approach real-world understanding. But researchers confused two domains, which, following Heidegger, we shall distinguish as "universe" and "world". A set of interrelated facts may constitute a universe, like the physical universe, but it does not constitute a world. The latter, like the world of business, the world of theatre or the world of the physicist, is an organised body of objects, purposes, skills and practices on the basis of which human activities have meaning or make sense. To see the difference, one can contrast the meaningless physical universe with the meaningful world of the discipline of physics. The world of physics, the business world and the theatre world make sense only against a background of common human concerns. They are local elaborations of the one common-sense world we all share. That is, subworlds are not related like isolable physical systems to the larger systems they compose but rather are local elaborations of the whole that they presuppose. Microworlds are not worlds but isolated meaningless domains, and it has gradually become clear that there is no way that they could be combined and extended to arrive at the world of everyday life.

In its third stage, roughly from 1975 to the present, AI has been wrestling with what has come to be called the common- sense knowledge problem. The representation of knowledge was always a central problem for work in AI, but the two earlier periods – cognitive simulation and microworlds – were characterised by an attempt to avoid the problem of common- sense knowledge by seeing how much could be done with as little knowledge as possible. By the middle 1970s, however, the issue had to be faced. Various data structures, such as Minsky's frames and Roger Schank's scripts, have been tried without success. The common-sense knowledge problem has kept AI from even beginning to fulfil Simon's prediction a quarter of a century ago that "within twenty years machines will be capable of doing any work a man can do."[55]

Indeed, the common-sense knowledge problem has blocked all progress in theoretical AI for the past decade. Winograd was one of the first to see the limitations of SHRDLU and all script and frame attempts to extend the microworlds approach. Having "lost faith" in AI, he now teaches Heidegger in his computer science course at Stanford and points out "the difficulty of formalising the commonsense background that determines which scripts, goals and strategies are relevant and how they interact."[56]

What sustains AI in this impasse is the conviction that the common-sense knowledge problem must be solvable, since human beings have obviously solved it. But human beings may not normally use common-sense knowledge at all. As Heidegger and Wittgenstein pointed out, what common-sense understanding amounts to might well be everyday know-how. By "know-how", we do not mean procedural rules but simply what to do in a vast number of special cases.[57] For example, common-sense physics has turned out to be extremely hard to spell out in a set of facts and rules. When one tries, one either requires more common sense to understand the facts and rules one finds or else one produces formulae of such complexity that it seems highly unlikely they are in a child's mind.

Doing theoretical physics also requires background skills that may not be formalisable, but the domain itself can be described by abstract laws that make no reference to these background skills. AI researchers mistakenly conclude that common-sense physics too must be expressible as a set of abstract principles. But it just may be that the problem of finding a theory of common-sense physics is insoluble because the domain has no theoretical structure. By playing with all sorts of solids and liquids every day for several years, a child may simply learn to discriminate prototypical cases of solids, liquids and so on and learn typical skilled responses to their typical behaviour in typical circumstances. The same might well be the case for the social world. If background understanding is indeed a skill and if skills are based on whole patterns and not on rules, we would expect symbolic representations to fail to capture our common-sense understanding.

In the light of this impasse, classical symbol-based AI appears more and more to be a perfect example of what Imre Lakatos has called a degenerating research programme.[58] As we have seen, AI began auspiciously with Newell and Simon's work at Rand and by the late 1960s turned into a flourishing research programme. Minsky predicted that "within a generation the problem of creating 'artificial intelligence' will be substantially solved."[59] Then, rather suddenly, the field ran into unexpected difficulties. It turned out to be much harder than one expected to formulate a theory of common sense. It was not, as Minsky had hoped, just a question of cataloguing a few hundred thousand facts. The common-sense knowledge problem became the centre of concern. Minsky's mood changed completely in five years. He told a reporter that "The AI problem is one of the hardest science has ever undertaken."[60]

The rationalist tradition had finally been put to an empirical test, and it had failed. The idea of producing a formal, atomistic theory of the everyday common-sense world and of representing that theory in a symbol manipulator had run into just the difficulties that Heidegger and Wittgenstein had discovered. Frank Rosenblatt's intuition that it would be hopelessly difficult to formalise the world and thus to give a formal specification of intelligent behaviour had been vindicated. His repressed research programme (using the computer to instantiate a holistic model of an idealised brain), which had never really been refuted, became a live option again.

In journalistic accounts of the history of AI, Rosenblatt is vilified by anonymous detractors as a snake-oil salesman:

Present-day researchers remember that Rosenblatt was given to steady and extravagant statements about the performance of his machine. "He was a press agent's dream", one scientist says, "a real medicine man. To hear him tell it, the Perceptron was capable of fantastic things. And maybe it was. But you couldn't prove it by the work Frank did."[61]

In fact, he was much clearer about the capabilities and limitations of the various types of perceptrons than Simon and Minsky were about their symbolic programs.[62] Now he is being rehabilitated. David Rumelhart, Geoffrey Hinton and James McClelland reflect this new appreciation of his pioneering work:

Rosenblatt's work was very controversial at the time, and the specific models he proposed were not up to all the hopes he had for them. But his vision of the human information processing system, as a dynamic, interactive, self-organising system lies at the core of the PDP approach.[63] The studies of perceptrons ... clearly anticipated many of the results in use today. The critique of perceptrons by Minsky and Papert was widely misinterpreted as destroying their credibility, whereas the work simply showed limitations on the power of the most limited class of perceptron-like mechanisms, and said nothing about more powerful multiple layer models.[64]

Frustrated AI researchers, tired of clinging to a research programme that Jerry Lettvin characterised in the early 1980s as "the only straw afloat", flocked to the new paradigm. Rumelhart and McClelland's book, *Parallel Distributed Processing*, sold six thousand copies the day it went on the market, and thirty thousand are now in print. As Paul Smolensky put it:

In the past half-decade the connectionist approach to cognitive modelling has grown from an obscure cult claiming a few true believers to a movement so vigorous that recent meetings of the Cognitive Science Society have begun to look like connectionist pep rallies.[65]

If multilayered networks succeed in fulfilling their promise, researchers will have to give up the conviction of Descartes, Husserl and early Wittgenstein that the only way to produce intelligent behaviour is to mirror the world with a formal theory in mind. Worse, one may have to give up the more basic intuition at the source of philosophy that there must be a theory of every aspect of reality – that is, there must be elements and principles in terms of which one can account for the intelligibility of any domain. Neural networks may show that Heidegger, later Wittgenstein and Rosenblatt were right in thinking that we behave intelligently in the world without having a theory of that world. If a theory is not necessary to explain intelligent behaviour, we have to be prepared to raise the question whether in everyday domains, such a theoretical explanation is even possible.

Neural net modellers, influenced by symbol-manipulating AI, are expending considerable effort, once their nets have been trained to perform a task, in trying to find the features represented by individual nodes and sets of nodes. Results thus far are equivocal. Consider Hinton's network for learning concepts by means of distributed representations.[66] The network can be trained to encode relationships in a domain that human beings conceptualise in terms of features, without the network being given the features that human beings use. Hinton produces examples of cases in which some nodes in the trained network can be interpreted as corresponding to the features that human beings pick out, though these nodes only roughly correspond to those features. Most nodes, however, cannot be interpreted semantically at all. A feature used in a symbolic representation is either present or not. In the net, however, although certain nodes are more active when a certain feature is present in the domain, the amount of activity not only varies with the presence or absence of this feature, but is affected by the presence or absence of other features as well.

Hinton has picked a domain – family relationships – that is constructed by human beings precisely in terms of the features that human beings normally notice, such as generation and nationality. Hinton then analyses those cases in which, starting with certain random initial-connection strengths, some nodes can, after learning, be interpreted as representing those features. Calculations using Hinton's model show, however, that even his net seems to learn its associations for some random initial-connection strengths without any obvious use of these everyday features.

In one very limited sense, any successfully trained multilayer net can be interpreted in terms of features – not everyday features but what we shall call highly abstract features. Consider the simple case of layers of binary units activated by feed-forward, but not lateral or feedback, connections. To construct such an account from a network that has learned certain associations, each node one level above the input nodes could, on the basis of the connections to it, be interpreted as detecting when one of a certain set of input patterns is present. (Some of these patterns will be the ones used in training, and some will never have been used.) If the set of input patterns that a particular node detects is given an invented name (it almost certainly won't have a name in our vocabulary), the node could be interpreted as detecting the highly abstract feature so named. Hence, every node one level above the input level could be characterised as a feature detector. Similarly every node a level above those nodes could be interpreted as detecting a higher-order feature, defined as the presence of one of a specified set of patterns among the first level of feature detectors. And so on up the hierarchy.

The fact that intelligence, defined as the knowledge of a certain set of associations appropriate to a domain, can always be accounted for in terms of relations among a number of highly abstract features of a skill domain does not, however, preserve the rationalist intuition that these explanatory features must capture the essential structure of the domain so that one could base a theory on them. If the net were taught one more association of an input–output pair (where the input prior to training produced an output different from the one to be learned), the interpretation of at least some of the nodes would have to be changed. So the features that some of the nodes picked out before the last instance of training would turn out not to have been invariant structural features of the domain.

Once one has abandoned the philosophical approach of classical AI and accepted the atheoretical claim of neural net modelling, one question remains: How much of everyday intelligence can such a network be expected to capture? Classical AI researchers are quick to point out – as Rosenblatt already noted – that neural net modellers have so far had difficulty dealing with stepwise problem solving. Connectionists respond that they are confident that they will solve that problem in time. This response, however, reminds one too much of the way that the symbol manipulators in the sixties responded to the criticism that their programs were poor at the perception of patterns. The old struggle continues between intellectualists, who think that because they can do context-free logic they have a handle on everyday cognition but are poor at understanding perception, and Gestaltists, who have the rudiments of an account of perception but no account of everyday cognition.[67] One might think, using the metaphor of the right and left brain, that perhaps the brain or the mind uses each strategy when appropriate. The problem would then be how to combine the strategies. One cannot just switch back and forth, for as Heidegger and the Gestaltists saw, the pragmatic background plays a crucial role in determining relevance, even in everyday logic and problem solving, and experts in any field, even logic, grasp operations in terms of their functional similarities.

It is even premature to consider combining the two approaches, since so far neither has accomplished enough to be on solid ground. Neural network modelling may simply be getting a deserved chance to fail, as did the symbolic approach.

Still, there is an important difference to bear in mind as each research programme struggles on. The physical symbol system approach seems to be failing because it is simply false to assume that there must be a theory of every domain. Neural network modelling, however, is not committed to this or any other philosophical assumption. Nevertheless, building an interactive net sufficiently similar to the one our brain has evolved may be just too hard. Indeed, the common-sense knowledge problem, which has blocked the progress of symbolic representation techniques for over fifteen years, may be looming on the neural net horizon, although researchers may not yet recognise it. All neural net modellers agree that for a net to be intelligent, it must be able to generalise; that is, given sufficient examples of inputs associated with one particular output, it should associate further inputs of the same type with that same output. The question arises, however: What counts as the same type? The designer of a net has in mind a specific definition of the type required for a reasonable generalisation and counts it a success if the net generalises to other instances of this type. But when the net produces an unexpected association, can one say it has failed to generalise? One could equally well say that the net has all along been acting on a different definition of the type in question, and that difference has just been revealed. (All the "continue this sequence" questions found in intelligence tests really have more than one possible answer, but most humans share a sense of what is simple and reasonable, and therefore acceptable.)

Neural network modellers attempt to avoid this ambiguity and make the net produce "reasonable" generalisations by considering only a prespecified allowable family of generalisations – that is, allowable transformations that will count as acceptable generalisations (the hypothesis space). These modellers then attempt to design the architecture of their nets so that they transform inputs into outputs only in ways that are in the hypothesis space. Generalisation will then be possible only on the designer's terms. While a few examples will be sufficient to identify uniquely the appropriate member of the hypothesis space, after enough examples, only one hypothesis will account for all the examples. The net will then have learned the appropriate generalisation principle. That is, all further input will produce what is, from the designer's point of view, the appropriate output.

The problem here is that the designer has determined by means of the architecture of the net that certain possible generalisations will never be found. All this is well and good for toy problems in which there is no question of what constitutes a reasonable generalisation, but in real-world situations a large part of human intelligence consists in generalising in ways that are appropriate to a context. If the designer restricts the net to a predefined class of appropriate responses, the net will be exhibiting the intelligence built into it by the designer for that context but will not have the common sense that would enable it to adapt to other contexts, as a truly human intelligence would.

Perhaps a net must share size, architecture and initial- connection configuration with the human brain if it is to share our sense of appropriate generalisation. If it is to learn from its own "experiences", to make associations that are humanlike rather than be taught to make associations that have been specified by its trainer, a net must also share our sense of appropriateness of output, and this means it must share our needs, desires and emotions, and have a humanlike body with appropriate physical movements, abilities and vulnerability to injury.

If Heidegger and Wittgenstein are right, human beings are much more holistic than neural nets. Intelligence has to be motivated by purposes in the organism and goals picked up by the organism from an ongoing culture. If the minimum unit of analysis is that of a whole organism geared into a whole cultural world, neural nets as well as symbolically programmed computers still have a very long way to go.

Notes

1 Wittgenstein, Ludwig (1982) Last writings on the philosophy of psychology, vol 1. Chicago University Press, Chicago, p 504 (66c) (Translation corrected)

2 Rumelhart, David E and Norman, Donald A (1981) A comparison of models. In: Hinton G, Anderson J (ed) Parallel models of associative memory. Lawrence Earlbaum Associates, Hillsdale NJ, p 1981

3 Newell, Allen (1983) Intellectual issues in the history of artificial intelligence. In: Machlup F, Mansfield U (ed) The study of information: Interdisciplinary messages. Wiley, New York, p 196

4 Newell, Allen and Simon, Herbert (1981) Computer science as empirical enquiry: Symbols and search. Reprinted in Haugeland J (ed) Mind design. MIT Press, Cambridge, Mass, p 41

5 Newell, Allen and Simon, Herbert (1981) Computer science as empirical enquiry: Symbols and search. Reprinted in Haugeland J (ed) Mind design. MIT Press, Cambridge, Mass, p 42

6 Thomas Hobbes (1958) Leviathan. Library of Liberal Arts, New York, p 45

7 Wiener, Philip (ed) (1951) Leibniz, Selections. Scribner, New York, p 18

8 Wiener, Philip (ed) (1951) Leibniz, Selections. Scribner, New York, p 20

9 Wiener, Philip (ed) (1951) Leibniz, Selections. Scribner, New York, p 10

10 Wittgenstein, Ludwig (1960) Tractatus logico- philosophicus. Routledge and Kegan Paul, London

11 Hebb DO (1949) The organisation of behaviour. Wiley, New York

12 Rosenblatt, Frank (1962) Strategic approaches to the study of brain models. In: von Foerster H (ed) Principles of self-organisation. Pergamon, New York, p 386

13 Rosenblatt, Frank (1962) Strategic approaches to the study of brain models. In: von Foerster H (ed) Principles of self-organisation. Pergamon, New York, p 387

14 Simon, Herbert and Newell, Allen (1958) Heuristic problem solving: The next advance in operations research. Operations Research 6:6

15 Ibid. Heuristic rules are rules that when used by human beings are said to be based on experience or judgement. Such rules frequently lead to plausible solutions to problems or increase the efficiency of a problem-solving procedure. Whereas algorithms guarantee a correct solution (if there is one) in a finite time, heuristics only increase the likelihood of finding a plausible solution.

16 David Rumelhart, James McClelland and the PDP Research Group in their recent collection of papers *Parallel Distributed Processing: Explorations in the Microstructure of Cognition*, vol 1 (MIT Press, Cambridge, MA, 1986), describe the perceptron as follows:

> Such machines consist of what is called a retina, an array of binary inputs sometimes taken to be arranged in a two- dimensional spatial layout; a set of predicates, a set of binary threshold units with fixed connections to a subset of units in the retina such that each predicate computes some local function over the subset of units to which it is connected; and one or more decision units, with modifiable connections to the predicates. (p 111)

They contrast the way a parallel distributed processing (PDP) model like the perceptron stores information with the way information is stored by symbolic representation:

> In most models, knowledge is stored as a static copy of a pattern. Retrieval amounts to finding the pattern in long-term memory and copying it into a buffer or working memory. There is no real difference

between the stored representation in long-term memory and the active representation in working memory. In PDP models, thought, this is not the case. In these models, the patterns themselves are not stored. Rather, what is stored is the connection strengths between units that allow these patterns to be re-created. (p 31)

[K]nowledge about any individual pattern is not stored in the connections of a special unit reserved for that pattern but is distributed over the connections among a large number of processing units. (p 33)

This new notion of representation led directly to Rosenblatt's idea that such machines should be able to acquire their ability through learning rather than by being programmed with features and rules:

If the knowledge is [in] the strengths of the connections, learning must be a matter of finding the right connection strengths, so that the right patterns of activation will be produced under the right circumstances. This is an extremely important property of this class of models, for it opens up the possibility that an information processing mechanism could learn, as a result of tuning its connections, to capture the interdependencies between activations that it is exposed to in the course of processing. (p 32)

17 Rosenblatt, Frank (1958) Mechanisation of thought processes. In: Proceedings of a symposium held at the National Physical Laboratory, vol 1. HMSO, London, p 449
18 Minsky, Marvin and Papert, Seymour (1969) Perceptrons: An introduction to computational geometry. MIT Press, Cambridge, MA, p 19
19 Lighthill, James (1973) Artificial intelligence: A general survey. In: Artificial intelligence: A paper symposium. Science Research Council, London
20 Rumelhart, David and McClelland, James (1986) Parallel distributed processing: Explorations in the microstructure of cognition, vol 1. MIT Press, Cambridge, MA, p 158
21 Minsky, Marvin and Papert, Seymour (1969) Perceptrons: An introduction to computational geometry. MIT Press, Cambridge, MA, p 4
22 Minsky, Marvin and Papert, Seymour (1969) Perceptrons: An introduction to computational geometry. MIT Press, Cambridge, MA, p 19
23 Rosenblatt, Frank (1962) Principles of neurodynamics, perceptrons and the theory of brain mechanisms. Spartan, Washington DC, p 292. See also:

   The addition of a fourth layer of signal transmission units, or cross-coupling the A-units of a three-layer perceptron, permits the solution of generalisation problems over arbitrary transformation groups. (p 576)
   In back-coupled perceptrons, selective attention to familiar objects in a complex field can occur. It is also possible for such a perceptron to attend selectively to objects which move differentially relative to their background. (p 576)

24 Rumelhart, David and McClelland, James (1986) Parallel distributed processing: Explorations in the microstructure of cognition, vol 1. MIT Press, Cambridge, MA, p 111
25 Rumelhart, David and McClelland, James (1986) Parallel distributed processing: Explorations in the microstructure of cognition, vol 1. MIT Press, Cambridge, MA, p 112

26 Minsky, Marvin and Papert, Seymour (1969) Perceptrons: An introduction to computational geometry. MIT Press, Cambridge, MA, p 231–232

27 Rumelhart, David and McClelland, James (1986) Parallel distributed processing: Explorations in the microstructure of cognition, vol 1. MIT Press, Cambridge, MA, p 112

28 For an evaluation of the symbolic representation approach's actual successes up to 1978, see Hubert Dreyfus, *What Computers Can't Do*, 2nd edn (Harper & Row, New York, 1979)

29 Newell, Allen and Simon, Herbert (1981) Computer science as empirical enquiry: Symbols and search. Reprinted in Haugeland J (ed) Mind design. MIT Press, Cambridge, Mass, p 197

30 Newell, Allen (1983) Intellectual issues in the history of artificial intelligence. In: Machlup F, Mansfield U (ed) The study of information: Interdisciplinary messages. Wiley, New York, p 10

31 Haugeland, John (1985) Artificial intelligence: The very idea. MIT Press, Cambridge, MA; and Boden, Margater (1977) Artificial intelligence and natural man. Basic Books, New York. Work on neural nets was continued in a marginal way in psychology and neuroscience. James A. Anderson at Brown University continued to defend a net model in psychology, although he had to live off other researchers' grants, and Stephen Grossberg worked out an elegant mathematical implementation of elementary cognitive capacities. For Anderson's position, see "Neural models with cognitive implications" in *Basic Processing in Reading*, ed Laberse D and Samuels SJ (Lawrence Earlbaum Associates, Hillsdale, NJ, 1978). For examples of Grossberg's work during the dark ages, see his book *Studies of Mind and Brain: Neural Principles of Learning, Perception, Development, Cognition and Motor Control* (Reidel Press, Boston, 1982). Kohonen's early work is reported in *Associative Memory – A System–Theoretical Approach* (Springer-Verlag, Berlin, 1977)

   At MIT, Minsky continued to lecture on neural nets and to assign theses investigating their logical properties. But according to Papert, Minsky did so only because nets had interesting mathematical properties, whereas nothing interesting could be proved concerning the properties of symbol systems. Moreover, many AI researchers assumed that since Turing machines were symbol manipulators and Turing had proved that Turing machines could compute anything, he had proved that all intelligibility could be captured by logic. On this view, a holistic (and in those days statistical) approach needed justification, while the symbolic AI approach did not. This confidence, however, was based on confusing the uninterpreted symbols of a Turing machine (zeros and ones) with the semantically interpreted symbols of AI.

32 Heidegger, Martin (1962) Being and time. Harper & Row, New York, sect 14–21; also Dreyfus, Hubert (1988) Being-in- the-world: A commentary on Division I of *Being and Time*. MIT Press, Cambridge, MA

33 According to Heidegger, Aristotle came closer than any other philosopher to understanding the importance of everyday activity, but even he succumbed to the distortion of the phenomenon of the everyday world implicit in common sense.

34 Wiener, Philip (ed) (1951) Leibniz, Selections. Scribner, New York, p 48

35 Winograd, Terry (1976) Artificial intelligence and language comprehension. In: Artificial intelligence and language comprehension. National Institute of Education, Washington DC, p 9

36 Wittgenstein, Ludwig (1953) Philosophical investigations. Basil Blackwell, Oxford

37 Wittgenstein, Ludwig (1975) Philosophical remarks. University of Chicago Press, Chicago

38 Wittgenstein, Ludwig (1975) Philosophical investigations. Basil Blackwell, Oxford, p 21

39 See Dreyfus, Hubert (ed) (1982) Husserl, intentionality and cognitive science. MIT Press, Cambridge, MA

40 "Der Sinn ... so wie wir ihn bestimmt haben, ist nicht ein konkretes Wesen im Gesamtbestande des Noema, sondern eine Art ihm einwohnender abstrakter Form." See Husserl, Edmund (1950) Ideen zu einer phanomenologie und phanomenologischen philosophie. Nijhoff, The Hague. For evidence that Husserl held that the noema accounts for the intentionality of mental activity, see Dreyfus, Hubert (1982) Husserl's perceptual noema. In: Dreyfus, Hubert (ed) Husserl, intentionality and cognitive science.

41 Husserl, Edmund (1982) Ideas pertaining to a pure phenomenology and to a phenomenological philosophy. Nijhoff, The Hague (translated by Kersten F)

42 Husserl, Edmund (1960) Cartesian meditations. Nijhoff, The Hague, p 45 (translated by Cairns D)

43 Husserl, Edmund (1960) Cartesian meditations. Nijhoff, The Hague, p 53 (translated by Cairns D)

44 Husserl, Edmund (1960) Cartesian meditations. Nijhoff, The Hague, p 51 (translated by Cairns D)

45 Minsky, Marvin (1981) A framework for representing knowledge. In: Haugeland, John (ed) Mind design. MIT Press, Cambridge, MA, p 96

46 Heidegger, Martin (1962) Being and time. Harper & Row, New York, pp 121–122

47 Edmund (1970) Crisis of European sciences and transcendental phenomenology. Northwestern University Press, Evanston, p 149 (translated by Carr D)

48 Husserl, Edmund (1969) Ideen zu einer phanomenologie und phanomenologischen philosophie, vol 5, book 3, Husserliana. Nijhoff, The Hague, p 134

49 Husserl, Edmund (1960) Cartesian meditations. Nijhoff, The Hague, pp 54–55

50 Husserl, Edmund (1969) Formal and transcendental logic. Nijhoff, The Hague, p 244 (translated by Cairns D)

51 Husserl, Edmund (1969) Formal and transcendental logic. Nijhoff, The Hague, p 246 (translated by Cairns D)

52 Husserl, Edmund (1970) Crisis of European sciences and transcendental phenomenology. Northwestern University Press, Evanston, p 291 (translated by Carr D)

53 Minsky, Marvin (1981) A framework for representing knowledge. In: Haugeland, John (ed) Mind design. MIT Press, Cambridge, MA, p 124

54 Newell, Allen (1983) Intellectual issues in the history of artificial intelligence. In: Machlup F, Mansfield U (ed) The study of information: Interdisciplinary messages. Wiley, New York, pp 222–223

55 Simon, Herbert (1965) The shape of automation for men and management. Harper & Row, New York, p 96

56 Winograd, Terry (1984) Computer software for working with language. Scientific American 142, Sept

57 This account of skill is spelled out and defended in Hubert Dreyfus and Stuart Dreyfus, *Mind Over Machine* (Macmillan, New York, 1986)

58 Lakatos, Imre (1978) Philosophical papers, ed Worrall J. Cambridge University Press, Cambridge

59 Minsky, Marvin (1977) Computation, finite and infinite machines. Prentice-Hall, New York, p 2

60 Kolata, Gina (1982) How can computers get common sense? Science 217:1237 (24 Sept)

61 McCorduck, Pamela (1979) Machines who think. WH Freeman, San Francisco, p 87

62 Some typical quotations from Rosenblatt's *Principles of Neurodynamics, Perceptrons and the Theory of Brain Mechanisms* (Spartan, Washington DC):

In a learning experiment, a perceptron is typically exposed to a sequence of patterns containing representatives of each type or class which is to be distinguished, and the appropriate choice of a response is "reinforced" according to some rule for memory modification. The perceptron is then presented with a test stimulus and the probability of giving the appropriate response for the class of the stimulus is ascertained ... If the test stimulus activates a set of sensory elements which are entirely distinct from those which were activated in previous exposures to stimuli of the same class, the experiment is a test of "pure generalisation". The simplest of perceptrons... have no capability for pure generalisation, but can be shown to perform quite respectably in discrimination experiments particularly if the test stimulus is nearly identical to one of the patterns previously experienced. (p 68)

Perceptrons considered to date show little resemblance to human subjects in their figure-detection capabilities and gestalt-organising tendencies. (p 71)

The recognition of sequences in rudimentary form is well within the capability of suitably organised perceptrons, but the problems of figural organisation and segmentation presents problems which are just as serious here as in the case of static pattern perception. (p 72)

In a simple perceptron, patterns are recognised before "relations"; indeed, abstract relations such as "A is above A" or "the triangle is inside the circle" are never abstracted as such, but can only be acquired by means of a sort of exhaustive rote-learning procedure, in which every case in which the relation holds is taught to the perceptron individually. (p 73)

A network consisting of less than three layers of signal transmission units, or a network consisting exclusively of linear elements connected in series, is incapable of learning to discriminate classes of patterns in an isotropic environment (where any pattern can occur in all possible retinal locations without boundary effects). (p 575)

A number of speculative models which are likely to be capable of learning sequential programs, analysis of speech into phonemes and learning substantive "meanings" for nouns and verbs with simple sensory referents have been presented in preceding chapters. Such systems represent the upper limits of abstract behaviour in perceptrons considered to date. They are handicapped by a lack of satisfactory "temporary memory", by an inability to perceive abstract topological relations in a simple fashion and by an inability to isolate meaningful figural entities, or objects, except under special conditions. (p 577)

The applications most likely to be realisable with the kinds of perceptrons described in this volume include character recognition and "reading machines", speech recognition (for distinct, clearly separated words) and extremely limited capabilities for pictorial recognition or the recognition of objects against simple backgrounds. "Perception" in a broader sense may be potentially within the grasp of the descendants of our present models, but a great deal of fundamental knowledge must be obtained before a sufficiently sophisticated design can be prescribed to permit a perceptron to compete with a man under normal environmental conditions. (p 583)

63 Rumelhart, David and McClelland, James (1986) Parallel distributed processing: Explorations in the microstructure of cognition, vol 1. MIT Press, Cambridge, MA, p 45

64 Rumelhart, David and McClelland, James (1986) Parallel distributed processing: Explorations in the microstructure of cognition, vol 2. MIT Press, Cambridge, MA, p 535

65 Smolensky, Paul (1988) On the proper treatment of connectionism. Behavioural and Brain Sciences

66 Hinton, Geoffrey (1986) Learning distributed representations of concepts. In: Proceedings of the 8th annual conference of the cognitive science society. Cognitive Science Society, Amherst, MA, Aug 1986

67 For a recent influential account of perception that denies the need for mental representation, see James J. Gibson, *The Ecological Approach to Visual Perception* (Houghton Mifflin, Boston, 1979). Gibson and Rosenblatt collaborated on a research paper for the US Air Force in 1955; see Gibson JJ, Olum P and Rosenblatt F "Parallax and perspective during aircraft landing", American Journal of Psychology 68:372–385

Chapter 4

Alternative Intelligence

Massimo Negrotti

Basic Assumptions and Theses

The past thirty years have presented many great challenges to our conceptions of science and technology and even of man himself. This fact is closely linked to the spread of computer technology and the power of that technology in improving our capacity to investigate not only natural phenomena but even human and social processes.

But this dramatic enhancement of our ability to deal with complicated and massive calculations has also led to the idea that the highest level of our nature, namely the mind, is near to being understood just by adopting the fascinating model of the computer.

This idea has grown both in social culture and in the scientific environment, perhaps for the same reason, that is, the apparent plausibility of the analogy between the computer and the human mind based on the fact that both are clearly able to do complex calculations in a logically precise manner.

Far from being a reliable starting point for a successful new tradition of research, the computer analogy, with its tacit assumptions of homology, is actually the product of a pragmatic philosophy which is, in its turn, the outcome of a way of looking at man which is intrinsic to advanced industrial societies.

In this paper I would like to contribute by demonstrating the following theses:

1. The aims and actual results of Artificial Intelligence (AI) have nothing to do with well founded replication of the human mind; indeed, AI can advance only if it abandons any such idea.
2. The conviction that AI is able to replicate the human mind is a cultural attitude which is quite consistent with advanced industrial culture.
3. The limits AI has to deal with are the same as current western culture is facing in its transition from the industrial to the post-industrial stage.

4. AI could have greater technological and scientific relevance if it accepted that the "intelligence" it wants to replicate is actually a new field of research and not a topic of a human science, as the so-called "cognitive science" would pretend.

If the above theses are true, then we shall deduce from them that current efforts to replicate the human mind by means of computer programs are not only hopeless but are wasting the resources of computer science. Since computer techniques are very powerful *in se*, but we have no reason to conclude that they represent the same tools that the mind uses in its own performance, we should conclude that we are dealing with a new object of research.

Therefore, a shift toward a new way of conceiving AI should emerge from such a criticism. But to do so, we need to shift from an information-based or symbolic-based conception of man to a truly knowledge-based one, i.e. from a pragmatical to a critical–rationalist point of view. Speaking in Popperian terms (Popper 1970), we need a sort of a new "demarcation principle" between the area proper to AI and that proper to humans. This doesn't require us to reject AI but simply to assign to the computer *sui generis* ways of working in order to perform tasks which usually require human intelligence.

I am deeply convinced that by doing so, we shall discover or invent models of a new kind of intelligence, compatible with the human mind but different from it in terms of both nature and power. The compatibility is due to the fact that the intelligence of the computer is the result of a human construction of computational structures and processes, and the novelty of its nature is due to the wide range of possibilities which come from the great complexity of the interactions among such structures and processes.

In this sense the intelligence of the computer looks like a real new object of research, that is an absolutely "pure" kind of intelligence completely formal and without cultural, biological and psychological motivations or constraints. We can build computer models to emulate the results of human mental processes but, in doing so, we gain knowledge about the possibilities inherent in the computer, and not about the nature of the human mind as such.

The knowledge we get from AI programs isn't necessarily important just because it helps us to understand the human intelligence but is just as powerful and intellectually interesting as any other scientific achievement.

Instead of carrying out projects just to give machines human intelligence, we would gain a truly new intelligent tutor able to help us in amplifying our efforts of knowledge, owing to its capacity to enhance the total variety of the strategies for solving problems.

But, as I have said, this shift requires a cultural change from a model in which knowledge is reduced to a rule-based information process to a model in which knowledge becomes once again a critical–rationalist process whose 'rules' are understandable not by means of computer programs but through philosophical research. The lack of continuity between the human mind and AI technology is the key point of the following pages, and could provide the first step towards explaining the apparent failure of the highly ambitious aims with which AI originally set out.

The Nature of Artificial Intelligence Projects

The original programme for AI was strong enough to provoke some kind of reaction from just about anybody: particularly philosophers, scholars of the humanities and computer scientists but also even the man in the street. However, the epistemological status of AI has been discussed much more by its opponents than by its supporters.

In fact it soon became clear that the "machine" which Herbert Simon, Allen Newell and John McCarthy had in mind was nothing more than a computer program, and not a material system. Because of this, even if it was discussed in terms of "physical symbolic systems" it is evident that the real enterprise of AI was the reproduction of intelligence or, rather, intelligent behaviour *in se*, that is without placing it in an intelligent system like the human body with its biological structure and environmental and cultural interactions. However, the assertion of the feasibility of a sort of physiological isolation of a mental faculty from the mind and the body was soon perceived as a pure dream promoted by early enthusiasm for the power of the computer.

What should be clear is that even today, AI projects are still basically attempts to implement computer programs developed to perform tasks which usually "require intelligence if performed by humans". Generally speaking, they aren't the only examples of such attempts, since the whole history of technology is the history of the transfer to particular machines of particular human physical abilities. Indeed, technology can be largely defined in terms of the attempt to capture the principles governing one or another of our biological abilities and to embed them in a different physical medium.

The scope of technology has been considerably enhanced by the application of cybernetics, deriving general models of control processes from living systems and applying them to the construction of machines that work in ways which would require intelligence if performed by humans.

The key point here is that, from the lever to the "brain wheels" of the nineteenth century and the most recent servomechanisms, technology has followed two basic strategies:

1. Discovering and then reproducing some process featured by the biological structure and dynamics of humans or animals.
2. "Inventing" something which doesn't exist in nature.

Often, if not always, the latter strategy is the result of the development of the former. AI is developing in a quite different way, starting (like many other contemporary technologies) from the second strategy and aiming for the first.

But I'm afraid that any attempt to derive models of human ways of thinking (conceived as a wider category than pure "reasoning") from machines invented to solve computational problems, has just about as much chance as would an attempt to understand human vision starting from the electron microscope. Computers weren't invented to emulate the human brain or mental processes, and computer science is not a human science at all in any real sense, since its object is the machine and not the human mind. For this reason, it can only hope to develop towards ever higher levels of specificity, that is, towards a progressively deeper understanding of what a computer can do and of its possible evolutionary path. In fact, the best results coming from AI are to be found in those fields such as Expert Systems or robotics, where the explicit emulation of human internal processes has been abandoned.

Since we lack a good knowledge of the human mind, AI programs are being designed without reference to scientific or philosophical theories, but on the basis of personal and partial models (though generally supported or influenced by some kind of logic or epistemology).

In this respect, both connectionism and the so-called "neuronets" are only, for the moment, attempts to go beyond the limits of current sequential computers. But, so far, the analogy between a connection machine or a neuronet program and the human brain is simply a construction of human imagination, without any serious reference to the reality of the biological basis of our mind. We have no direct evidence about the ways our brain works. However, a prudent starting point could be to conceive of it as a machine which performs both sequential and parallel tasks. If we think that "conscious control processes operate serially and in stages" and that "those that operate subconsciously, as with higher levels of skill, can operate in parallel with a conscious control process" (Singer and Gerson 1979) then we get a first step in the modelling process – but only in order to build something which produces results like a brain and not a copy of it.

We cannot derive the conclusion that the same performances are developed in the same way in our brain from the fact that neuronet programs seem to be able to learn and to develop toward effective performances (though at a lower level than conventional AI programs).

We need a great deal of knowledge about the human brain before we can seriously try to reproduce it. Otherwise, we have no way of "verifying" our models. Computer models as such can only give us high or low computational performances and, generally speaking, the more powerful they are, the further away they and the programs which execute them are from being good models of the mind. They relate, rather, to a very fascinating "new" world of intelligence which we should understand as it is and develops, and not in so far as it appears to produce human-like behaviours. The outcome of a good AI program is a *product* of our mind and not a *mirror* of it.

Our mind is quite able to adapt itself to the material and functional nature of machines, and more generally of the physical world, and even if we had to deal with totally different computers, we would still probably get something interesting from them. It is highly improbable that in building the current generation of computers and the AI programs which run on them we have uncovered anything very much of the intimate nature of our mind or our brain.

If an alien visitor were to attempt to study the human mind by observing our computers, it would certainly get to understand many things about our mental skills. But it would be wrong if it tried to derive a model of the way in which our mind reasons from the way in which computers currently work. For example, if it looked at a sorting program and then discovered that such a problem has been solved with very different algorithms (such as the "cheap sort", the "bubble sort" etc.), it would be very hard pressed to understand which of them was the "true" sorting method actually used by the human mind. Fortunately, the ways in which our computers work are, more than a "part" of our actual way of reasoning, a proof of our ability in representing, as actors, in our mind different more or less intelligent entities and our capacity to reason as if we were they.

The field of AI is a drama school in which people learn to think like computers rather than where computers learn to reason like people. And while the humans make enthusiastic efforts to arrange and predict the actual behaviour of the machines, the latter persist in repeating their own characteristic behaviour: one which is consistent with their nature, without any motivation or pleasure in playing a human role.

This doesn't mean that such programs are in no way useful in understanding the human mind but only that they have no intrinsic capacity to reproduce the whole of human intelligent behaviour: they only produce results which normally are produced by human intelligence, but in a different, and therefore new way.

I think that, in this regard, the arguments proposed by John Searle (1984) and Ajit Naranayan (1986) are conclusive. According to Searle, the simple fact of getting the same result from a man and from a computer doesn't mean that the two systems are structurally the same thing or that they perform the task in the same way. This is a well known pitfall of behaviourism. According to Naranayan, the models proposed by AI researchers are self-verified, in the sense that the implementation of the models can in no way be accepted as an attempt to falsify a theory. They work (when they do work) for the simple reason that they are built to work in a particular manner, but this does not constitute experimental evidence that mental processes have been replicated: these systems reproduce only the models which they contain.

In other words, programs are not theories but models in which procedures are built and which the computer follows to produce some kind of result.

Due to the great diversity of origins and objectives in the AI field, formal scientific method has a rather low profile in this discipline. Nevertheless, AI efforts are ostensibly aimed at actually discovering ways in which humans think and reason. To do so, that is, to reach actual though tacit scientific goals, AI adopts the *ad hoc* method of "implementability", instead of the classical theoretic– experimental one. This is not a novelty in our century (nor would it even be a problem if AI were to be defined as a pure technology), since both Freudian psychology and historicist sociology, among others, have claimed the need for an *ad hoc* method in order to explain human facts. However, none of these fields has developed a powerful and convincing body of general knowledge.

Implementability is, at the same time, a scientific and a technological principle by means of which a model (not a theory) is true if it works as it is intended to work. The experimental stage is replaced by the running of a program, and it is sure that, if it works the first time, it will continue to work well under the same conditions. In other words, the "good number of experiments" needed to certify the plausibility of an hypothesis, is replaced by the indefinite recurrence of a behaviour determined by a program.

In fact, at this point we don't really need the implementation at all. Even without putting it in a computer, the model on which the program is based should be enough to satisfy the main objective, namely the persuasion of having reproduced a true mental behaviour. Being tautological, the "implementability" of the program doesn't add any supplementary value to the model.

The implementability principle only has the power to improve the acceptability of a model within the AI community, and sometimes in the market, replacing the reproducibility criterion with that of the reliability of a well programmed system.

The impressive performance of some programs, perhaps designed just to create such an impression, appears to play a purely psychological role in the claims of "strong" AI.

In a sense, AI researchers seem to have learned the lesson coming from a certain sociology of science which describes the results of scientific research as a social construction due to a negotiation activity among scientists (Bloomfield 1988). On the other hand, while adopting *de facto* this point of view like a "truth" principle, AI people appear to go so far beyond its implicit conventionalism, as to argue (at least from the standpoint of "strong" AI) that their programs actually implement real mental states. This position simply reopens the problematic issue of how such a claim can be supported with some kind of evidence conceived in terms of a classical methodology.

Let me now conclude this section with a further critical argument. After thirty years of research and after the most penetrating critiques of the claims of AI, the original aims of this discipline have been greatly modified. At the very least, we could say that AI has tried to give itself a less ambitious image by reverting to a more "classical" status. This step is manifestly openly demonstrated by the rise of a parallel field named cognitive science. My feeling is that the only function of this change has been to allow AI researchers to continue along the same old road by assigning to the new *ad hoc* "science" the role of giving scientific respectability to AI achievements or projects. But in fact, if one reads the abstracts of the Turing Institute, the various working papers of AI departments or the proceedings of AI Conferences, one will find no trace of the well known distinction between a "strong" and a "weak" AI.

The AI literature reports a large and growing number of projects or already implemented programs which are basically attempts to improve the performance of previous programs, for example by shifting from one kind of logic to another or from one programming language to another. This work usually makes no reference whatever to cognitive science, suggesting that when AI is successfully making real advances, AI people are content to build up a new and specific tradition of research and design. The main issue here is the persistence of misunderstandings about the status of these projects.

From my point of view, AI programs are technological tools for transferring to machines that kind of ability which is coherent with their essential nature. In other words, AI programs reflect human efforts to understand machines in order to give them some kind of ability by means of software strategies. These strategies, in their turn, embody a real but unusual aspect of human reasoning which the machine can amplify and develop in a kind of complexity unmanageable by the human mind, but whose essence is actually implemented in the human mind itself. Thus the computer can be said to be "intelligent" owing to its capacity to repeat or execute human "programs". But such programs, or strategies, are structurally different (and a reduction) from the ways man normally adopts to solve his problems. They demonstrate the aptitude of humans to reason like computers rather than the aptitude of computers to reason like humans.

In this sense AI is nothing but an evolutionary development of Computer Science, i.e. an attempt to improve the power of the machine by means of strategies which are consistent with its nature and which are able to produce behaviour which is not limited to numeric computation. The actual novelty of AI, as compared to traditional Computer Science, consists in the ambitious level of its targets, and not in the discovery of ways humans could follow to reach them.

This is the reason for my belief that AI is really intelligence and, at the same time, really artificial. It is a new field of technological research and not a human science. Its advances are constrained by intrinsic limits in reproducing human faculties, but they could be of great concern if cultural evolution were to reject or modify the early and unfounded premises of AI.

The Cultural Roots of AI's Claim to Legitimacy

Our culture is above all a re-productive culture. Contemporary advanced industrial societies are involved in many processes aimed at expanding individual rights and allowing the greatest collective fruition of material goods and services. These processes, deeply linked to the requirements of democracy, are mainly based on the technological capacity:

1. to extend our natural senses (McLuhan 1964) and organs by means of ever more powerful devices, and
2. to reproduce such devices in great quantities.

The combined results of these aspects of technology is the amplification of the individual's ability to act on the external world and to retrieve information from it. As I have maintained elsewhere (Negrotti 1975) this development of technology has encouraged the psychological appropriation of technological devices and sensitivity to the growth of individual power. Our culture, with its strong belief in the power of science to redeem man from poverty and ignorance, has been ready for at least the past century to sanction such an extension of the individual ego.

Culture and technology have developed reinforcing each other as parts of a unique system governed by positive feedback (Maruyama 1963). Technology has improved our capacity to go around the world; to produce and to take care of physical dimensions like temperature, humidity, light; to cover great distances by means of physical tools which expand our arms or eyes; to collect and store many kinds of acoustic, visual, symbolic information and so on. Western culture, in its turn, has given legitimacy to these facts, shifting from theological or metaphysical premises to positivistic and pragmatistic ones, thus giving the necessary cultural basis to the effort of extending the range of human capabilities.

The brain is the latest organ which technological development has tried to amplify. Beginning with calculators, advances in electronics seem to have given humans even this possibility, and the ability of electronic devices to do mathematical calculations, the most formal and rule-based performance carried out by the human mind, has unfortunately persuaded many people that the "electronic brain" is no longer a pseudo- scientific pipedream but a genuinely achievable aim.

The decline of cultural imperatives regarding the metaphysical nature of man and its divine similarity, (and their redefinition as "anti-progressive prejudices"), has helped to establish the legitimacy of numerous scientific or technological enterprises which in the past would have been condemned as sinful. The claims of AI to be able to reproduce not only limited formal capacities of the mind, but, in its strong version, even real mental states and psychological processes (Sloman and Croucher 1982) makes it one of the most crucial fields in this regard.

Today, even its most sceptical opponents have no strong moral argument to use against AI: its legitimacy is generally accepted in principle and the only "prejudice" concerns its feasibility. But such a synergic co-evolution (Sommerhoff 1968; Gallino 1987) could be very dangerous on a cultural level, since it appears to be an unregulated process.

It would be very interesting, for instance, to predict the possible consequences of a generally recognised failure of AI. Due to its close interaction with culture, such a failure could reverse the current trend, already slackened by impressive failures in certain technological fields such as industrial chemistry, nuclear plants or aerospace enterprises. Our culture could quickly turn back to pre-industrial models, passing through a stage of irrational and frustrating searching for existential guarantees.

This unhappy evolution could be avoided by anticipating final failure through a self-limiting redefinition of AI, allowing the technology to develop a new type of demarcation principle related to the most plausible limits of technological rationality. This would mean, after all, giving back to the human complexity, on the one hand, its own rights and to the new technology on the other its instrumental importance.

The difficulties which this self-limiting process has to face are the same as those our culture is already encountering in its all-too-rapid transition to a post-industrial era (Bell 1980). Despite the fact that it is perhaps the most frequently cited premise, to this transition, computer science and AI have no role in the establishment of the new era, since they are deeply linked to a pragmatic and mechanistic view of man, which is, in turn, a basic premise of industrial society.

The so called post-industrial society should be characterised not by a non-productive way of life but by a different way of production. It is not the production process as such which is central, but just these new ways. It is surely true that the new ways of producing will be much less "material" than those, of, say, twenty years ago, but they are based on an information processing which is aimed at emulating specific mental faculties as they are here and now, and, therefore, there is no pressure to promote or encourage new cultural models. Apart from their obvious capacity for relieving humans from physical fatigue or complex and standardised jobs, there is no reason to think that the diffusion of computers and AI devices might be seen as a key factor in bringing about the transition from the present culture to a more intellectual one. On the contrary, as I have pointed out, AI devices are oriented towards a sort of philosophy whose purpose is that of building up models of mind suitable to existing types of technology and to actual ways of thinking. The actual aim of AI is to discover ways of building machines reliable enough to replace workers, experts and perhaps teachers, and not to enhance the range and the scope of problems of daily or professional life. In any case, the market itself would not accept any device which demanded too much mental effort, and the achievements of computer science and AI are really pursued with the aim of reducing such efforts completely. As Karatsu has said in presenting the Japanese project for a Fifth Generation computer, "the new machine may be put into our daily work quite naturally, just as if it were air" (Karatsu 1981).

Although the computer is potentially very powerful in stimulating creativity, its current use and improvement outside of the scientific field is only directed towards solving well-known problems and not to helping humans to discover the problematic nature of reality. Three surveys on the way AI people perceive the relationship between humans and machines, carried out by myself and my group during three international conferences (Negrotti 1986), have shown that a large proportion of AI researchers themselves agree with the idea that creative behaviour is more significantly to be found in the human capacity to *discover* problems than in problem *solving* activity.

Since creativity, particularly the ability to discover original problems, is the key point of critical thinking and, therefore, of the intellectual way of life (Negrotti 1984), the orientation of computer applications towards problem solving does not stimulate any real change at all in our culture. Such a use of the computer is, however, quite consistent with the philosophy of industrial society whose intrinsic purpose is to solve problems and to distribute the best solutions in the market.

AI at a Crossroad

The current debate on the nature of AI seems to be based on the idea that the epistemological quality of this technology could be a relevant variable in determining its future advances. According to this implicit assumption, the future of AI is likely to be linked to the cultural acceptance of the dominant solutions to three key problems:

1. The nature of understanding
2. The role of rules in performing intelligent tasks
3. The efficacy of future AI devices in relation to the solutions adopted to problems 1 and 2.

In fact, the balance between problems 1 and 2 will have no relevance if it does not lead to any concrete improvements in real devices. In other words, because the success of AI is always, in the end, a matter of public or cultural approval, whatever solutions to the problems of the nature of understanding and the role of rules in intelligent behaviour eventually prevail among AI people, it will be culturally validated on the basis of its real effectiveness. Since current western culture is looking for increasingly powerful tools to solve ever more complex problems, their "true" nature will simply not be an important issue when it comes to their acceptance and use. The destiny of technological truths is accomplished in the market-place and not in university classrooms. I think that even in a substantial part of the scientific and technological community, the final criterion against which the achievements of AI will be assessed will simply be their effectiveness in solving problems which normally require intelligence and large bases of knowledge. This is, in any case, the reason which explains the success of expert systems.

I'm not saying that these issues have no relevance. On the contrary, they are actually key factors in deciding what is an AI device, although it isn't clear what influence this decision could have on what an AI device can do.

I think that insistence on the claim that an AI program has all the necessary characteristics to be a true mind is both a matter of great interest in itself and, as we have seen, a noteworthy cultural influence, but at the same time it acts as a brake on the development of AI and, particularly, on the development of a fully autonomous discipline dedicated to a really new field of research.

The problem of the nature of understanding is very illuminating in this regard. The claim that real mental states can be reproduced in computer programs, which is the obvious premise to support the proposition that computers can understand, has been discussed in considerable depth (Searle 1984). My feeling is that in the famous debate around Searle's attack on the so called "strong" AI (and even on the "weak/strong" AI), we are dealing with intellectual positions which cannot be assessed by means of new advances in the attempt to develop effective AI programs. So we are facing a stimulating paradox: even if AI programs were to exhibit more and more power in performing "intelligent" tasks, this fact would have no influence on beliefs about the nature of their particular kind of intelligence. Searle's position, which asserts that mental states are an emergent product of the biological structure of the brain, would be the same even if he were placed in front of a more powerful program than those he knows today. On the other hand, the position of those who have tried to answer Searle's very penetrating arguments by maintaining that "understanding" refers to a system property would be the same even if AI programs couldn't be improved at all.

Both these positions, as I have maintained above, cannot be falsified: they simply say that, in Searle's version, even if a computer works very well in a complex field and produces human-like results, it lacks a mind due to its non-biological nature; while his opponents' version argues that effective and human-like working is the proof that we are dealing with a reproduction of the human mental way of working. I don't see how it would be possible to test both these positions, particularly, through further advances in AI programs.

AI advances do not depend, in this case, upon the nature of understanding but only upon the success of human understanding of the nature of the machine. Consequently, AI advances are dependent on the success of the attempt to transfer at all costs human ability to the computer, adapting projects to the characteristics of the machine and not to those of the human mind. At the end of this process, the computer really can reproduce human mental performances but only the ones we have designed on the basis of its capacities by forcing ourselves to behave like it.

The problem of the role played by rules in human intelligent behaviour could appear to have a rather more direct influence on the development of AI, since computers cannot do anything except through formal rules.

In this case, the problem concerns particularly the technology of expert systems since this is a field where AI cannot advance without a direct investigation on human mind processes. In other words, after having extracted all the rules of which the human expert is aware, no computer-oriented solutions can be found to simulate those missing part of the reasoning processes which not even the expert can express explicitly.

If it could be conclusively demonstrated that, beyond certain thresholds, the rules an expert follows aren't expressible or that, in the Dreyfus' version, the human expert doesn't follow rules at all, then the current impasse in the development of more powerful expert systems could point to a definitive arrival point for this technology.

Unfortunately, even the question of whether an expert follows rules or not isn't falsifiable on a scientific level. As we shall see in the next section, clearly not all mental performance of an expert's reasoning is formally expressible, but what kind of process happens in this sort of *silent reasoning*? Is the simple fact that the expert cannot express the rules sufficient reason to conclude that his mind doesn't follow any? On the other hand, if he does follow rules, why can't he express them?

These are key questions for two main reasons. First of all, because the answer to the question about the nature of silent reasoning determines just what an AI designer should reproduce in his program (with the constraint that, if this kind of reasoning isn't rule-based, then it is not implementable).

Secondly, if one thinks that an expert follows rules even in "silent reasoning", then the AI researcher (in this case the so-called "knowledge engineer") will have to deal with the problem of how those "special" rules can be extracted from the expert's mind. Clearly this problem cannot be solved with improved AI techniques: it might be solved only by means of psychological procedures which either aren't currently available or are in a very crude state of development (Hart 1988).

In the end, AI products are programs, i.e. symbolic specifications of what an electronic processor should do in order to perform a physical process interpreted by humans in terms of computation, selection, deduction and so on. Their theoretical nature is totally irrelevant in view of the fact that the AI community do not set up experimental environments to test their theories: they only describe procedures which must perform tasks whose theoretical nature should be, but generally isn't, already tested otherwise.

The conceptual difference between simulations and AI programs should help to understand this aspect of the question. Simulation is possible if and only if an already tested theory of a process is available (or, failing that, at least an accurate description of it). So, if we know that an event A causes an event B with a well described relation with variables C, D and E, then we can easily simulate such a causal process in order to see what amount of B we could expect by varying the amounts of C, D and E.

In an AI program not only do we not know the process of the mind at all, but we are only interested in reproducing event B on the basis of alternative models whose choice is made just by evaluating their power to reproduce it.

Furthermore, in practice AI models are generally oriented towards the performance of an "intelligent" task, and not towards producing scientific explanations of mental processes. If an AI researcher were able to find a new and more powerful programming solution for a novel problem of understanding, he could instruct a computer to do it, but the machine has no power to verify the model as if it were a theory of human understanding. The program performs a task because it is built to work that way. There is no reason to think that humans follow the computer way of performing the same task. The computer way of performing a task is the result of the programmer's ability to discover all that is necessary in order to force the computer to work in that manner. But in doing so, the programmer concentrates on the computer's capabilities, and not on those of human mind.

This is why we can think of AI as a genuinely new field of research and not as a pseudo-experimental extension of a human science. Its contribution in improving human understanding of the human mind (Miller 1978) is thus quite random and unpredictable: we cannot exclude it and we cannot depend on it.

Nevertheless, on a sociological level such considerations have no great effect. Owing to its growing ability to give the market just what it is looking for, AI could indeed spread in our life "as if it were air". Cultural approval, as we have seen, will depend on the power of AI devices and not on their "true" nature. The artificial nature of AI devices could be correctly understood by people just depending on the public perception of the epistemological foundation of the new technology.

Only the recognition that AI is a technological field (or a "science of the artificial") and not a scientific area which has finally discovered the real nature of human understanding and reasoning, could avoid a cultural misunderstanding which might result in very serious consequences regarding the ways of regarding human beings, their ethical values, their responsibility and their intellectual freedom.

I have no qualms about accepting the evidence, if any were forthcoming, that human thought is a physical process, though I'm persuaded to the contrary. I'm afraid, however, of witnessing a cultural abandonment of western values on the basis of "findings" that are nothing but "intelligent", and therefore effective, software machines able to drive hardware machines to perform useful tasks.

We should be aware of this danger, the probability of which is deeply linked to the present tendency of culture to give legitimacy only to that which demonstrates effectiveness and pragmatical reliability.

This attitude is a point of convergence of both AI and culture, since at the same time the former is looking for a "verifiable" model of the human way of thinking as it is here and now, the latter offers openly to AI the mainstream to follow, that is, the same pragmatical criterion AI people try to satisfy with their projects.

In this situation, general culture and the sub-culture of AI people constitute a self-amplifying system which lacks clear targets and solid foundations, having reduced the search for human nature to a group of beliefs appropriate to the increasingly attractive aims of technology.

Some Remarks on the Arguments of Searle and Dreyfus

Just because I fundamentally agree with Searle's position regarding the nature of AI programs when compared against human understanding, let me now propose some remarks on his argument against the possibility that different structures can cause the same process. My argument is not oriented to support the idea that computers can "understand" like human minds, but only to avoid the risk that too strong an opposition to the claims of AI could give rise to new misunderstandings about the nature of technology and perhaps also the nature of human beings.

My feeling is that the position according to which only the biological structure of the brain can cause mental states and processes (Searle 1988) belongs to an overridden positivistic way of looking at reality. Like the positivistic sociologist Emile Durkheim, who maintained that only social facts can explain other social facts (Durkheim 1895), Searle seems to think that structures which produce particular kinds of events are linked to them in an exclusive causal way. This leads directly to a monocausalistic way of thinking which contrasts with the contemporary view of reality and its complexity. In any case, it's quite possible to demonstrate that different structures can produce the same process.

Searle himself, on the other hand, agrees with the possibility that if we could duplicate the causes, consequently we could duplicate the effects (Searle 1984), but in the field of mental performances he is inclined to maintain that we can only set up a system able to give rise to thinking capacities if we can physically duplicate a nervous system with neurons and dendrites. His disagreement with the claim that computer programs which are only able to manipulate symbols could be said to "think" and "understand" can therefore come as no surprise when he starts from premises which postulate such close relationships between the natures of causes and effects.

In any case, we can distinguish "hard" and "soft" versions of the above thesis. The "hard" version seems to say that "only identical structures can produce identical processes", where for "identical" we should intend "unique". In other words, the hard version is aimed to maintain that only Socrates can think like Socrates. It seems to me that this version is quite obvious and, in this sense, we should even recognise that no human mental status or process is "identical" to another. Incidentally, if we were to assert the strong point of view, we would consequently also have to accept a totally unfounded solipsistic idea of man. The simple fact that humans succeed in communicating with each other should be enough to reject such an idea.

The soft version of Searle's argument says that only structures of a certain class can produce certain processes, and therefore only a brain can produce mental states. This thesis can be accepted or rejected according to the answer one gives to the question: which components of the process are strategic in order to guarantee that we have produced it? If our answer is "all", then we have implicitly decided to accept the idea of an exclusive relation between the process and its structural cause. But if our answer were to indicate a subset of components whose occurrence is enough to indicate the production of the process, then we should admit that in many cases different structures can produce the same processes.

Our answer will clearly depend on our ontological conceptions about what is essentially a fact.

First of all we should be clear that we are speaking about a system which through some kind of process performs a task. In fact, what Searle has in mind when he refers to digestion is the name we give to the final task performed by processes caused by the structure of the intestines. He cannot obviously maintain that such a final task cannot be performed by other kind of structures, but only that, in doing so, another kind of structure would perform the task through different processes. In other words, given a non-biological structure, we can get from it some sort of computational or reasoning performance but we cannot claim to have demonstrated that this final task has been reached by means of the same internal processes which happen in the human mind. Consequently, the names we give to such tasks as "understanding", "reasoning" and so on are quite ambiguous since they refer to the final outcomes of very different processes.

Nevertheless, and to remain in a biological field, if we think that all of the kidney's internal processes are involved in allowing it to perform dialysis then we shall have great difficulty in recognising that an artificial kidney performs some of the internal processes of a real kidney. We could say the same for an artificial breast or for an artificial heart. To the contrary, if we are inclined to think that the essential function of the structure of the kidney is an empirically well-described process which in its turn permits a final outcome named "dialysis", then we will have no difficulty in admitting that structures which are very different from those in natural systems (in terms of both architecture and physical material) can produce the same essential processes and the same final outcomes.

Obviously this is true if and only if we have empirical evidence about the nature of the processes which allow the final task to be performed. The simple ability to get a performance from a machine which is identical to one carried out by a human has nothing to do with knowledge of the internal processes which allow the human to perform the same task.

Therefore the real problem is that we don't know the "internal" processes of thinking or understanding, so that we can't decide what is essential to them.

What I'm suggesting with the concept of "essential processes" isn't that the ability of AI partially to replicate the essential processes of human mental behaviours is enough to demonstrate its capability of adequately reproducing real mental behaviour. As we have seen in the previous sections, there is (unlike the various biological examples cited above) no empirical evidence to support such a claim. What I'm saying is that if we can demonstrate that different structures can produce essentially identical processes, then we must accept that the alternative methods we use to impart intelligence to computers cannot be rejected as possible models of human intelligence simply on the basis of structural or material heterogeneity.

If one says that the heart is essentially a pump and wishes to describe the minimum set of characteristics such a pump should have in order to replace a human heart, why should we suspect that the resulting structure of the artificial heart couldn't cause the same and essential processes of a natural one in performing its final task, i.e. the circulation of the blood? In this case we not only reproduce the final performance by means of a "black box" strategy, but also the essential internal processes which enable the final outcome to be attained.

From this point of view, I think that we are in the same situation with regard to computers. Their computational processes are often, though not always, performed following the same explicit rules which humans follow in their work. Furthermore, when the designer writes a program to perform a task according to some kind of rule base, he extracts from his internal mental processes just that subset of rules which is essential to allow the logical or mathematical calculations to work, trying to adapt that subset to the symbolic and formal capacities of the computer. In doing so, the designer himself is producing those processes in his mind as if he were a computer, and it is just these redefined and unusual mental processes which the computer will reproduce to perform the task, even if on the basis of a different physical structure. Such mental processes are "redefined and unusual" because they are only formal and lack intentionality, background knowledge and so on, but, at the same time, we cannot reject the idea that they are the essential processes caused by the mind's structure when it performs certain kinds of very formal tasks.

According to the weak AI arguments as stated by Searle, though a computer program cannot be said to reproduce mental states, it is however a necessary condition in order to get such states. Putting this another way, the mind cannot be modelled by avoiding a formal and syntactical stage of description. Searle's answer to this version of the argument says that, synthetically, mental states are the products of physical and not formal-computational processes.

The "weak" AI position is indeed truly unfounded. But if we look at the "redefined and unusual" mental processes which the programmer transfers to the machine, we can say that those processes, and only those, are really reproduced by the program – despite the structural differences. Even a formal theory of human mind can in this way be transferred to the computer, but it will reproduce only that theory, i.e. that way of theorising the human mind, and nothing else.

The syntactical level probably isn't the first stage to give the computer deeper mental states, but *in se* it is already a true mental one: the same as humans produce in themselves when they are concerned with very formal tasks. In addition, when performing very formal tasks, humans need to protect themselves from troubles, from psychological motivations or problems, in a word from everything outside the walls of the closed system they are working in.

This is really the actual nature of a computer environment. The best thing to say is that the formal level is, at the same time, the lowest and most expensive level of human thought (pure rule-based intelligence) and the highest level a computer can reach.

This tendency of humans to reason like computers is very important to understanding not only the terms of the current debate on AI but also the more general meaning of science and technology.

Scientists and technologists are always involved in a sort of auto-reductionism when they work, since we cannot pretend to capture the whole of reality on the basis of an empirically oriented methodology. The same occurs when we program a computer: we know that, in order to get something useful from it, we must abandon the idea of having to deal with a human interlocutor.

The result is a reduction of the concerned area (content) and the reasoning tools (form). With the objective thus redefined, every AI program works well and, like any other machine, shows some level of intelligence. But to pass a non-domain-specific test, an AI program should be produced by an effort to understand the whole reality of the mind, and the complete understanding of the whole of nature is something which is beyond the capabilities of scientists.

The specificity of computer technology is consistent with the sectorial tradition of science and technology, that is the attempt to understand a single dimension (or a system of dimensions, if we follow a systems approach) at any one time. The dimension (or system of dimensions) appropriate to working with a computer, is that of formal reasoning, i.e. that particular kind of thinking activity which, though not essential, I believe, in order to describe human thought, is one of the defining features of human intelligence. This gives further support to my opinion that AI is both really intelligence and really artificial. Its intelligence derives from the fact that the computer, like every other machine, really demonstrates intelligent behaviour in the domain for which it is programmed. Its artificiality derives from the fact that the intelligence shown by the computer isn't connected with thought. While humans may make efforts to force themselves to deal "with and only with" formal rules, the computer doesn't have that sort of choice. It is unable to connect itself with something which isn't formal for the simple reason that when it works, it doesn't "reduce" anything: it is just what it does, and that's all.

By the way, if we agree with the position above, it should also mean that we have already agreed with the idea that formal rules have no semantic content. Or is it rather just the ability of the computer (and other technological tools) to perform formal processes which suggests that formal rules are quite independent of semantic content?

This means, as I have maintained in the previous sections, that the crucial expression "as if" (having in mind the concept of human thought) which we adopt to describe the computer's performance, should really be reversed: in order to get intelligent performances by the machine, the programmer should reason as if he were a computer. The final result is that this imposed but really new human way of reasoning is effectively and completely transferable to the machine.

In many circumstances, the redefined ways of performing a task coincide with the original human ways (as in some, but not all, examples of mathematical calculations) and in others with an essential subset of its components (as in reasoning programs). But in any case the computer will reproduce exactly what the programmer has in his mind and in the same way. After all, this is the real meaning of the sentence "The computer does just what we tell it to do".

AI has no empirical evidence to support the claim that, in executing a program which reproduces mathematical calculations or a reasoning process, the computer replicates the ways in which a human might work if he were not involved in the problem of transferring the process to a machine. Indeed, it seems rather improbable in any case. Despite this reservation it is true to suggest that AI is really able to transfer to the computer mental processes that are redefined by humans in order to fit the machine's capacities, and these new mental processes are really reproduced by the program.

The problem now becomes "To what extent does such a redefinition of the way to perform a task coincide with the essential nature of the original mental process?". As we have seen, in mathematical calculations or in a rule-based task, the coincidence could be very high, while in all other traditional projects of AI it is surely very low or unpredictable. For instance, the Turing Test is based on an excessively weak principle of essentiality: indeed it bypasses the problem completely.

Giving coherent answers is obviously not the essential purpose of the processes implied in human understanding. Getting coherent answers from a computer means only that the machine works effectively according to a program which gives it this behavioural capacity. That is, according to our argument, the computer will work at reproducing real mental processes of the programmer, but these are, in their turn, very far from being an essential subset of those usually involved in human understanding. For example, it is very difficult to define what is essential in "background" knowledge. In fact we don't know much at all about human understanding and therefore we cannot decide what its essence might consist of.

The above discussion has tried to demonstrate that computer programs always reproduce human ways of calculating or reasoning because programs are redefined and unusual but nevertheless real human processes which the programmer first executes in his mind as if he were a computer. Secondly, I have maintained that we cannot reject the idea that, in some circumstances, programs can be said to really reproduce even the essential processes involved in usual (that is "natural" and "cultural") human reasoning, under the sole constraint that they essentiality consist of formal rules. But we simply haven't any evidence to indicate when, outside of formal domains, human thought is only a rule-based performance. Therefore, the reproduction by the computer of real and usual mental states is a quite random possibility.

At this point, the discussion encounters the position (Dreyfus and Dreyfus 1986; Dreyfus 1988) according to which human expertise develops towards a mental behaviour which doesn't follow any rules.

In this case, I will defend the thesis that, by its very nature, AI is condemned to work with rules and that, though not all human mental processes appear to follow rules, it is quite reasonable to represent them by rules. The effort of AI, in this case, should be directed to setting up systems which, under certain conditions and limits, can perform like humans, but in a way which is recognised as different.

The Dreyfus brothers' argument is that both an experienced car driver and a professional expert don't solve problems by means of rules but through a complicated, though unconscious, process of discriminating among thousands of situations. In doing so, the expert reacts rapidly to an internal perception of reality which is oriented to find quickly the best solution according to his previous experience. Furthermore, if one questions the expert with the object of identifying the rules on which his performance has been based, he could be forced to regress to the early stages of his apprenticeship in order to give an expressible and rigorous answer. Since we lack a conclusive theory or model of such abilities of the human mind we cannot hope to give computer programs the same capacities. I think that nobody could disagree about two points:

1. Neither experienced car drivers nor experts consciously consult a rule table when they need to decide about the most suitable behaviour
2. We just don't know what really *does* happen in their minds

My comments are only aimed at supporting the idea that, at least in principle, whatever might happen in our minds when we are in the situations cited above, our decisions are taken on the basis of an IF-THEN process (perhaps based on a sort of "biological syntax") or, in any case, are capable of being represented in this way, and this is, in the end, the actual nature of a rule.

I can state my point of view in the following terms: if every machine is the result of a theory (or of a process of evolution which can be understood by building a theory), then either our mind isn't a machine or we have to deal with a sort of non-theory-based machine. But this seems absurd to me, since it would be indistinguishable from a random aggregate. The fact that we often cannot account for our own intelligent behaviour, doesn't mean that our mind isn't following structurally embedded rules.

We could maintain the same behaviourist criticisms here that we have accepted against the claims of AI. Indeed, even if it is true (since we know their internal structure and operations) that machines such as "neuronets" may behave intelligently without following rules, we still cannot say in the case of humans that if they aren't able to express the rules they are following, then they aren't following rules at all.

Even in supposed discriminating or matching processes, when the solution or the decision is the result of the nature of the problem itself which addresses and activates a stored and well-experienced answer, we have to deal with a process which can be represented as a rule.

This possibility, obviously, leads us to the question, previously discussed, about the plausibility of getting the same effect from different processes.

I could try to synthesise my thought as follows:

Rule-based decision making works like this:
"If the situation is A, then choose action B."

Matching-based decision making, in its turn, can be described as the direct activation of B by the configuration of situation A. No rules of the former type are consulted and therefore no rules can be elicited from the expert except in the tautological form:

"I selected action B since it appeared to me to be the best one".

But we cannot reject the idea that, even in his mind, the expert doesn't act in a sort of stimulus-response manner or by means of an unconscious retrieval as Dreyfus inclines to think: the "decision" to select action B should be in some way confirmed or approved by a higher level of regulation. In fact, the more the awareness declines, the more both a car driver and an expert lose their ability.

In any case, due to the fact that no situation is totally identical to another (apart from formal games like chess) the process can be represented in the following way:

"If situation A matches stored pattern B more than any other, then choose action B."

The discrimination and evaluation process does develop as a rule-based one in any case, since the regulatory level needs to choose just one alternative at any time, and this implies a "decision" process (or, rather, a control process) according to criteria of some kind.

This doesn't mean that we could easily get an explicit description of his mental behaviour from the expert: there is no empirical evidence to encourage such a claim. On the other hand, it is possible to consider that rule-based reasoning and matching aren't separate processes, in the sense that the natural trend might consist of translating matching processes in terms of explicit rules. This is what really happens in the evolution of any professional field, when experts try to identify the constants and regularities among their own matching experiences, for instance in the course of writing a handbook on their own specialisms. The handbook on which a beginner learns is often the best product of his expert- teacher. Otherwise we couldn't account for the progress of professions.

However, it is the unfortunate truth that experts' rules are normally, rather than rarely, broken – particularly by the experts themselves! Therefore no rule can be used by a novice to become as powerful and skilful as the original expert. That is a truly unresolvable problem since we don't know any rules which describe an individual's deviation from, bypassing or re-combination of the rules.

All the same, in a professional field, expertise based intuition, even if doesn't follow explicit rules, could in principle be represented through a model of choice among stored alternatives regulated by selection criteria.

This model could be integrated with the explicit rule-based one or it might be built up by a learning process. From my point of view just this learning process, with its very great complexity and large amount of interaction with the external world, is the most difficult to understand or to reconstruct and not the use of the structure of stored patterns which it produces.

In the end, both Feigenbaum (1983) and Dreyfus agree, though with very different feelings, with the possibility that the expert's mind works by discriminating among thousands of facts (or patterns of facts). This means that an expert's work is in any case representable as the consultation of a sort of "look- up table" of rules and/or patterns. The very difficult task is, consequently, that of reconstructing the ways (or the rules?) an expert follows in order to build up and dynamically develop this "table" and not that of modelling the ways followed in using it. I think that in building his "look-up table" of expertise, the expert's mind activates several different processes and that they are, furthermore, strongly influenced by all internal and external events and even by randomness.

But the work of a "knowledge engineer" has to deal with ready made "look-up tables" and for this reason his task is that of extracting such a structure from the expert, perhaps reducing it to a more manageable set of classes. It could be a very complex and fatiguing task, but it is the only hope of integrating and enhancing a pure rule-based system.

Although they are arguing from different starting points, the views of both Searle, and Dreyfus and Dreyfus lead to the conclusion that, though the human mind is a machine, human intelligent behaviour doesn't follow theories or rules.

I have tried to support the idea that the lack of explicit theories or rules doesn't mean that we cannot understand our intelligent behaviour (that is, our problem solving activity) by means of theories or rules. If we are machines, then we are built on the basis of a theory (or of an understandable evolution) and we follow rules, just as a computer does.

The only way to avoid this conclusion is to recognise that we are more than intelligent "solving machines" and that our nature allows us to act even against the "theories" which govern our mechanical system – for instance, through problem finding activity, which cannot be explained either by means of rules or by means of common sense or matching procedures since all three, like more or less complex machines, lead the system, by their very nature, to already established conclusions and not to the "new", which is implicit in every original problem.

References

Bell D (1980) The social framework of the information society. In: Forester T (ed) The microelectronics revolution. Blackwell, Oxford

Bloomfield BP (1988) Expert systems and human knowledge: A view from the sociology of science. AI & Society 2(1)

Dreyfus HL (1988) Si puo' accusare Socrate di cognitivismo? Nuova Civilta' Delle Macchine 1(1/2)

Dreyfus HL, Dreyfus SE (1986) Mind over machine: the power of human intuition and expertise in the era of computers. New York Free Press, New York

Durkheim E (1895) Les regles de la methode sociologique, 14th edn. Presses Universitaires de France, Paris

Feigenbaum E, McCorduck P (1983) The fifth generation. Addison-Wesley, Reading, MA

Gallino L (1987) L'attore sociale. Einaudi, Torino

Hart A (1988) Sistemi esperti: Dall'ingegneria della conoscenza all'intelligenza artificiale. Gruppo Editoriale Jackson, Milano

Karatsu (1981) What is required of the Fifth Generation computer – social needs and its impact. In: Proceedings of international conference on Fifth Generation computer systems. Japan Information Processing Development Center, Tokyo, pp 87- –100

Maruyama N (1963) The second cybernetics: Deviation amplifying mutual causal processes. General Systems 8:233–241

McLuhan M (1964) Understanding media, the extension of man. McGraw-Hill, New York

Miller L (1978) Has artificial intelligence contributed to an understanding of the human mind? A critique of arguments for and against. Cognitive Science 2:112–145

Naranayan A (1986) Why AI cannot be wrong. In: Gill KS (ed) Artificial intelligence for society. Wiley, Chichester

Negrotti M (1975) Sociologia dell'ambiente tecnico: Saggio sull'equilibrio futuro del sistema cultura-tecnica. Angeli, Milano

Negrotti M (1984) Cultural dynamics in the diffusion of informatics. Futures 16(1):38–46

Negrotti M (1986) The AI people's way of looking at man and machine. Applied Artificial Intelligence 1(1):109–116

Polanyi M (1962) Personal knowledge. Routledge & Kegan Paul, London

Popper KR (1970) Logica della scoperta scientifica. Einaudi, Torino

Searle JR (1984) Menti, cervelli e programmi. CLUP-CLUED, Milano, p 65

Searle JR (1988) La scienza cognitiva e la metafora del computer. Nuova Civilta' Delle Macchine 1(1/2):53–61

Singer RN, Gerson RF (1979) Learning strategies, cognitive processes and motor learning. In: O'Neil HF, Spielberger CD (eds) Cognitive and affective learning strategies. Academic Press, New York

Sloman A, Croucher M (1982) Perche' i robot potranno avere emozioni. In: Negrotti M (ed) Intelligenza artificiale e scienze sociali. Angeli, Milano

Sommerhoff G (1968) Purpose, adaptation and directive correlation. In: Buckley W (ed) Modern systems research for the behavioral scientist. Aldine, Chicago

Sommerhoff G (1969) The abstract characteristics of living systems. In: Emery
FE (ed) Systems thinking. Penguin, Harmondsworth

Chapter 5

Artificial Intelligence as a Dialectic of Science and Technology

Ephraim Nissan

Bipolarity

In the framework of a discussion about the epistemology of computing, Bernard Stiegler (1986) employs a metaphor based on the myth of Epimetheus and Prometheus. According to that myth, Epimetheus endowed animals with various qualities, but forgot man. Unfledged and defenceless, to survive, man had to be endowed with reason by Prometheus, who sacrificed himself in the process.

This metaphor is going to be transposed here into the following idea, different from Stiegler's: "The 'AI-er' is an Epimetheus who yearns to become Prometheus for the machine".

Because of the very nature of the different interests addressed by the two terms in the binomial "science and technology", the technologist relishes his or her Epimethean role. This is justified by rational industrial criteria which are themselves justified by reference to the socio-cultural pattern which has produced, for example, Edison (and for which see Jenkins 1987, sect. II).

So far, computer technology has endowed the machine with new attributes, just as the myth has Epimetheus endowing the spectrum of animal species with various combinations and "dosages" of faculties that are suitable for fitting them into the natural environment: but without the powers of reasoning. Computer science has not yet produced any actual system, whether scientific prototypes or industrial applications that breaks out of the bounds imposed by Epimetheus' gifts.

Not only that, but nowadays we are witnessing a trend in computing which aims at the "mainstreaming" of AI methods in computer practice, adapting them by making them more similar to traditional algorithmic programming. The idea is that you can describe objects in cohesive clusters or adopt the AI technique of defining and searching a constrained space of possibilities, with purely practical aims and no cognitive preoccupations (or with preoccupations that are simply motivated by ergonomic considerations).

The "aristocrats of AI" may turn up their noses at such down-to-earth interests when wearing their "basic research" hats, but that doesn't actually seem to stop them taking an interest in applied projects as potentially profitable sidelines! Scientific and technological interests each have a specific dignity: admitting the criteria of practice is not degradation. It is not tantamount to the guilt of Peer Gynt, who in Ibsen's drama wears a tail to gain acceptance in the country of the Trolls.

Whatever computer system we might consider, whether actually implemented or merely proposed as feasible, we are forced to identify no more than Epimethean task-appropriate adaptation, and we are reluctant to consider such systems as already intelligent (without quotes). This does not necessarily imply mind/mechanism or soul/matter dualism. Dissatisfaction with given AI artefacts seems to parallel the criteria of Promethean eschatology, which are practically impossible to meet from the point of view of cognitive desiderata. Realistically, such criteria have to be drastically simplified to be attainable step by step, and then they have to be gradually redefined more tightly while we progress on the alternative platforms of widening the technical "can-do" space and of gaining more scientific insight. The arbitrariness of technical representation shapes and provisionally delimits scientific conceptions, but the latter in turn provide feedback for technological developments. Awareness that scientific conceptions are a product of social constructivism, not just an objective product of either occasional serendipity or methodical sweat, helps to protect science from excessive enthusiasm. However, new adepts do not always appreciate that fact: which can explain why in certain domains (e.g. linguistics), AI often becomes an obtrusive tool or even a new theory of its own, instead of being recognised as being a versatile non-partisan testbed where representation subserves theory but does not replace it.

Different research taxonomies of AI are surveyed by Hall and Kibler (1985) and by Ringle (1979, 1983). AI is most often conceived as fitting somewhere in a spectrum, the two poles of which are:

A focus on the simulation of cognition
An effective but cognitively indifferent tool

The contrast between science and technology – as we witness it in AI – only serves to indicate the extent of the ground which must be covered; this is made clear when we draw an analogy with the history of science and technology during the positivist era, when distances between the two were thought to be smaller than they later proved to be (and when developments in the 20th century were predicted by extrapolating into "triumph" current "militant" conceptions of the 19th century). Nowadays, there is the factor of impatience, as Latour (1986) has pointed out: "used to leading, engineers find it disquieting to follow [popular expectations]".

What is most specific in the contrast inside AI between technological opulence and scientific eschatology is tightly bound to a terminological choice that stressed only one element of the binomial: by naming the discipline "artificial intelligence" (or, less explicitly and more modestly, AI), the ground to be covered has been approached from the wrong end. A practical concrete down-to-earth choice (the nearest end) could have been: defining a cumulative open-ended metric: "callidiority" (from the Latin callidior: "smarter than").

This metric has both the merit and the fault of sparing technology the scathing criticisms which have been attracted by the ambitions of cognitive science, since the "callidiority" metric compares only past achievements, not absolute standing relative to some "Omega Point". Yet such a metric could risk ungluing the binomial. For technology, it may mean sinking into a swamp – in the eyes of AI scientists – similar to that which COBOL administrative data processing has become for up-to-date programmers. Production- system based commercial products would be replicated *ad nauseam* (a sort of this-worldly relic of a mortal fallen angel), whilst remaining deaf to the *memento mori* admonitions of underfunded basic research. Many AI-ers fear that such an "AI Winter" could stem from premature industrial disillusion after a brief period of feverish fashionability. On the other hand, ungluing the binomial is a scenario that cognitive scientists, AI researchers and the scientific culture of AI cannot afford to accept. Indeed – and this is the fundamental importance of AI – AI as implemented or to be implemented is, nowadays, the testbed that makes theories materialise. Intellect hopes in the advantages of matter. Once we have started considering it feasible to bring the Heavenly Jerusalem down to earth, not to lose hold becomes a cultural imperative.

Mainstreaming in Computing

Mainstreaming – i.e. AI becoming a mainstream practice in computing – is both consistent and at odds with conceiving AI as a leading edge technology within computing.

Consistency stems from the metaphor of a new leading edge delimiting an expanding technology. Such an over-broad definition of AI is found among some of the people involved, and has been elaborated time and time again as AI has proliferated. For example, Guzman Arenas (1983) (having adopted a definition of applied artificial intelligence (AAI) as encompassing methods for the computational solution of complex real-world problems) asked, rather tautologically: "Could it be that I have been developing a complex program to solve an important problem, and that I am not using the tools offered by AI?" Such a definition depends on what is considered to be a "complex problem". Familiarity breeds contempt, and some techniques that once belonged to AAI are not now considered to do so. This is one way in which AI is reduced simply to the margins of computing technology.

However, viewing AI just as the edge of computing is at odds with analytic – not just ostensory – definitions of AI. The currently traditional paradigm of AI, if it is to be seen in a historic perspective, must have a discernible specific focus, or even a technical (not just prestige-driven) perspective of programming, prescribing an agenda for the programmer, instead of merely labelling his or her product.

The technical paradigm is analytically defined once we identify the role that an explicit search space has in problem-solving techniques. Moreover, a useful distinction – valid for expert systems – is viewing data, rules and control (the latter applies rules to data) as separate components, but actually this is only one popular approach: for instance, in object-oriented systems you can have rules and control embedded in objects that eventually trigger each other.

A taxonomy of quite crisply defined approaches, rooted in the general class of pattern-directed inference systems (PDIS) was defined by Hayes-Roth et al. (1983) complementarily to Waterman & Hayes-Roth (1978), but this classification is too general with respect to AI technology, as mere grammar-driven systems such as compilers are also included in the hierarchy.

Impact on Human Skill

One of the intriguing facets of knowledge-based systems is their twofold potential, on the one hand for relieving humans of the need to practice knowledge-based skills directly and on the other hand for enabling human experts to gain insights into deeper knowledge by relieving them of lower-level sub- tasks in the process of discovery. The history of technology is not always encouraging in this respect, as there are instances where technological innovation allowed de-skilling (skill requirements dwindled and workers no longer developed complex skills) followed by downward social mobility (see Braverman 1975; More 1980). Thus, Drummond (1987) points out that during the years 1843–1914, locomotive production at Crewe works evolved through an explosion of scale and the division of labour from "an advanced engineering centre where the hand skill of the tradesman was aided only by the machine tools that were present" in 1843 to a situation in 1914 where the role of a typical employee was reduced to that of "a skilled machine worker who, though still requiring some skill, found his range of skill and work limited by the continued introduction of machine tools and by the increased division of labour".

The role of the technologist as an innovator can bring about an impact on the quality of work, not only in the long run, but also in the very short term: in the 1870s, Edison and other inventors catering to the interests of major telegraph corporations were determined to de-skill the operator's role and undermine the strength of unionism among operators (Jenkins 1987).

Office automation today is sometimes seen as threatening to de-skill white collar work, while effective use of decision support systems is likely to cause a reduction of the number of levels in the management hierarchy. There is even the paradox within the knowledge engineering community that the development of meta-tools and shells for constructing expert systems is often intended to remove the need for a knowledge engineer mediating between the domain expert knowledge provider and the computer system.

However, there is much in knowledge engineering which gives it the potential for enhancing instruction (Nissan 1989a), technical practice and even the process of discovery.

Since 1986/7, Dr Alex Galperin (of the Nuclear Engineering Department of Ben Gurion University) and I have been developing the Heuristic Refueller: an expert system that generates good configurations of fuel in the core of a nuclear reactor. It emulates the skills of a fuel manager during critical "downtime" periods at nuclear plants. Refuelling periods with the plant shut down are very costly, and the Expert Refueller allows the reduction of downtime. The motives behind this project are firstly that this is an important industrial application and secondly that there is a benefit in terms of augmenting the expertise of the domain expert, and finally there is the possibility of making a contribution to AI. A technical description of the expert system is given by Galperin and Nissan (1988, 1989).

The system is not yet a commercial or industrial tool, but it has been under investigation for some time and has been successful in locating families of good configurations that refuelling optimisation experts had never thought of before. We have, in fact, managed to develop an integrated human–machine knowledge-based system that learns. Human experts analyse the geometrical intension (characteristic patterns) and physical significance of families of selected configurations (the extension) that the expert system has found. They then exploit this new knowledge to provide feedback. New rules (previously unknown to the experts) are induced and added manually to the rule set of the expert system, which then runs once more and discovers further, even more interesting, families of configurations. A "moving cloud" effect on search results in improved performance at problem solving and discovery. Located families are visualised by a scanner in a peaking/efficiency plane and successive runs tend to move into a secure zone below a certain peaking threshold.

The expert system contains a rule set of mandatory rules and a subset of heuristic hints, and it is the latter which is developed by feedback. It can also be replaced by a rule set simulating conjectured rules derived from the published authors in the literature of the domain. In these cases, the expert system visualises where such solutions fit into families of (often far superior) solutions. Both security and efficiency are obtained, thereby disproving an old engineering "folk-theorem".

Initial concerns, from the perspective of knowledge-engineering technology, related to resource allocation in terms of representational choices in managing a large search-space. Further aspects of this expert system include extension with explanation (by augmenting rules into frames with properties appropriate to explanation), and tutoring. For the purposes of the present discussion, it is interesting to observe that the human domain expert is integrated into a system that also incorporates an expert system, and it is this integrated system that learns: learning is not totally automatised. The ambition of automating the entire process would be of interest to the science of machine learning within the framework of AI, but it is not necessary in order to make a useful tool for supporting discovery in the expert domain of refuelling optimisation in nuclear engineering. AI tools should be considered in relation to the environment in which they will be applied. Thus, Woods (1986) focuses on the joint human–machine cognitive system, instead of just the artificial tool.

The Challenge of Quantity

To be able to extend representation as well as to make it portable, it is useful to separate knowledge and the uses of knowledge according to purposes and contexts. One approach to such separation is the adoption of a blackboard organisation with a dynamically defined flow of control, where different sub-domains of knowledge are embodied in different co- operating sources of knowledge interacting through a shared data structure (the blackboard), and where even the application of knowledge – though complex in itself – can be encoded as separate knowledge sources (Nii 1986, p 103).

A very important criterion in AI – both for industrial purposes and for setting the goals of specific endeavours in basic research – is the avoidance of representing knowledge deeper than may be necessary to achieve the goals of the project in hand. Irrelevant knowledge should not encumber reasoning in an AI tool employed for a specific purpose. For example, the common sense about objects falling if dropped should correspond to the naive knowledge of real-life fact, with no need for recourse to scientific theories of gravity.

Besides, with large knowledge bases, the use of general methods of representation involves a penalty being incurred in terms of efficiency. For particular cases, simplification is called for: preferably as adopted by the artificial agent itself. This is the domain of knowledge compilation: let human developers resort to flexible and intuitively appealing representations, while constructing the knowledge base, and let a compiler transform the resulting knowledge base into efficient code. One more step, not practical yet, in this open area of research is cognitive economy, with systems automatically improving their performance by changing representations and access, and compiling knowledge according to experiment-based predictions of the opportunity and nature of changes without the developers having to anticipate how knowledge will be used in particular cases (Stefik et al. 1983; Lenat et al. 1979).

The problems of encoding huge quantities of knowledge – in particular common-sense knowledge, that is, the knowledge humans employ most frequently – are discussed by Lenat et al. (1986) from the perspective of the ongoing CYC common-sense knowledge base project of MCC (Austin, Texas). Instead, from the viewpoint of AI as simulating human cognition, Cherniak (1988) epistemologically questions the testability of a huge program with ambitions of simulating the mind, a program that can be expected to be "inhumanly unmanageable from a resource- realistic approach to cognitive science … an impossibility engine, in that it would be practically unfeasible for us fully to comprehend and evaluate it". Cherniak goes on to point out that he does not propose an impossibility proof, but instead observes that because of our own human limitations, in front of a hypothetical mind-program embody-ing a model as unwieldily structured as the human mind (as opposed to hypothetical models yielding the full range of functions of human intelligent behaviour), "our stance towards it might end up a little like that of coral animals towards the vast reef they have built", but that modelling built up from the neural level could nevertheless be expected to converge in complexity at the same level. Resources for computational reasoning are starting to be reflected in suitable theories: at the University of Michigan, Ann Arbor, Yuri Gurevich has been challenging traditional approaches to logic that ignore resource limitations, and has developed a logic computational model that accounts for the quantitative limit of computational resources.

Purpose (In)Dependency of Representation

Divergent purposes for a knowledge base with the same core involve the need for the representation of knowledge to be adapted for given controls, or else a penalty is incurred in terms of bulky chunks of knowledge being accessed and searched, even if we admit that task-specific control components embody knowledge of what they should look for.

Let us consider the contrast between the consulted knowledge base and the control exploiting it in the ONOMATURGE project (Nissan 1985a–c; 1987a; 1989b; 1991a–c). ONOMATURGE, developed since 1983, is an expert system for word formation: given a definition of a concept, ONOMATURGE coins Hebrew "candidate" neologisms to express it, and evaluates their quality in terms of morpho-semantic transparency for fluent Hebrew speakers. Representation in the lexicographic frame- base is structured according to a rule-based meta-description – a description of attributes – of the internal structure of frames (that in ONOMATURGE are passive, deeply- nested relations, i.e. trees of properties). Expertise in the specific domain of word formation is embodied in the control component of ONOMATURGE and in a rule set for derivational morphology. The lexical database consulted is general instead and should be considered as a stand-alone component from the viewpoint of machine dictionaries. Indeed, each lexical entry in the database is described by a tree of properties that concerns only in part a given application, such as word formation in ONOMATURGE. Most properties in the schema (Nissan 1991b) are not exploited by the present version of control of ONOMATURGE: the database potentially subserves other tasks in computational linguistics that involve semantics, morphology and the lexicon. Certain properties are concerned only when the task is affected by historical knowledge about the lexicon, pragmatics or morphology (Nissan 1986; 1991c). Some architectural changes are involved if the database is conceived as having to subserve a multilingual task. Nissan (1991c) describes the schema of a multilingual Semitic dictionary: an architecture, a representation in terms of graphs and an attribute testing meta-description for the database. They account for the relation between constellations of semantic concepts and constellations of derivatives (related by roots and morphological derivational patterns, parallel in a given family of languages). Architecture in the multilingual lexicon and in the lexical database of ONOMATURGE differ, and choices are justified in terms of multilinguality versus monolinguality. Language kinship is exploited. Here, too, a taxonomy of choices could be defined, according to cognitive or lexicographic or machine translation practical interests. For example, for the purposes of machine translation, the exploitation of language kinship does not seem useful.

Even in the specific domain of ONOMATURGE itself – word formation – uses are bound to differ: in its present version, control generates neologisms as being of interest for institutional language planning, an activity of interest in societies that have to preserve or develop their language. This use motivated conceiving the control as a system for generation rather than for analysis, or for both: the latter case is interesting for basic linguistic research, while analysis is of interest for natural language processing (NLP) when having to handle terms unknown to the lexicon of the parser. The latter use, in turn, can be dichotomised: the practical goal of making NLP robust is not the same as the important goal of making NLP models cognitively more plausible. ONOMATURGE, as subserving lexical innovation for the purposes of language planning, has to evaluate how well native speakers are going to cope with the term (guessing its meaning correctly) on meeting it for the first time: thus the ONOMATURGE model relates morphological derivation to semantics, socio-linguistics, typicality of features etc., in order to evaluate formation transparency. It emerges that such evaluation would be enhanced by the addition of an analysis phase after the currently implemented generation phase. Not only that, but this kind of evaluation, with suitable modifications, could fit into the framework of text-generating systems (e.g. abstract-generators or explainers) and allow apt wording according to assumptions about the epistemic and linguistic background of the intended audience. However, describing the typicality of semantic features and knowledge about the distribution of knowledge about the lexicon or semantic concepts or properties among professional communities, or in age-classes of the general population of a given culture involves the representation of an explosion of knowledge (Nissan 1987b).

In a different project, I have been investigating creative aspects of alternative explanations: with two students of mine, Zvi Kuflik and Gil'ad Puni, I have developed ALIBI, a rather primitive prototype of a planner synthesising alibis. It spoils imputed actions, specified in an input "police report" of connotational interpretations (e.g. "stealing" is reduced to "taking" as in given objective circumstances); then alternative explanations of the imputed behaviour are put together and displayed. In the database of the system, semantic knowledge is stated about connotations (in terms of legality), component actions and effects. Action verbs are hierarchically decomposed into constitutive actions. Because complex actions are involved at run-time in the generation of an alibi, the planner core is recursively applied to semantic knowledge and relates effects to actions after having related actions to "atomic" constitutive actions. This way of conceiving the use of semantic concepts is very different from their use in word formation, but there is an intersection of attributes that could subserve both tasks, given suitable control components.

ONOMATURGE is subserved by a frame manager, RAFFAELLO (Nissan 1986; 1987c,d; 1988; 1991d: see also "Formalism and Society", below) that we also used for another application, namely hospitality management (Nissan 1987e). RAFFAELLO handles large frames with a possibly very deep tree of properties. However, its present status reflects a situation where frames are loaded with all of their properties. What I have explained before about knowledge bases intended for use by different tasks, just sharing interest in intersections of attributes, suggests that an interface between tasks (or experts) and a global shared knowledge base should be developed. Such an interface would cause only relevant fragments of frames to be loaded and according to opportunity it would allow the reconstruction of a tailor-made special interest frame out of miscellaneous fragments or of large disparate chunks.

Meta-models of Expert Behaviour

Artificial intelligence can be of some help in trying to analyse very large processes that it would be unfeasible to simulate in detail, such as the development of certain sciences and of variants of expert behaviour therein. The example to be described here is a meta-model of trial and error in Etruscology, the science that for two centuries has been trying to interpret Etruscan, an ancient language of pre-Roman Italy, of which hundreds of inscriptions are extant in an alphabet that can be read. The lexicon and grammar of the language are practically unknown. I have developed (Nissan 1991e) a knowledge analysis which is intended to provide the basis for a meta-model of the interpretation of Etruscan, based on protocols of principled interpretation trials published in the domain literature. The search space is very large, but the odds are favourable for satisfactory partial matching in given lexical instances (or even better for sub-strings of a continuous string with no indication of word separation, as is frequent in Etruscan inscriptions). Moreover, this is dangerous ground for using induction to reconstruct grammar and cultural analogy to hypothesise semantics. The meta-model of interpretation as I have outlined it, considers competing partial interpretations of Etruscan as trying to climb to local optima in a universe of paradigms being constructed by learning. Two main phases are identified in the process:

1. Attempts to select among known languages a candidate model with respect to which to reconstruct deviation. This is attempted by reduced runs of phase II. Overall paradigm shifts occur in phase I. Promise evaluation is hampered in phase I by the cumulation of errors in confidence transmission between investigators.

2. Once a candidate model is selected (one language or a family of phylogenetically or historically closely related languages), phase II focuses search for relatively small discrepancies. A blackboard architecture is considered suitable for representation of integrating learning methods. There are some analogies with speech processing, e.g. because the lack of word separation motivates island-based word hypothesising. However, while English speech processing refers to a description of English (a known language), for interpreting Etruscan, learning has instead to bridge between two components: (i) the model of interpretation of Etruscan itself, the description (lexicon and grammar) is the paradigm being constructed in the partial solution space, and is used as a constraint in order to maintain coherence. Nevertheless, the paradigm is defeasible by a certain threshold of counter- examples. Induction is not indulged in, other than by strictly regulated comparison with; (ii) the description (lexicon and grammar) of a known language, selected by phase I as a model of deviation.

It is crucial that an established set of fixed rules of phonetic/phonologic or morphological correspondence should not be departed from. Simulating the spectrum of the specific expertise models of linguistic inquiry in Etruscology (as opposed to a general undetailed schema of those models: the meta-model) looks unfeasible unless a group of experts and knowledge engineers would be willing to devote a substantial portion of their professional life to the development of a running simulator of the various directions of research.

Indeed, the present status of Etruscology (which is not the same as extant results) developed from two centuries of work of researchers with certain competencies who pursued very different directions, especially in what I have called phase I. Their linguistic knowledge was in each instance almost unique. Resulting from the cumulation of linguistic knowledge in one or more languages as an object of scientific inquiry, such knowledge was affected by given stresses, imprecisions and limitations and presumably the linguist's competency exploited synergies between the domains learned. Not only did each linguist know a different set of languages (so partitions of the set of all languages involved should be accounted for), but their knowledge was biased. Therefore implementation should be based on simulated professional person-alities of characters conceived as reflecting a "typical" set of Etruscologists. Such meta-modelling in the considered domain is interesting even from the viewpoint of AI and not just (and arguably more than) for Etruscology: indeed, some interesting phenomena in search are typified, and this looks like a fertile ground for investigating machine learning in connection with blackboard architectures. The latter embody distinct areas of linguistic/epigraphic exper-tise, triggered according to a control whose flow (especially in phase II) is defined at run-time.

Formalism and Society

The extension of human abilities has implications for the dynamics of human culture. One can argue that, during the last century, while trying to provide what he claimed was a scientific rather than ideological basis for political thinking, Marx adopted hierarchical models for social organisation because hierarchies are relatively simple structures that at his time could be formally managed for the purposes of planning. It is needless to point out the impact of this choice on human life in hierarchically managed societies. The way we can organise ourselves through formal models is potentially enhanced by tools supporting intellectual activities, and the evolution of the latter offers options for what we are actually going to do with them: nowadays complex dynamic structures are modelled in computing that are moderately or intensively parallel and account for multiple sources of initiative. The blackboard representation as known from knowledge engineering and other schemata of parallelism allow us to model universes where several agents co-operate or compete and to intervene in terms of the formalism.

From another perspective, Ghandchi and Ghandchi (1985) discuss the technological basis of certain social structures and the potential social impact of knowledge-based tools outperforming humans at certain tasks.

Conclusions

In "Bipolarity", above, I have discussed "Prometheic" ambition in AI, as opposed to down-to-earth progress according to the "callidiority" metric. This contraposition roughly corresponds to the opposition of science and technology, or of cognitive simulation versus cognitively indifferent practical purposes. On the technological side, I discussed, in "Mainstreaming in Computing", the view of AI as a potential mainstream direction in computing practice. Then the thread of technology leads to consideration of the potential impact of AI on human skill (see "Impact on Human Skill", above). Resource realism is important in AI for both technology and science; quantity as a limit to feasibility was discussed in "The Challenge of Quantity", with a mention of

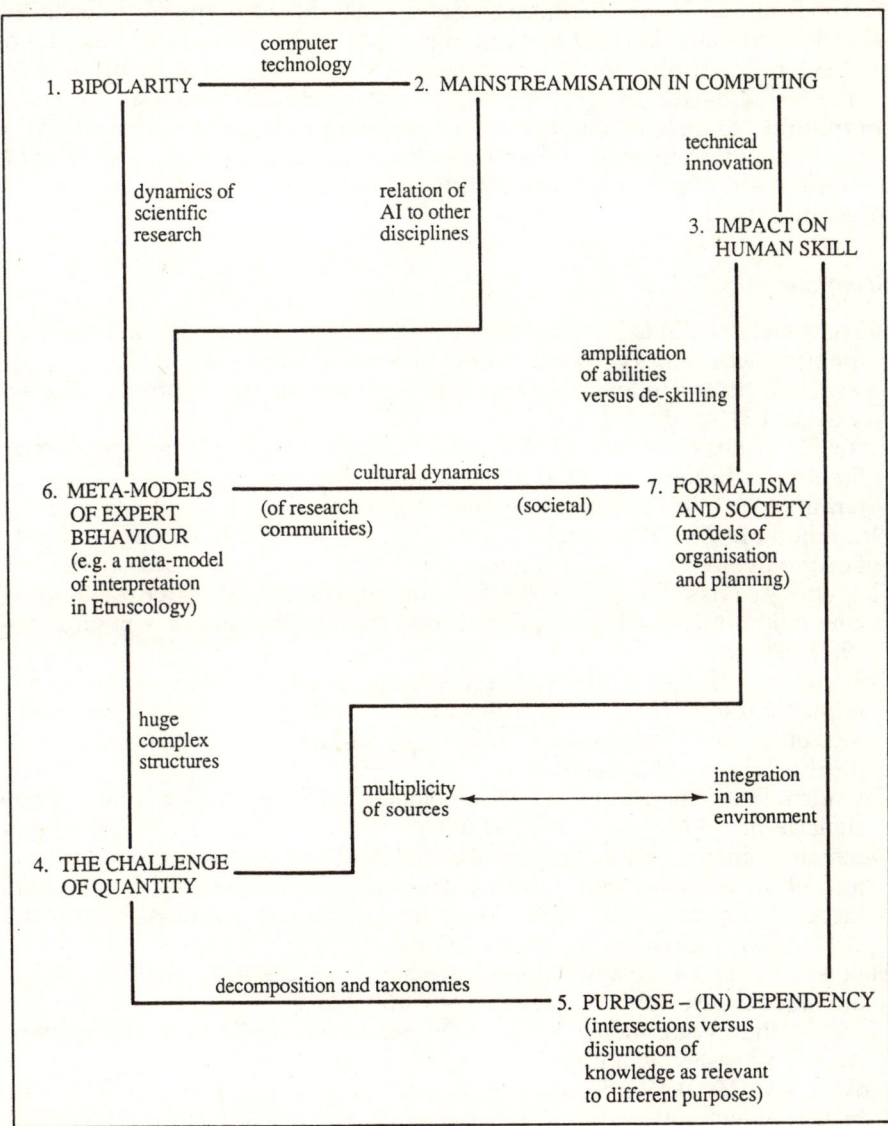

Fig. 5.1. Relationship between the topics discussed.

problems of rationalising representation. "Purpose (In)Dependency of Representation" goes on along the thread of large scale problems of representation and points out that elements in taxonomies of domains or purposes can happen to share intersections of relevant knowledge, while representations face problems of flexibility if use is intended as subserving different tasks and domains. "Meta-models of Expert Behaviour" discusses ambitions as upgraded to (meta)-modelling the cultural dynamics of given scientific disciplines, as opposed to models of individual or standard expert behaviour. "Formalism and Society" continues the societal thread of the sections on the impact on human skill and meta-modelling by individuating the extent – as attained by culture – to which reasoning can handle models of complex structures, a factor in the making of socio-political thinking. AI has a contribution to offer to simulation and planning in large scale distributed or concurrent environments, and thus it potentially has a say in the way humans organise their gregarious dimension. Fig. 5.1 depicts connections among the topics discussed.

References

Braverman H (1975) Labor and monopoly capital: The degradation of work in the twentieth century. Monthly Review Press, New York

Cherniak C (1988) Undebuggability and cognitive science. Communications of the ACM 31(4):402–412

Czap H, Galinski C (eds) (1987) Terminology and knowledge engineering Frankfurt. Indeks Verlag (Proceedings of the international congress on terminology and knowledge engineering, Trier, 1987)

Drummond D (1987) Building a locomotive: skill and the work force in Crewe Locomotive Works, 1843–1914. Journal of Transport History 3rd ser 8(1):1–29

Galperin A, Nissan E (1988) Applications of a heuristic search method for generation of fuel reload configurations. Nuclear Science and Engineering 99(4):343–352

Galperin A, Nissan E (1989) Discovery as assisted by an expert tool: a refinement loop for heuristic rules in an engineering domain. In: Proceedings of the 16th convention of Electrical and Electronics Engineers in Israel (IEEE). Tel-Aviv, March 1989

Ghandchi HM, Ghandchi JA (1985) Intelligent tools: the cornerstone of a new civilisation. AI Magazine 6(3):102–106

Guzman Arenas A (1983) Applied artificial intelligence: an emerging technology of widespread use. Informe Technico, Departamento de Engineria Electrica, Centro de Investigacion y de Estudios Avanzados del Instituto Politecnico Nacional, Zacatenco (Mexico)

Hall RP, Kibler DF (1985) Differing methodological perspectives in artificial intelligence research. AI Magazine 6(3):166–178

Hayes-Roth F, Waterman DA, Lenat DB (eds) (1983) Building expert systems. Addison-Wesley, Reading, MA

Jenkins RV (1987) Words, images, artifacts and sound: documents for the history of technology. British Journal for the History of Science. 20(64):39–56 (part I)

Latour B (1986) Technologos, vol 3. Laboratoire d'Informatique pour les Sciences de l'Homme, Paris, pp 3–5 (editorial)

Lenat DB, Hayes-Roth F, Klahr P (1979) Cognitive economy in artificial intelligence systems. In: Proceedings of the 6th IJCAI conference, pp 531–536

Lenat D, Prakash M, Sheperd M (1986) CYC: Using commonsense knowledge to overcome brittleness and knowledge bottlenecks. AI Magazine 6(4):65–85

More C (1980) Skill and the English working class, 1870–1914. Croom Helm, London

Nii HP (1986) Blackboard systems. Part Two: Blackboard application systems. Blackboard systems from a knowledge engineering perspective. AI Magazine 7(3):82–106

Nissan E (1985a) Could an expert system perform what Schonberg couldn't for Moses: word-coinage in the Bible's tongue? ONOMATURGE, a lexical mint. In: Proceedings of the Cognitiva '85 conference, vol 1. CEST, Paris, pp 95–100

Nissan E (1985b) The representation of synonyms and related terms in the frames of an expert system for word coinage. Part I: The twelve chairs and ONOMATURGE. Part II: On lions, leopards and ONOMATURGE. In: Rault J-C (ed) Proceedings of the 5th international workshop on expert systems and their applications, vol 2. Avignon, 1985, pp 685–703 and pp 705–741

Nissan E (1985c) On the architecture of ONOMATURGE, an expert system inventing neologisms. In: Brunet E (ed) Methodes quantitatives et informatiques dans l'etude des textes – Computers in literary and linguistic research. Proceedings of the 12th conference of the Association for Literary and Linguistic Computing. Nice, June 1985. Champion-Slatkine, Paris, pp 671–680 (Volume in honour of Charles Muller)

Nissan E (1986) The frame-definition language for customising the RAFFAELLO structure-editor in host expert systems. In: Ras Z, Zemanovka M (eds) Proceedings of the 1st international symposium on methodologies for intelligent systems, Knoxville, Tennessee. ACM Press, New York

Nissan E (1987a) ONOMATURGE: an expert system for word formation and morpho-semantic clarity evaluation. Part I: The task in perspective and a model of the dynamics of the system. Part II: The statics of the system: The representation from the general viewpoint of knowledge-bases for terminology. In: Czap H, Galinski C (eds) (1987) Terminology and knowledge engineering Frankfurt. Indeks Verlag, pp 167–176 and pp 177–189) (Proceedings of the international congress on terminology and knowledge engineering, Trier, 1987)

Nissan E (1987b) Exception admissibility and typicality in proto-representations. In: Czap H, Galinski C (eds) (1987) Terminology and knowledge engineering Frankfurt. Indeks Verlag (Proceedings of the international congress on terminology and knowledge engineering, Trier, 1987)

Nissan E (1987c) Knowledge acquisition and metarepresentation: attribute autopoiesis. In: Ras Z, Zemanovka M (eds) Methodologies for intelligent systems. North-Holland, Amsterdam, pp 240–247 (Proceedings of the 2nd international symposium on methodologies for intelligent systems)

Nissan E (1987d) Data analysis using a geometrical representation of predicate calculus. Information Sciences 41(3):187–258

Nissan E (1987e) The Wining and Dining Project. Part II: FIDEL_GASTRO, an expert system for gastronomy and terminal food-processing. International Journal of Hospitality Management 6(4):207–215

Nissan E (1988) NAVIGATION: the metarepresentation-guided component of RAFFAELLO for retrieval from deeply-nested relations. In: E. Nissan, ONOMATURGE: An expert system for word formation (in press)

Nissan E (1989a) Artificial intelligence in higher education. Part I: Education for AI, from courses in computer science to courses in application domains. Part II: AI for education; present trends as sources for a concept of knowledge representation. In: Osthoek H, Vroeijensteijn (eds) Proceedings of the 5th EARDHE congress on higher education and new technologies, Utrecht, 1987. Pergamon, London, pp 67–98 and pp 249–262

Nissan E (1989b) Derivational knowledge and the common sense of coping with the incompleteness of lexical knowledge. In: Proceedings of the international symposium on communication, meaning and knowledge versus information technology. Lisbon, 13–15 Sept 1989

Nissan E (1991a) ONOMATURGE: An expert system for word formation (in press)

Nissan E (1991b) Attributes in the lexicographical knowledge- base of ONOMATURGE. Part I: Overall organisation of lexical entries and acceptations. Part II: Going deeper inside the topology. In: Schmidt KM (ed) Concepts, content, meaning, vol. 2. JAI Press, Greenwich, Conn (The Society for Conceptual and Content Analysis by Computer, supplementary volume in the series Advances in computing and the humanities)(in press)

Nissan E (1991c) Structure and representation for a multilingual Semitic machine dictionary: Issues in engineering a lexicon meant for symbolic manipulation. In: Schmidt KM (ed) Concepts, content, meaning, vol. 2. JAI Press, Greenwich, Conn (The Society for Conceptual and Content Analysis by Computer, supplementary volume in the series Advances in computing and the humanities)(in press)

Nissan E (1991d) A metarepresentation-driven tool as used in training to build expert systems. In: Bar-On E, Scherz Z (eds) Intelligent training (tutoring) systems. Ablex, Norwood, NJ

Nissan E (1991e) A knowledge analysis of Bernadini Marzolla's Indoglottal interpretation of Etruscan: for a metamodel of interpretation. In: Sinha RMK, Nissan E (eds) Computing and India's (or Indian-related) scripts, a special section in: Nissan E (ed) Advances in computing and the humanities, vol 1, Language and speech. JAI Press, Greenwich, CT

Ringle M (1979) Philosophy and artificial intelligence. In: Ringle M (ed) Philosophical perspectives in artificial intelligence. Humanities Press, Atlantic Highlands, NJ

Ringle M (1983) Psychological studies and artificial intelligence. AI Magazine 4(1):37–43

Stefik M, Atkins J, Balzer R, Benoit J, Birnbaum L, Hayes-Roth F, Sacerdoti E (1983) The architecture of expert systems. In: Hayes-Roth F, Waterman DA, Lenat DB (eds) (1983) Building expert systems. Addison-Wesley, Reading, MA, pp 89–126

Stiegler B (1986) La faute d'Epimethee. Technologos, vol 3. Laboratoire d'Informatique pour les Sciences de l'Homme, Paris, pp 7–16

Waterman DA, Hayes-Roth F (1978) Pattern-directed inference systems. Academic Press, Orlando, FL, pp 3–22

Woods DD (1986) Cognitive technologies: the design of joint human–machine cognitive systems. AI Magazine 6(4):86–92

Chapter 6

Biological and Artificial Intelligence

Alberto Oliverio

What is Intelligent Behaviour?

The analogies and differences between biological and artificial intelligence are today an object of discussion, controversy and working hypotheses. The search for analogies is based on the ways in which information is first recorded and then processed, generalised and retrieved. "Simplified" models of the nervous system have been put forward in order to explain these problems on the neurophysiological level. These may take the form of the nervous system of an invertebrate such as a worm or a snail, the circuitry of the spinal cord, complete with its excitatory and inhibitory components or, at a level of increasing complexity, the set of palaeoencephalic structures which modulate the "intelligent" behaviour of a species (the so-called "instincts") or, in the obvious case of the cerebral cortex, whose columnar arrangement makes it a powerful information analyser and processor.

These models differ greatly from one another as regards both their underlying nervous structures and the "intelligent" functions which they perform. These range from inhibitory– excitatory circuits, such as the sensory-motor reflex (as in the case of the nervous system of a worm, or many of the functions carried out by the spinal cord in vertebrates) to the sophisticated memory, generalisation and analysis processes carried out by the cerebral cortex. The term "intelligence" is therefore used somewhat ambiguously, with the result that similarities and contrasts between biological and artificial intelligence frequently refer to a wide spectrum of structures and functions having little in common. However, the problem is not merely semantic. In fact, biologists often assess "intelligent" activities in terms relating not to neurophysiological criteria – and thus to structures, circuits and nerve networks which are "analogous" to those of artificial intelligence – but to evolutionary criteria. They thus refer to a series of adaptive modifications in which close relations between structures and functions result in the "plastic" modifications which are typical of biological brains but which are rare in artificial ones.

Can the problem be limited and common ground established for neurobiologists and computer scientists by considering only the processes of memory and problem solving? The limitations of this solution, which is linked to a more restricted approach, lie in its assumption that the biological structures to which memory and cognitive activities are related have a certain "rigidity" of their own which makes them not unlike the material substrates on which the processes of artificial intelligence are based. However, this view of the nervous system is, in fact, a simplification. It involves rigid nervous structures and localised functions rather than ones which are plastic and not strictly delimited, and a view of the nervous system in "localisationist" terms and of the brain through reference to neomechanistic metaphors. It is therefore worthwhile going over some of the crucial points of the debate on relations between biological and artificial intelligence and examining in particular the concepts of "plasticity" and "localisation", which are often based on metaphors derived from other disciplines: most recently robotics and information theory. This metaphorical aspect of approaches to the working of the nervous system often leads to a vicious circle, in which computer-type metaphors regarding the brain stimulate research into artificial intelligence, based on concepts and models of the nervous system which are more metaphorical than real.

The Plasticity of the Nervous System

The first point to be considered is the essentially biological concept of plasticity. The considerable ambiguity characterising the term arises for two reasons. It is applied to different aspects of the cerebral function, and therefore used to indicate different features; and it has been used in the past to indicate that the brain managed somehow to evade those "laws", or ideal principles, which described it as rigidly organised, and therefore impervious to structural modification. The mechanisms were, however, quite unknown, and so the term seemed annoyingly ambiguous. Let us, therefore, examine the different uses and meanings of the term "plasticity", the ideal principle it contradicted in the past and its current meaning in the language of modern neurosciences (Oliverio 1983).

Plasticity for the Evolutionist

Students of behaviour and the nervous system who have tried to fit the long evolutionary path of vertebrates into a single framework often point out how the course of evolution has led from rigidly structured nervous systems and behaviour to nervous structures and activities of a more plastic kind. Thus, the more primitive chordate species (essentially those with spinal cord structures) are equipped with a nervous system which corresponds to rigid "programming" and allows mainly reflex actions. Reptiles, on the other hand, possess palaeoencephalic structures and a limbic system and display instinctive behaviour which, though corresponding to a programme common to the species, also allows individual experience. They are therefore characterised by a nervous system and by behaviour of a slightly less rigid and slightly more plastic kind than that of primitive chordates. Finally, mammals, especially primates, being equipped with a well-developed cerebral cortex, display their ability to modify their behaviour, to evade the rigidity of genetic programming and thus be more plastic.

According to this evolutionistic framework, which holds all the fascination characteristic of universal theories and has been strongly supported by Paul MacLean (1955), the evolution of the nervous system proceeds from the simple to the complex, and by transition from reflex actions to the instinctive actions typical of a species, and thence to learning, or actions characteristic of the individual: a range from greater rigidity to great plasticity. This way of defining plasticity has its strong points, but also its weaknesses. While instinctive behaviour is certainly less rigid than reflexes, the behaviour typical of a certain species, i.e. its instincts, is also affected by experience, learning and memory. It develops and is influenced by relations with the living environment.

Environmental Input and Cerebral Plasticity

In about the mid-sixties, a group of comparative psychologists from Berkeley, led by Mark Rozenweig (Rozenweig and Bennett 1969) carried out an experiment which was, in some ways, heretical with respect to the theories of the brain current at that time. The brain was, in fact, regarded as practically impervious to the effects of the environment. Programmed by genes, provided with a predetermined number of neurons and incapable of mitosis after birth, the brain appeared to present certain predetermined structural characteristics, relations between neurons and circuits which were regarded as invariants absolutely immune to modification. The experiment devised by Rozenweig involved the immersion of two groups of rats in two different environments, one rich in stimuli and the other poor. Raised in the two different environments, the animals proved to be deeply affected by their different juvenile experiences, in that the brains of the "enriched" rats were heavier, were characterised by a thicker cortex, by a greater number of cells in the glia and by neurons equipped with a greater number of dendritic spines (the slender elongations forming synapses between one neuron and another). The results obtained by Rozenweig and his colleagues basically show that brain structure is not completely predetermined, but is susceptible to considerable structural modification, which may involve behavioural differences: such as the greater learning ability characteristic of the adult rats which had been reared in an enriched environment. In this case, plasticity has a different meaning from that which characterises the evolutionist's viewpoint: it indicates that cerebral structures have dynamic characteristics rather than the static ones ascribed to them by the traditional view.

Plasticity and Epigenesis

The new concept of the brain introduced by Rozenweig has already been confirmed and extended by the studies of David Hubel and Torsten Wiesel

(1973) on the dynamics of nerve connections between the eye and the IV layer of the visual cortex in the course of development. The configuration of the visual cortex could be described as striped: to use more technical terms, it is subdivided into "columns of ocular dominance". Each visual cell decodes information transmitted by a small part of the retina of the eye to which it is connected. If no light falls on that point, the cell "sees" nothing. This sensory field is connected to only one eye, the right or the left. If we move slightly along the IV layer of the visual cortex and examine a cell next to the previous one, we find that its sensory field comes from the other eye. The IV layer of the visual cortex is, in fact, composed of adjacent columns of cells arranged in such a way that if the sensory field of one column is in the left eye, then its neighbour, slightly less than half a millimetre away, will respond to light impinging on the corresponding point in the right eye. These columns alternate along the whole length of the visual cortex, which therefore presents a striped pattern since it alternately gathers information from one eye or the other.

This strange architecture of the cortex is not found in a new-born animal, and at that age, each eye projects its image over virtually all of the cells of the IV layer, forming an enormous number of synapses with many nerve cells without having a striped pattern. However, the situation soon changes as the fibres of the two eyes begin to compete: in a small part of the visual cortex, the right eye will begin to gain the upper hand and to drive out the left; in another, the left will triumph. Gradually in the course of infancy, the fibres of the two eyes will form increasingly localised synapses in one stripe or other of the cortex. Researchers do not know how this striped pattern is programmed, but do know that it arises through competition between synapses, ensuring that a synapse connecting a certain point of the right eye to a cell in the IV layer will get the better of a synapse from the corresponding point of the left eye. Thus, the synapses "struggle" and either establish themselves or succumb. They follow no predetermined rules – save that of the columnar arrangement – but behave in a plastic way, with consequences that may be either positive or negative according to complex interaction between genetic factors, environmental stimuli and internal factors. According to this view, plasticity underlies the epigenetic processes of the nervous system.

Plasticity as a Repairing Phenomenon

Seen in this light, plasticity appears to have characteristics which are primarily aimed at the stabilisation of the nerve network and at attaining a state of equilibrium rather than playing a dynamic role in the repair of damage or deficiencies. However, this function does not necessarily clash with that of stabilisation, and is based on the same dynamic processes related to the budding of the axon, to synaptic growth and to competition between neurons, as indicated by Patricia Goldman's studies of the repair of lesions to the central nervous system during the foetal stage (Goldman-Rakic 1981).

Goldman has studied the effects of cerebral lesions in rhesus monkeys six weeks before birth. While lesions to the frontal cortex of the adult animal lead to virtually irreparable lasting damage, prenatal lesions result in no noticeable functional consequences after birth, as processes of compensation take place during the foetal stage. In fact, the frontal lobe is linked through a functional circuit to the caudate nucleus of the same hemisphere and to that of the contralateral hemisphere. In animals subjected to lesions of the frontal lobe at the foetal stage, a massive re-innervation of the caudate nucleus of the damaged hemisphere (the left, for example) was implemented by the intact frontal lobe (e.g. the right). In this way, the lack of afferents from the damaged frontal cortex in the left caudate was compensated by an increase in connections between the intact frontal lobe (the right) and the left caudate. In fact, the dendritic spines of the neurons of the intact frontal lobe are free to form synapses with the neurons of the left caudate, not innervated by the frontal cortex of the same side.

Goldman's experiments also indicate, like those carried out on hemispherectomised children, the existence of precocious plasticity phenomena. In the case of hemispherectomy performed on new-born babies or older children, the remaining hemisphere is able to take over a function for which it is not normally competent. In the case of lesions of the frontal cortex, on the other hand, re-innervation phenomena occur through an increase in connections with other neurons. However, plastic phenomena are not limited to the prenatal phase, as one might be led to suppose. Under the category of "plastic" come also the phenomena which occur throughout life, such as habit, memory and the attempts at repair which take place in the adult brain after damage to the central nervous system.

Neuronal Plasticity and the Recording of Information

The first aspect, that of plasticity in memory and learning, is prominent in Erik Kandel's (1976) research on *Aplysia*, a sea-slug with a fairly simple nervous system. If the siphon through which it emits water is lightly stimulated, the slug retracts its branchiae ("gills"). If the stimulus is repeated regularly a number of times, the *Aplysia* becomes habituated to it, i.e. it ignores the stimulus and no longer retracts its branchiae. Habituation, as Kandel has demonstrated, is a modification of behaviour: a simple form of short-term memory which depends on plastic alterations to the synapses of the nerve circuit controlling the reflex action of retracting the branchiae. When the siphon is touched, the sensory neurons are stimulated and transmit an excitatory stimulus to the motor neurons which innervate the muscles used to retract the branchiae. The use of a thin electrode to record the electrical activity of the neurons causing the branchiae to retract, reveals that in the course of habituation to the stimulus, the post-synaptic potential (i.e. the electrical activity of the membrane of the motor neuron) diminishes gradually as the sensory neurons send the motor neurons electrical charges in response to the stimulation of the siphon. Kandel has demonstrated that these phenomena are caused by an increase in potassium ions, a decrease in the so-called "calcium channels", and a cascade of biochemical events, leading to a decrease in the neuron's activity. In short, habituation and other forms of adaptation are, in the last analysis, plastic phenomena linked to modifications in the activity of the synapses.

To conclude, nerve plasticity has different facets and carries out different functions. But the different types of plasticity underlie a new way of viewing the brain, an authentic change in philosophy, that has taken place in recent years. Even concepts such as the "map" of sensory or somato-motor functions have changed from what they were in the past. Once cortical maps of sensory or motor functions – which offered an approximate and out-of-scale representation of peripheral territories at the level of the motor or somato-sensory cortex – were held to be invariant, subject to slight variation among individuals of a species, but constant in time as regards the individual. However, in recent years it has emerged that cortical maps (the homunculus) are subject to considerable variation within a single animal species and to great "plastic" fluctuation during an individual's lifetime. As a result of these fluctuations, a given peripheral territory (e.g. one finger of one hand) may be represented at the cortical level to a greater or lesser extent according to its functional activity.

Localisationism or Holism?

The phenomena of cerebral plasticity indicate how necessary it is to re-evaluate the over-deterministic and locationist view of the brain that can be expressed today in such metaphors as "the brain is a computer" and was based in the past on metaphors drawn from other fields: Cartesian mechanistic metaphors, electrical metaphors after the discoveries of Volta and Galvani, the mechanistic– thermodynamic variety of the late nineteenth century (Loeb's "thinking machine"), the telephone (the brain and its "relays") and finally the computer. Metaphors are obviously not devoid of positive implications, and their heuristic value should not be underestimated. But most metaphors regarding the brain stem from mechanistic–deterministic concepts that can hardly be reconciled with cerebral plasticity.

The argument that the principles of cerebral functioning are similar to those of the computer is in line with the strictly localisationist views of Franz-Josef Gall, the Viennese phrenologist, who maintained that every human faculty – from love to religion – was localised in the cerebral cortex. The idea that different cerebral functions were localised found considerable support in the discoveries of the French neurologist Paul Broca and others in this field. They demonstrated that the loss of a particular cerebral function subsequent to vascular or traumatic lesions could be related back to damage to specific cortical regions. The localisationists also claimed that the different areas or functional units of the brain were depositories of mnemonic images – visual images or objects or auditory images of words – associated with their functions. According to these views, recognition involved the coupling of the images formed at the level of the sensory receptors with images previously recorded and deposited in specific centres of the memory. Similarly, remembering depended on the activation of previously recorded images. For example, in 1869, Charles H. Bastian described a case of "verbal deafness" in a patient able to hear the words but not to understand or distinguish single words or phrases. Bastian attributed this deficiency to loss of the "auditory images" of the words. The patient's spoken language was intact, as the "motor schemata or images" had not been damaged.

Disputes between localisationists – from Broca, C. Wernicke and H. Jackson to W. Penfield, E. Ross, K. Heilman and E. Robins – and holists – from K.

Goldstein, I. Pavlov, H. Head and K. Lashley to E. Roy John and R.W. Thatcher
– have continued with alternating fortunes up to the present day. A position
attempting to reconcile the two sides, first adopted by C. Wernicke in the
nineteenth century and now taken up again by E. Kandel, views some "basic"
functions, such as the motor or somato-sensory functions as being localised or
organised "in-series" (and thus more vulnerable). The more general processes,
like memory and learning, are not regarded as localised and are supposed to
respond to a "parallel" logic, in that they involve different nuclei and layers
(see Kandel 1985, p 85). However, to say that a function is localised does not
mean to say that it is not plastic, just as to claim that some functions like
memory are organised "parallel" to the cortex does not necessarily imply that
there is no participation in them by various cerebral "levels", such as the
subcortical structures involved in emotion.

Freud and Dream Memories

Israel Rosenfield (1988) has recently observed that localisationist views were
attacked by Freud, who stressed that dreams have a fragmentary meaning, and
that the same "image" or memory did not have an absolute and specific
significance in a dream, but could have a number of connotations. A face, for
example, could refer to a woman or a man, to a loved one or to a mere
acquaintance. Freud regarded this lack of specificity in dream memories as due
to the lack of contextualisation in dreams and in particular to the absence of a
critical point of reference, i.e. the emotions. His views attracted little attention
until the late 1930s, when Papez was able to delineate the so-called limbic
system – a group of subcortical structures which modulate our emotional lives.
Neurologists have since demonstrated how the various nerve nuclei of this
system play an important part in memory processes, enabling a memory or
image, in itself neutral, to be "attached" to a particular emotional context
whereby it is given a specific connotation. In short, as Rosenfield (1988) and
others point out, memory is not a localised and specific process, but one of
generalisation and categorisation.

There is actually much evidence in favour of memory being strictly
dependent upon context and relating to individual strategies rather than a
stimulus-specific process of codification identical in all individuals. For
example, the Soviet neurophysiologist N. Bernstein (see Kandel 1985) has
demonstrated that movements are never identical and that they involve the
action of different muscles. When drawing a circle by hand, we use different
muscles according to whether the circle is drawn in the air with the arm held
straight out in front of us or with the index finger pointing to the ground.
Bernstein's studies, like Freud's work on dreams and emotions, indicate that a
brain does not record a specific piece of information in a "memory warehouse",
but the capacity (or procedure) for carrying out movements in different
circumstances. In this case too, the process is not specific but forms part of a
generalising strategy.

There are many other findings in line with this conceptual approach which
cast doubt both upon essentially localisationist interpretations and on analogies between biological and electronic brains as regards the process of

recording specific memories. For example, David Marr (1982) has challenged the classic approach to human memory used in the field of artificial intelligence with regard to visual recognition. The significance of a circle or a square may vary according to the context in which the figures are inserted, just as the recognition of a particular shape may be possible without reference to a stock of fixed memories. Moreover, in using simulation programs on the computer, Marr has noted that recognition of a particular shape does not come about through its immediate coupling with a previously codified stimulus, but through a series of intermediate steps which permit the brain to "calculate" the salient features of an object and arrive at the formation of a so-called "primal sketch", which involves the activation of general strategies and diffused centres rather than specific strategies and localised centres.

Memory as a Categorisation Procedure

A further example of the importance of the processes of categorisation and generalisation is furnished by Alvin Lieberman's (1982) studies of language. He has demonstrated that the sounds we perceive as parts of language – such as the phonemes [ba], [di] etc. – are merely categorisations of acoustic signals based on the motor patterns (lip and tongue movements etc.) required to produce a particular phoneme. We do not actually hear the single sounds produced by our acoustic apparatus, but a generalisation or categorisation of these sounds in the form of a phoneme. Each individual phoneme represents a "packet" of information which has no significance in itself, but which acquires one – is contextualised – in relation to the phonemes preceding and following it. In the final analysis, recognition of a word or phrase should be bound up with recognition of the way in which the sound is produced (its motor articulation), and the same types of movement are recognised as different phonemes according to the context. For example, suppose that a viewer watches someone articulating the sound /di/di/di on a TV with the volume turned down while a recorder at a distance from the TV transmits the sound /ba/ba/ba. The viewer will perceive /da/da/da if he looks at the screen and /ba/ba/ba if he looks away and only listens to the recording. Ability to recognise phonemic structures in different contexts is the basis of the so-called parallel distributed processing (PDP) machines, or sequence analysers which can "learn to speak" and which suggest that language may be structured in terms of the motor activity necessary to produce certain phonemes in different contexts, and not in terms of specific linguistic or grammatical rules.

The examples in favour of a contextual and computational approach are many: suffice it to maintain Land's theory of colour (1977) and the classic experiment in which, using only black and white images, it is possible to recreate the original scene by exploiting the differences in light intensity through which the brain distinguishes different colours. These examples cut the localisationist approach down to size and cast doubt on analogies between biological and artificial brains. There is, however, another aspect to be considered which is not bound up so much with the presence or absence of rigid, predetermined hardware where numerous functions of biological brains are supposed to be localised, as with the procedures underlying the recording of specific memories in the nervous structures. The primary strategy of neurobiologists has, in fact, been that of seeking the modifications which single experiences may involve at the synaptic level: the process whereby memories are "fixed" – from the large-scale of imprinting to habituation in *Aplysia* or memory in the goldfish. Now a great deal of experimental evidence unquestionably exists which suggests that experience leads to modification on the level of synaptic structures and thus to modification in the neuronal network. It is, however, doubtful whether each individual input or memory leads to specific modifications in a particular neuron or group of neurons, because the deterioration or death of individual neurons would then involve the selective loss of specific memories. This would have evolutionary disadvantages, as the consequences over the years would be extremely serious.

Biological Brains and Individual Variability

The "microlocalisationist" view of the memory – and therefore of brain–computer analogies – is today challenged by supporters of epigenetic theories, such as Jean-Pierre Changeux (1985) and Gerald Edelman (1987). The latter in particular maintains a "neuronal Darwinism" which views cerebral activity as highly individual and claims that no two brains react identically to the same types of stimuli. He maintains that analogies with conventional computers are misleading, in that they ignore a fundamental principle underlying biological brains: the individual variability bound up with both genetic and environmental factors. And if variability has an important role in terms of cerebral functioning, there must be a Darwinian principle of selection for the nerve structures or groups of neurons which react more than others to particular stimuli. However, as in the case of dream images, which can have different significance and reference, one group of neurons can codify different stimuli/ memories. Edelman's views are based on simulation experiments carried out with the computer. These groups of neurons are arranged in layers or "maps", and it is through the interaction of different maps (linked to initial sensory input and to motor output) that information is categorised.

While Edelman's studies attempt on the one hand to represent models of the brain through simulation with classic computers, they also form part of a broader attempt to apply knowledge of the brain to the functioning of machines. In 1982, W. Little and subsequently J. Hopfield noted that the mathematical formulae of statistical mechanics could be applied to analysis of formal neuron networks. This led to the study of the so- called "neuronal" machines, based on networks of "neurons" interconnected by "synapses" in which information is not stored within a single memory cell but through a configuration of the network, i.e. the state of relations between a number of neurons. Memorisation – of a shape, for example – takes place through modification of the significance of the connections in such a way that the "attractors" of the network, i.e. the stable configurations, represent the shape. The machine will subsequently be able to recognise similar shapes by evolving towards one of the configurations which illustrate the memorised shapes. The production of the so-called connection machines, which are built on the basis of research carried out by D. Hillis at MIT, exploits an extremely high degree of connectivity between processors, i.e. a characteristic of the human brain. But this does not mean, despite the constant use of biological metaphors in the field of connection machines, that formal neuron networks resemble biological nervous systems with their cognitive and emotive features. Some of these may obviously be simulated, but the overall strategies of biological and artificial intelligence cannot be superimposed. Nevertheless, our doubts as to the legitimacy of analogies between brain and computer will have the consequence of reactivating a moribund approach to cerebral functions such as memory and also of fertilising the field of artificial intelligence with ideas that are somewhat different from the traditional ones.

References

Changeux JP (1985) L'Homme neuronal. PUF, Paris

Edelman GM (1987) Neuronal Darwinism. Basic Books, New York

Edelman GM, Gall E, Cowan WM (1984) Dynamic aspects of neocortical function. Wiley, New York

Goldman-Rakic PS (1981) Development of plasticity of primate frontal association cortex. In: Schmitt, Worden, Adelman, Dennis (eds) The organization of the cerebral cortex. MIT Press, Cambridge, Mass

Hildreth EC (1984) The measurement of visual motion. MIT Press, Cambridge, MA

Hubel DH, Wiesel TN (1973) Ferrier Lecture: Function architecture of Macaque monkey visual cortex. Proceedings of the Royal Society (Biol.), London, pp 1–59

Hubel DH, Wiesel TN (1979) Brain mechanisms of vision. Scientific American 241:150–162

Kandel DH (1976) Cellular basis of behavior: An introduction to behavioral neurobiology. Freeman, San Francisco

Kandel DH, Schwartz JH (1985) Principles of neural science. Elsevier, New York

Land EH (1977) The retinex theory of color vision. Scientific American 237:108–128

Lewin R (1982) Neuroscientists look for theories. Science 216:507

Lieberman AM (1982) On finding that speech is special. American Psychology 37:148–166

MacLean (1955) The limbic system and emotional behavior. Arch. Neural Psychiatry 73:130–134

Marr D (1982) Vision. Freeman, San Francisco

Oliverio A (1983) Genes and behavior: An evolutionary perspective. In: Rosenblatt, Hinde, Beer, Busnel (eds) Advances in the study of behaviour. Academic Press, New York, pp 191–220

Rosenfield L (1988) The inventions of memory. Basic Books, New York

Rosenzweig MR, Bennett EL (1969) Effects of differential environments on brain weights and enzyme activities in gerbils, rats and mice. Developments in Psychobiology 2:87–95

Computers, Musical Notation and the Externalisation of Knowledge: Towards a Comparative Study in the History of Information Technology

Henrik Sinding-Larsen

Introduction

It's easy enough to state that computer technology has an important impact on our society and culture and that what we have seen so far is only the beginning. It's also easy to describe countless examples of computerisation of various private and public work processes. However, it is very difficult to give an account of what is happening from a more comprehensive perspective. The social sciences lack concepts and theories for understanding and describing this kind of cultural change. So, what's happening? Are we witnessing a cultural revolution or just a limited technological change? Is computerisation a historically unique phenomenon, or is it just a new form of something we have experienced before? In what sense is "artificial" intelligence (AI) a manifestation or expression of "natural" intelligence?

In order to understand what computers are doing to our society, I believe that it is necessary to establish a broad historical and comparative perspective. We need a global, cultural history of information technology.

One problem that arises when we try to compare our present situation with the past is that much of our understanding of computers is based on newly coined terms like "artificial intelligence", "high-level programming languages" and so on. It is difficult to make a sensible comparison between so-called artificial intelligence and biological intelligence if the meaning of the term "intelligence" does not remain constant in the two contexts. The same is true for natural language versus programming languages. To gain a general understanding of what is new and what is old, we need terms and theories which encompass both computers and more traditional technologies. We must be able to show whether or not computerisation is a special case of something more general.

In order to evaluate the long-term future impact of computers, we must look at historically documented changes following similar inventions. But which inventions from the past *are* actually comparable with the computer?

We sometimes encounter attempts to compare the present situation with the great Industrial Revolution of the last century (Bolter 1984). But in fact this revolution was mainly a product of new energy technologies, like the steam-engine, electricity and the internal-combustion engine. Not even the telephone or the printing press are really comparable with the computer, because they did not imply new ways of representing knowledge. They only made the already written and spoken work more accessible in space and time. This is, of course, no mean achievement, but while it's true that computers have greatly stimulated the same development, that isn't their most revolutionary attribute. Perhaps the most strikingly unprecedented quality of computers is their ability to simulate and thereby represent natural and mental processes that formerly could not be described or expressed.

It is common to semiotic systems before the computer that they can only describe the static structure of a process. A recipe, for instance, is static, and contains no "motion" until someone uses kitchen utensils and lets the structure of the recipe guide the process of cooking. Similarly, a novel is the static structure of a story which is set in motion and brought to life through the process of reading. On the other hand, computer programs store descriptions of structures which can guide physical processes directly by means of computers. Running programs are processes that represent processes. This makes the computer an entirely new tool of description. Therefore, to make historical comparisons, we must look to other periods when new systems for representing knowledge appeared. And we have to look for a vocabulary which is suited for the comparison of systems of representation.

The rest of this chapter is divided into three parts, though some themes overlap. I will start out by presenting some basic concepts and an outline of a more general history of information technology. The second part, which is the main part, contains an exploration of the history of musical notation as a particularly interesting and (in this context) relatively unexplored case of knowledge representation. Towards the end, I shall focus on possible future consequences of computerisation within this historical perspective.

Externalisation of Knowledge as a Historical Process

As part of a general theory for understanding the cultural history of information technology, I have introduced the expression "externalisation of knowledge". In using the concept of "externalisation", I want to denote a historical process whereby knowledge previously stored in human beings (i.e. intracognitively) is transferred to a storage medium outside the human mind (i.e. becomes stored extracognitively). The concept of externalisation, therefore, may characterise a process of change in society's management of information.

We can employ the theory of externalisation of knowledge to divide cultural history into information technology epochs. In this way, the characteristics of three main epochs may be discerned:

1. Externalisation of knowledge is made possible through a spoken language and a social organisation of specialists. This is the most radical step, and the one which made us human in the first place. But in mankind's first period, communication and accumulation of ideas were to a large extent limited by the ephemeral nature of speech.
2. Externalisation of knowledge is made possible through descriptions expressed in various forms of writing intended for human interpretation. The accumulation and concentration, as well as the distribution of knowledge were greatly enhanced by the invention of various means of writing.
3. Externalisation of knowledge is made possible through descriptions expressed in various forms of programming languages intended for machine interpretation.

The new form of externalisation in any period does not replace previous forms but supplements them. As a first elaboration of the idea of externalisation, I will present some examples from the three epochs.

Externalisation of Knowledge and the Social Organisation of Specialists

One of the characteristics of human culture is that we live in groups in which not all individuals possess the same knowledge. It is true that there is a certain division of knowledge (largely based on age and sex) among other social animals, but on the whole, individuals of an animal species are much more homogeneous than humans with regard to the knowledge that is necessary for survival and reproduction. In human cultures based on hunting and gathering, age and sex are the predominating organising principles for the division of knowledge. But the great majority of other cultures manage their collective knowledge through a number of specialists who pass on their knowledge from generation to generation. Early examples of specialists are medicine men (and women) and political leaders. Nowadays we have a large number of "professions".

Externalisation of Knowledge Through Writing Made for Human Reading

Amongst humans, knowledge is never just stored mentally (cognitively) in relation to an unprocessed natural environment. From the earliest times, houses, tools, clothes and parts of the cultural landscape have been material manifestations of knowledge, and have always been essential for learning. But in pre-literate societies, man-made physical objects which "mean something" will be considerably fewer than in a society where writing is used as a storage medium for knowledge. Precisely because this distinction is so crucial, it is meaningful to use "pre-literate societies" as a category. The process whereby a society becomes literate offers interesting comparative material in order to understand what occurs during other profound information technology revolutions. This is the case for modern literacy processes in the Third World, but it is especially interesting to look at the endogenous literacy processes that occurred in Mesopotamia and Egypt.

The ancient civilisations which became literate not only developed writing to store the "spoken word", but a whole range of semiotic systems, such as various types of maps of the sky and the earth, counting systems, monetary systems, architectural diagrams, maps for town planning and a series of other drawing systems for description and design. In early Sumerian as well as Egyptian cultures, these representational systems seemed to develop more or less simultaneously.[1] This was the second great stage in the externalisation of knowledge; this time externalised in relation to both individuals and groups. Writing as a process of externalisation was based upon the description of structure. For instance, the law consists of structures for court procedures, while medical books can impose structure on the practice of diagnosis and treatment. But in their externally stored form, all texts are static, and they will only have an impact when human beings realise their structures through processes of action.

A semiotic system that developed in the middle of the age of writing and constituted an important exception was the mechanical clock. In this case, not only is the structure for the measurement of time externalised (or represented) but also the process itself. A man-made process, the movement of the arms of the clock, is a dynamic representation (simulation) of another process (the movements of the sun, the beating of the heart or other "natural" manifestations of time). If we attempted to live without a clock, in a "clockless society", we would soon notice that our externalised management of knowledge of time has to become re-internalised.

Externalisation of Knowledge Through Computer Programming

It is, however, with the advent of computers that the third great process of externalisation began: that is, the externalisation of knowledge processes. In contrast to writing, which could only be read by human beings, computer programs store descriptions of structures which can guide physical processes directly by means of computers. Robots are the most obvious and comprehensible evidence that computers store knowledge of processes. But even a pocket calculator is an example of how structures (algorithms for reckoning) operate on numbers without requiring us to be conscious of them.

Typical of the sorts of things we regard as knowledge are the structures which guide us when we are carrying out specialised tasks. Since structures can be stored in written form, we do not need to remember all of them: we can look them up in a book and just follow the procedure given by the text. But we cannot escape the fact that we must understand the structures in order to be able to carry out the operation. We cannot use a recipe as a structure without having some idea about the process of cooking. We must possess knowledge about both the structure and the process and, generally, if we perform an action often enough following a written description, we will get to "know it by heart". This is not the case with knowledge stored in the form of computer programs. In this case, both the structure and the process can be stored and we can have operations carried out without us human beings having to understand or to be aware of what is happening. The process of externalisation is more complete at this stage. Today, children can perform mathematical operations which Einstein would have found hard to solve.

This dissociation of competence and performance is one main reason why many companies and organisations invest in the development of expert systems. They hope to economise on the expensive expertise of specialists by allowing less expensive and less experienced personnel to take decisions which, without a knowledge base system, would lie outside their area of competence.

In the Norwegian Central Office for Social Security, a legal expert system has been implemented for handling housing benefit claims. The relevant laws and regulations operate as a hidden structure in the computer program. The structure is not static like a text, but produces a sequence of questions about sex, age, income and expenditure of the members of the household, and eventually determines the amount of financial support to be awarded in accordance with the law. This is an externalisation of process and as such must be considered in a completely different light from written law texts. Legal expert systems in public offices can easily lead to personnel handling claims without actually understanding the rules applicable to a particular type of claim.[2]

The computer is a new means or tool for the externalisation of knowledge. As we increase the use of this medium it will change the relationship between internalised and externalised knowledge. But the process of externalisation is not simply moving knowledge from the inside to the outside. The knowledge is transformed in the process, often in an irreversible way. In order to get a better understanding of this, we shall dig deeper into that process of externalisation that started when some monks in the Middle Ages tried to freeze their knowledge of Gregorian chants by means of painted signs on parchment. The following glimpses from the history of music may be valuable as a background for an understanding of the present computerisation of knowledge.

Notation and Music: The History of a Tool of Description and the Domain it Describes

Musical notation may not have the cultural importance of writing or computers, but it is exactly this limited and specialised position which makes its history well-suited as a "test case". In addition to this, its early development is relatively well documented, since musical notation has been a controversial topic from its inception. On the other hand, the early development of writing occurred at a time lacking other recording systems which could be used to discuss and comment on this new invention.

My interest in notation started several years ago when I was doing anthropological fieldwork among Norwegian country fiddlers. I was struck by their generally strong and articulated resistance to any kind of musical notation. Later I discovered that there were some interesting parallels between the fiddlers' scepticism about notation and the fears that many professionals express about artificial intelligence and knowledge engineering. So let us start where it all began, in the Middle Ages.[3]

From Mnemonic Device to "Programming Language": Music and Musical Notation as a Case of Co-evolution

Pope Gregory I (*c.* 540–604) dispatched monks to most regions of Western Europe to preach Christianity and expand the monastic orders. The use of liturgical chants, later known as Gregorian chants, was an integral part of their worship and missionary work. In the scriptoria of different monasteries, monks copied these religious texts onto parchment, the most advanced information technology of the time. The question of standardisation was important as these hymns were part of the papal plan to establish a unified Roman Church in Western Europe. The unification project was greatly enhanced by the marriage of clerical and secular power on Christmas day 800, when Pope Leo III crowned Charlemagne as the first Christian emperor since antiquity.

The cultural impact of the monastic parchments was not limited to the expansion of a newly invigorated religious faith. The content of the texts was perhaps less important than the written language itself. Literacy and Latin were, in many respects, the basis for the new Christian civilisation. Both language and religion were subject to standardisation with the spread of the psalms and scriptures.

The monks used writing to co-ordinate the chants, so that everyone would sing the same words regardless of the monastery they belonged to. This golden age of chant composition is considered to be the period from the fifth to the eighth centuries. Contemporary texts from this period have been found, but they contain no indications of the melodies, as these were composed and maintained within a purely oral tradition (Parrish 1959). The desire to standardise texts by means of an alphabet for the notation of words was, from the ninth century, extended to a desire for an "alphabet" for the notation of music. The aim was to facilitate the learning and secure the standardisation of melodies.[4]

Fig. 7.1. is a section of one of the oldest preserved sheets of written music. We may discern the possible precursor of musical notation, namely accents indicating when the voice should move up and down in pitch. The notes, or neumes, as they were called, gave rather inaccurate information about the pitch or duration of each tone. This is a problem for present-day research and interpretation. It was not a problem for the ninth-century monks, however, as the early neumes were never used as an independent source for learning music. They were only a mnemonic device within an otherwise oral or internalised tradition.

The earliest systems of notation developed simultaneously in several European regions. The results were different "dialects" of notation, some persisting for several centuries. The monasteries that "invented" notational systems distributed treatises ("manuals") explaining the code as well as giving the rationale behind their systems. The situation was clearly competitive, not unlike the competition we see today in the field of electronics. It was generally agreed that the situation would eventually lead to standardisation, but nobody knew when this would happen or which system would be victorious. The "war" was not settled until the mass production of the printing houses replaced the scribes of the monasteries.

In the beginning, notation was intimately linked to the tradition of religious plainchant. Notation of instrumental music did not appear until several centuries later. The monks primarily wanted a sign system for the description and promotion of an existing vocal tradition. They were largely unaware of the fact that the tool of description they developed with the aim of preserving a tradition would become a major agent of change, transforming the very music they wanted to preserve.

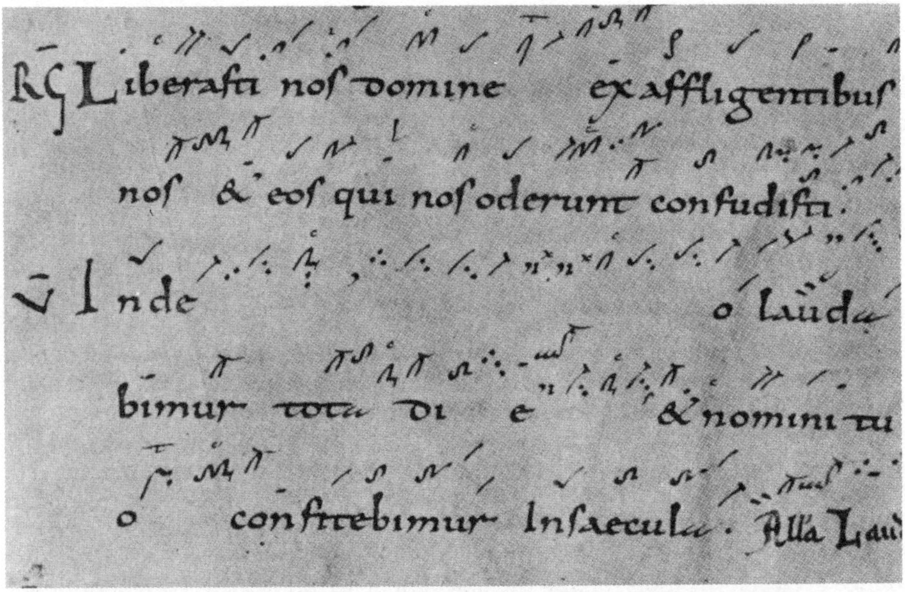

Fig. 7.1. Musical notation from the end of the 9th century. (Parrish 1959, plate II.)

However, some of the inventors were sharply aware of the fact that they lived in a decisive period in the history of music learning. In the late tenth century, Guido d'Arezzo refined a system of notation to make it more suited for learning new and unknown songs directly from parchment. One of his inventions was a better system for referring to the notes. He proposed both the alphabetical C,D,E,F,G and the well known do-re-mi- fa-sol. In a letter (approximately 1032) to a fellow monk in his former monastery, he evaluates his invention, which he, in accordance with medieval humility, attributes to God. His visions of how he and his helpers will be rewarded for this invention are rather less humble:

Therefore I, inspired with charity by God, have, with the greatest haste and care conferred not only on you but on as many others as I could the favour given by God to me, all unworthy as I am; so that the ecclesiastical *songs which I and all those before me learned with the greatest difficulty may be learnt with the greatest ease by men to come,* and they may wish eternal health to me and you and my other helpers and may ask God's mercy to grant a remission of our sins, or at least that a small prayer may come from the gratitude of so many. For is those *men who have up to now been barely able in ten years to gain an imperfect knowledge of singing from their teachers* intercede for their teacher most faithfully with God, what do you think will be done for us and our helpers who *produce a perfect singer in the space of a year, or two at most?* (cited in Cattin 1984, p 176; my emphasis)

We can find the same optimism about entering a new era where learning will be easy and accurate among many researchers within the fields of artificial intelligence and computer-based education. And in the same way, as we shall see later, the inventors mainly see the gains in efficiency, and have a less clear view of how the traditional domain is likely to be transformed (or lost).

Guido d'Arezzo did no more than systematise a few conventions concerning the representation of musical knowledge. This was enough to make him famous throughout the Latin world. In 1030, Pope John XIX called him to Rome to give a demonstration of his Antiphonary (book of liturgical chants). Guido tells about this encounter:

John of the highest apostolic seat, who now governs the Roman church, hearing the reputation of our school, and how *by our Antiphonary boys were learning songs they had not heard*, was much astonished, and invited me by three messengers ... And so the Pontiff rejoiced greatly at my arrival, making much conversation and asking various questions; and often *turning over our Antiphonary as if it were some prodigy*, and pondering the rules forming the preface, he did not cease or move from the place where he was sitting until he had satisfied his desire by learning one versicle that he had not heard, so that he suddenly recognised in himself what he scarcely believed in others. What need of more words? (cited in Cattin 1984, pp 176–177)

This is the account of a demonstration of a new information technology. It was invented by a previously unknown monk in a relatively small and unknown monastery. It was eagerly adopted by the clerical authorities in Rome and became a powerful tool in their centralising work. The use of notation developed slowly, and for a long time the description and perpetuation of oral traditions dominated. But the power of this new semiotic system was greater than was necessary simply for the efficient teaching of an existing repertoire. Gradually, it became a tool for composers exploring new possibilities for the design and organisation of polyphonic choral music. The tool was developed to describe an existing domain of knowledge, but its power to create and prescribe new kinds of knowledge changed its original domain of description.

Detailed control of musical activities requires a high degree of correspondence between the tools for and the object of description. This correspondence developed gradually in a way that we could think of as co-evolution.[5] The mutual development of musical notation as a tool of description and music as the domain to be described continues for a period of about seven centuries, from the ninth to the seventeenth (Parrish 1959, p xiii). This picture of just two evolving units is a simplification. The actual co-evolution was certainly more complex, involving at least several other aspects of music-making, such as instruments, aesthetic theory and the organisation of musical performances.

A possible chain of evolutionary steps could have been:

1. The originally simple notation creates the new possibilities for experimenting with three and four part choral singing
2. These experiments stimulate the refinement of the notational system
3. Experiments are extended to instruments, which gradually become standardised to facilitate the performance of complex harmonic modulation
4. Complex social organisation of large orchestras (e.g. the performance of symphonies) becomes the frame for an aesthetic ideal

The "actors" of this co-evolution may have a possible parallel in the current development of computerisation: formal languages ("tools of description and prescription"), computers ("instruments for realisation of formal descriptions"), computerised work settings ("complex social organisation"), all contributing to the "aesthetics" of formalised knowledge.

A new tool of description (notation) makes it possible to make explicit (i.e. to give external reality to) structures that had previously been implicit in the process of music making. The external fixation of melodic and rhythmic structures (patterns) make it possible to inspect and isolate them as conceptual entities and give them names. This was more difficult and at times impossible when the patterns were hidden in the ongoing flux of live music. Aggregate patterns that are discerned in the externalised description may themselves become elementary building blocks in higher levels of complexity. The externalised descriptions may also be used to identify simple patterns that connect structures and processes that previously were considered to be unique. This may in turn lead to a simplification and thereby strengthening of the notational system.

At the end of the seventeenth century, there was a halt in the development of both notation and instruments. Since J.S. Bach, there has been no major change in the traditional orchestral string instruments, in the system of notation or in the scales.[6] Music, however, continues its development, inside the frames set by the instruments, the notation and the standard twelve-step scale. It is difficult to give reasons why standardisation appeared when it did, and why these particular systems have proved so viable. Semiotic systems seem to be relatively open to change in certain periods, but can be remarkably stable at other times.[7]

In the examples that follow, we shall see small glimpses from a centuries-long process, in which scores gradually evolved to contain more and more musical information. Apparently, and paradoxically, this happened as each single note or sign came to contain less and less information. More emphasis was placed on the expressive power stemming from the combinatorial properties of the semiotic system, its syntax, and less on the complex meaning of each element. From a more or less approximate and analogue description of melodic movements, notes became exact digitalised symbols in a well-defined system.

In Fig. 7.2, text and notes are connected, so that the different syllables of the words are placed along a line, moving analogously to the melody. This way of intervening in the writing system did not last long, but it is a good illustration of the way early notation was inseparably tied to the words of the chants. The notation was only a means to render the melodic aspects of the lyrics. Much of the musical information was still hidden in the words and the oral tradition. As a consequence, the notation did not need to be explicit and unequivocal.

The pitches in Fig. 7.3 are symbolised both by a "melodic line" moving up and down in an analogous manner, and by the "Guido d'Arezzo letters", a,b,c,d,e,f, and g.[8]

As we may see from Fig. 7.3, the same note letters are placed approximately on the same horizontal line. Thus, the pitch is indicated by double information: its vertical placement and the note designation in the form of a letter. This was simplified by using only a vertically placed dot (the note head) indicating the pitch (see Fig. 7.4). The letters still continue to be used as an oral means of referring to the graphically depicted notes.

We shall now take a closer look at how the evolution of systems of notation, polyphonic music and instruments influenced each other.

Figs 7.2 and 7.4 both show notations of early polyphonic music (i.e. music with two or more parts or voices). The description of the music is still quite

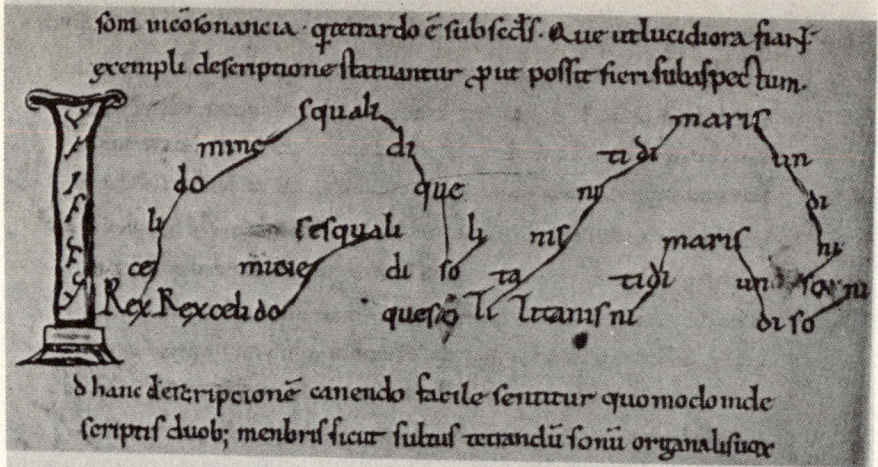

Fig. 7.2. Musical notation, 11th century. (Parrish 1959, plate XXa.)

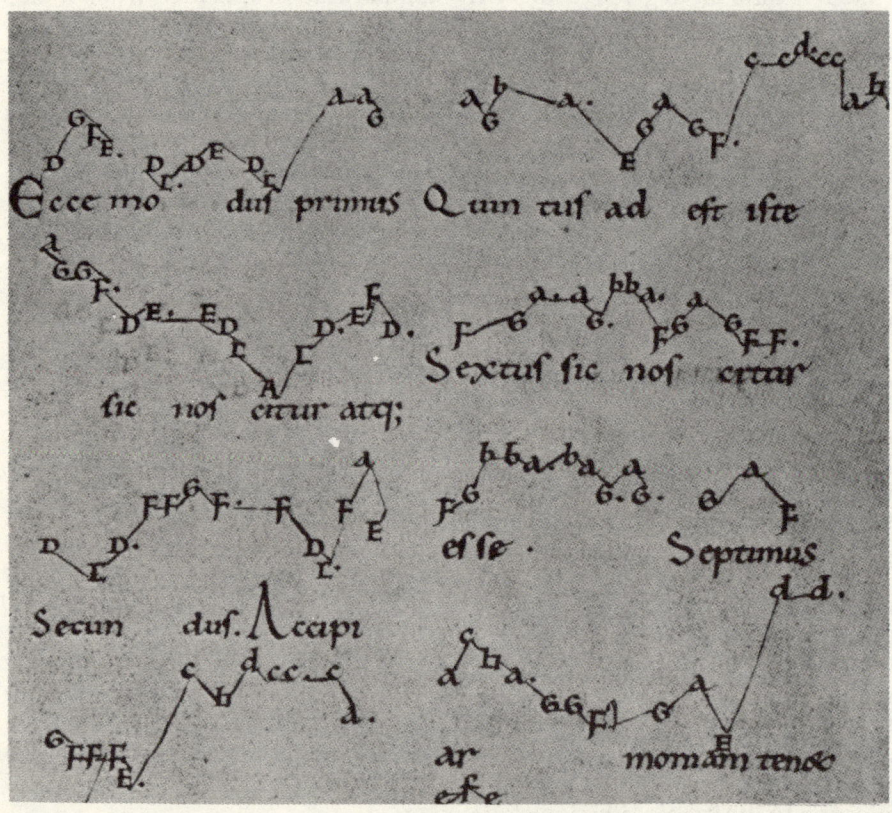

Fig. 7.3. Musical notation, end of 11th century. (Parrish 1959, plate V.)

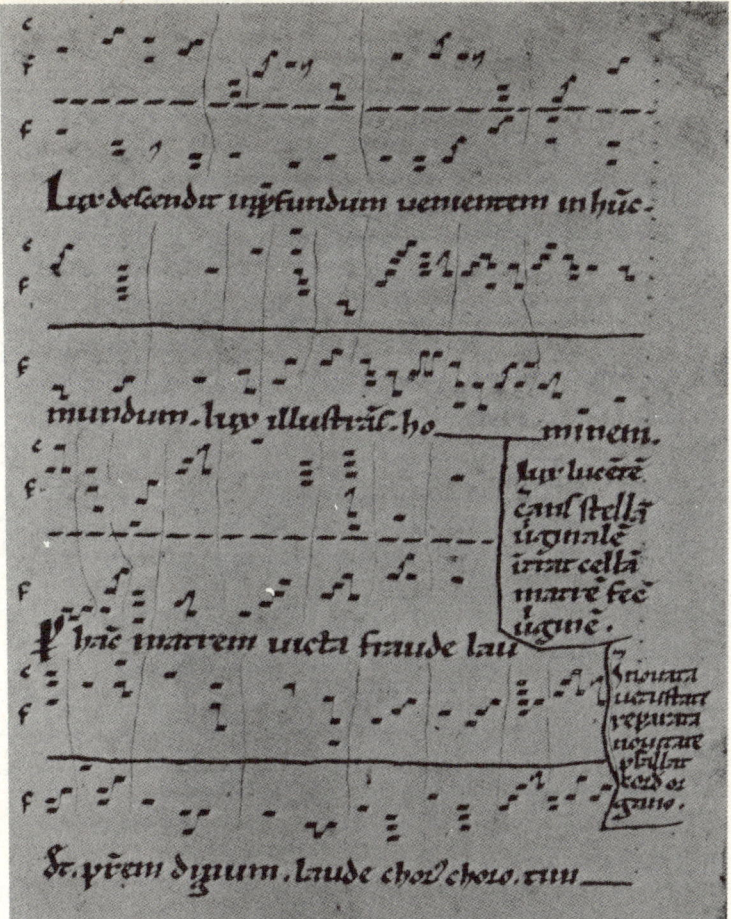

Fig. 7.4. Musical notation, 12th century. (Parrish 1959, plate XXII.)

imprecise as far as the dimension of time is concerned. There is no systematic use of barlines to help indicate the basic rhythm punctuation, and the note symbols give only a very limited selection of different duration values. Moreover, some of the early notes had context-dependent duration values: the same note could signify different durations depending on the value of the surrounding notes (Parrish 1959, p 73).

Polyphonic music requires a synchronisation of several different melodic lines. The musicians would then need a system of notation continually informing them about their exact location in the music in progress. Barlines and notes giving exact duration values give essential information in these matters. Such a degree of precision was not crucial in early notation, because the melodies were monodic (one-part, plainsong) and learned mainly through oral tradition.

The vertical placement becomes more accurate with the introduction of staves made up of horizontal lines. The degree of precision was measured against efficiency and finally staves with five lines each became standard.

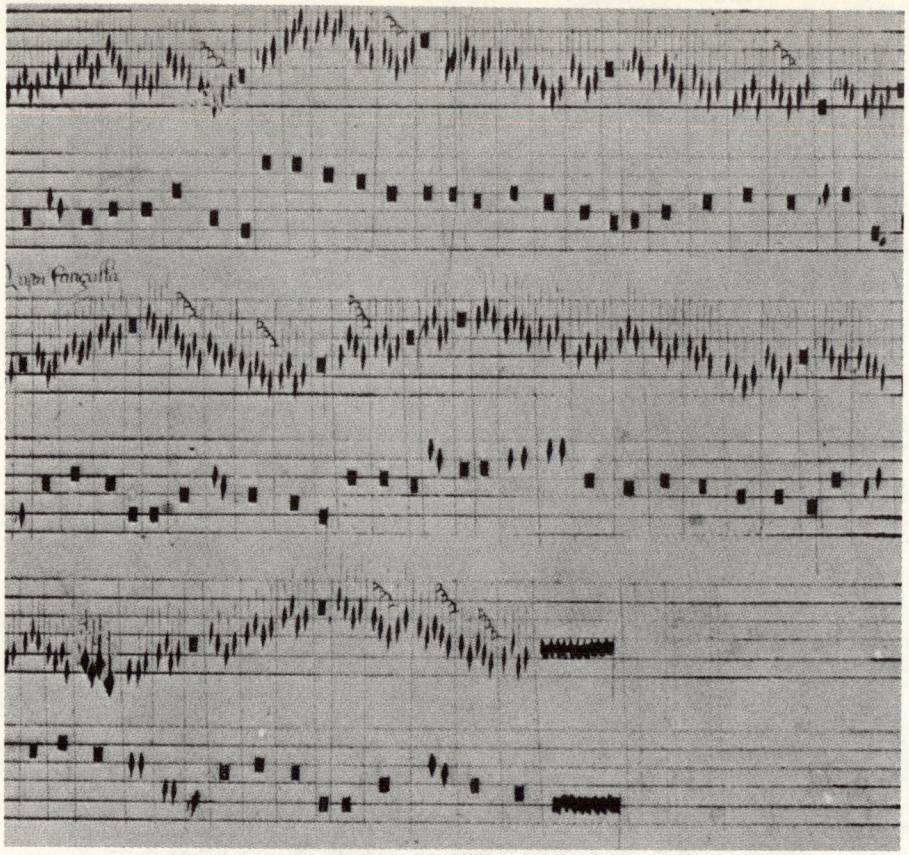

Fig. 7.5. Musical notation, 15th century. (Parrish 1959, plate LX.)

Fig. 7.5 is the notation of a song by Landini arranged polyphonically for a keyboard instrument. There are six lines in each staff. Although it may look somewhat compact, the notation is unambiguous, clear and much closer to modern notation that the previous examples.

Most of the evolution of medieval systems of notation can be seen as a struggle for the creation of independent (context free) sets of written semiotic contrasts for each of the musical dimensions, duration (rhythm) and pitch (melody). In the first centuries of this evolution, a certain text could impose a certain scale and melodic mode which in turn imposed a certain rhythm, which in turn imposed a certain performance style. In fact, many of the musical elements that we recognise today as the basis of any practical musical education did not exist as independent conceptual entities; they were performed, but they could not be referred to because they were integrated aspects of different "aesthetic packages".

In this situation it would be a redundancy to symbolise every dimension separately. However, when the composers wanted to co-ordinate the singing of several parts with different melodic and rhythmic patterns, the temporal precision of the notational system was crucial. In 1320, Philippe de Vitry invented several new notational conventions that made it possible to describe

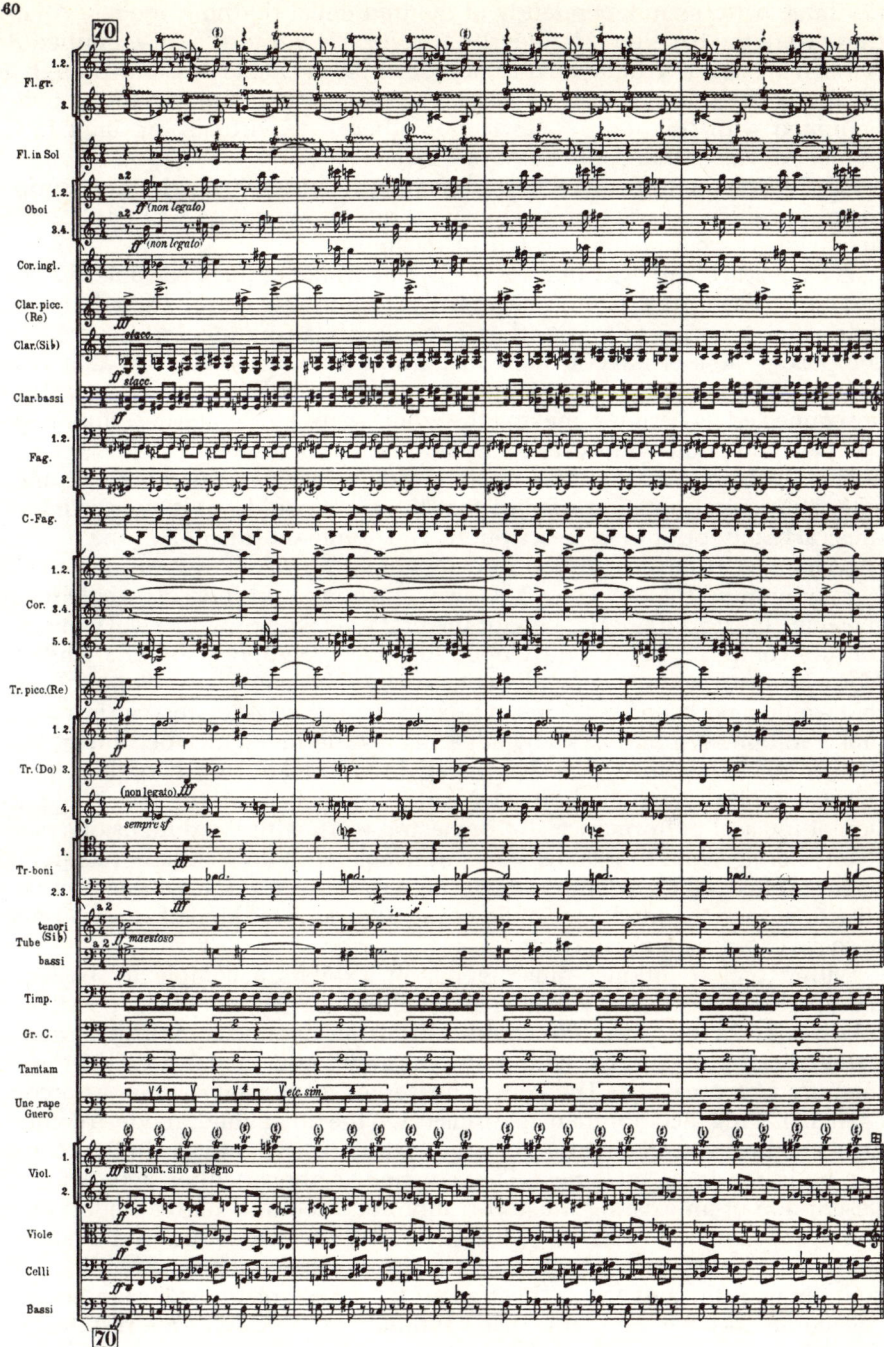

Fig. 7.6. Page 60 from *The Rite of Spring* by Stravinsky.

rhythmic patterns independently of the traditional rhythmic modes. Among these were the bar sign (Hindley 1971, p 70). He wrote a treatise entitled *Ars Nova* on the new rhythmic and harmonic complexity made possible through his notation. This was a decisive step in the co-evolution of music and notation. Equipped with this tool of description, there was virtually no limit to the number of voices that could be co-ordinated.

Fig. 7.6 is taken from an orchestral score by Igor Stravinsky. In this example, the composition is not described by one or two five-line staves, but by 32 staves of five lines each, making a system of 160 lines.

The musical complexity of *The Rite of Spring* would be inconceivable in an oral tradition. Each part is not necessarily technically more difficult for the individual musician to master than a medieval dance tune, but the medieval composers did not have at their disposal a semiotic system capable of co-ordinating so many musicians simultaneously. In *The Rite of Spring*, all 160 lines are connected by barlines, making the whole score a 137-page description for a complex polyphonic musical performance.

That such musical complexity could not be achieved without the aid of external musical notation implies that the work could not have existed as a musical reality prior to its description. The dominant function of the notation has changed from description and mnemonics to composition and design ("programming the orchestra"). However, the composition of "orally inconceivable" music did not happen for the first time with Stravinsky. The twelfth century composer Perotin developed four-part polyphony in Paris while the Notre Dame cathedral was under construction. His music was of a complexity that would have been very difficult to conceive as well as to preserve in a purely oral tradition. We may acknowledge this as the moment when music, as a domain to be described, was definitively influenced by its tool of description.

The complexity of polyphony also had consequences for the social organisation of musical performance. An orchestral work with the dimensions of *The Rite of Spring* would be equally inconceivable without a strictly hierarchical orchestra headed by a composer. (If the score is an externalisation of musical structure, then the conductor could be regarded as some kind of externalisation of social coordination and control.)

Within oral traditions, music generally exhibits a complexity based on modularity, in such a way that each "module" is easy, or at least possible, to rehearse and remember. We could call this an organic complexity. Musical patterns can only survive within an oral tradition if they can be kept in the memory of a musician. The constraint serves, at the same time, as a check against making incomprehensible music. On the other hand, modern composers sometimes use geometrical or other extra-musical patterns in the score as the basis for their melodies. The notation is then neither a tool for the description of an existing musical reality nor a tool for the realisation of the composer's musical ideas, since the vision of the music as sound did not exist prior to its notation. Complexity can be designed independently of the sounding result, and the orchestra can by means of the externalised score collaborate in what we would call a synthetic complexity. One result of this liberation from the constraints of memory has been profound ruptures in style, such as serialism and other modernistic experiments.

The new electronic instruments illustrate this very clearly. In the case of programmed synthesisers the description of the music is identical to its performance. The limitations of the musician as a human performer are eliminated, and performance is only limited by the conceptual ability of the composer (programmer). The result can be immensely complex, although it may sometimes be difficult to identify it as music at all. Although he played a part, it would be unfair to blame Guido d'Arezzo for this!

Fields of Complexity

Many textbooks present the history of music as a development from simplicity to complexity. This is quite correct in certain respects, but as a general conclusion it is mistaken. Rather it is a question of one kind of complexity being replaced by another, or complexity in one dimension or domain being replaced by complexity in another. For example, improvisation results in a kind of musical complexity that disappeared from orchestral performances as the orchestras grew to ever larger size. An orchestra presented with a score of the complexity of *The Rite of Spring* would collapse in disorder if each musician were to add or disregard notes according to his or her mood. The performance as a totality may become extremely complex, even though the task of every musician may be simple. Classically trained musicians of outstanding quality may often respond like helpless amateurs to a demand for improvisation.

There seem to be some general trends in the development of semiotic systems for description and prescription of human activity. Each elementary symbol in early musical notation was more composite and complex, i.e. contained more information, than each note in modern systems. As a semiotic system develops, the elementary contrasts tend to be simplified in ways that make them more suitable for combination into more complex statements. If the symbols are simple and context- independent on an elementary level, then they can more easily be combined to produce complexity on a composite level. The syntactic (grammatical or combinatorial) aspects of the semiotic system will accordingly increase in importance.

I think this is valid in most or all processes of externalisation, since the same tendency can be observed in a whole range of fields: the letters of the phonemic alphabet can be combined into more numerous and more complex words than the signs in a pictographic system. Each industrial worker building a moon rocket can learn and accomplish his job more easily than a traditional carpenter building a house. The ultimate simplicity of the electronic binary code has produced an unforseen complexity of computer applications. The modern complexity seems to appear at more composite levels than "primitive" complexity, but this does not mean that its total complexity is greater.

Some time ago, I received a leaflet that showed how experts in artificial intelligence do not share my view of the evolution of knowledge. It was an invitation to participate in the Second International Symposium on Commercial Expert Systems in Banking and Insurance. The chairman, Professor John Campbell of University College London introduced the conference theme with these words:

Knowledge is the key to success. Knowledge is growing exponentially. Ninety per cent of mankind's knowledge has been produced over the past 30 years.

If we define knowledge as the ability to survive in a sustainable sort of way in a natural environment, then I think it would be closer to the truth to state that 90% of mankind's knowledge has been lost over the past 30 years! But if we add some more of the text cited above, we can also see more of the context within which its statements make sense:

> The right knowledge at the right time is crucial for competitiveness in today's global market ... Today already a number of systems automate expert reasoning for business advantage. For their future successful application, however, a better view of knowledge management and engineering is necessary.

It is my hope that the historical reflection put forward in this chapter will make it more difficult to make statements about the progress of knowledge in such a categorical way.

Musical Notation as the Creator of "Wrong Notes"

Scales with a great variety of (and greatly varying) intervals are found in many orally transmitted musical traditions. A scale with twelve identical steps is only found in the Western classical tradition. The traditional way of tuning fixed pitch instruments became inadequate when both instruments and compositions were to an increasing degree made for polyphony. The tuning had to be standardised to exploit the full range of the tonalities made possible by notation. This was especially important for keyboard instruments. A major work by J.S. Bach (*Das wohltemperierte Klavier*) is dedicated explicitly to the exploration of harmonic transformations made possible by the newly tempered tuning of his keyboard instruments. A simplification (standardisation) at the level of the elementary pitch intervals was the basis for an increased complexity at the more composite harmonic level. This standardisation of scale was unnecessary in earlier periods because the music was concentrated on a few closely related tonalities (keys). If one attempted to use non-standard intervals within the "new" polyphonic music, the result would sound dissonant, or "false".[9]

Through the prestige power of bourgeois music, the equalised twelve-step scale was adopted as the standard for all music, making some of the tones regarded as correctly pitched in traditional scale systems "false notes". Standard scales and complex harmonies became a hallmark of bourgeois music appreciation. The system of notation was mentally coupled to this particular scale. All notes that could not be placed within this system were considered false. This will be illustrated by an example from an encounter between classical and folk music. The story, as well as the other references to Norwegian folk music, are based on my thesis on the cultural history of Norwegian folk music (Sinding-Larsen 1983).

A Millimetre from the Tradition

Some time in the 1880s, the country musician Olav Brenno played the folk instrument *langeleik* for tourists at a hotel in the Norwegian mountains. The old

Norwegian *langeleik* is a string instrument in the dulcimer family. The pitch of each note in the *langeleik*'s scale is determined by the position of its frets. The principle is basically the same as for the guitar, with one important difference: the intervals of the scale on a *langeleik* are not necessarily standardised, as they are on a guitar.

After the performance, a member of the audience walked up to the musician and praised the music. However, the tourist, referring to his position as an organist, insisted that two notes of the *langeleik* were "false". He offered to correct this by moving the relevant frets a few millimetres. Olav Brenno agreed to this, without knowing how miserable the outcome would be. The classically tuned scale imposed by the organist was incompatible with Brenno's conception of and way of remembering his tunes. When he tried to play his "correct" instrument, he did not recognise the tunes and "lost track". In the end, he gave up playing the *langeleik*.

Several decades later, after the turn of the century, when Brenno had become an old man, he was contacted by two young scholars of folk music, who recognised the cultural value of the old scales. They helped him to move the frets back again to their original positions, They also gave him back some of his self-confidence by redefining the "false" notes as a valuable cultural trait. Brenno resumed his *langeleik* playing and many of the tunes came back to his memory after almost a generation in oblivion. The dominance of the standardised scale was, in this case, absolute because it was embedded in the sound producing instrument.

The "imperialism" of the standardised scale is more subtle but it is obvious enough in a text written in 1850 by the Norwegian musicologist L.M. Lindemann. The citation below is taken from the introduction to a collection of folk songs that Lindemann himself had collected and transcribed. Observe the extent to which the notation of the music is intimately linked to the standardised scale:

The problem of transcribing the melodies does not only consist in the lack of distinction and clarity of the old people's way of singing. Far worse is the fact that one is repeatedly presented with notes that are a quarter of a step higher or lower pitched than the appropriate ones; i.e. notes that are placed exactly in between our half-tone steps. It is the task of the collector to determine to which note, the higher or the lower, they belong. [...] By frankly confronting the old people with two alternatives, the singer can be *guided to a choice of his own* as to which tone should be considered the right one. (cited in Dal 1956, p 182, my emphasis)

In this case it is obvious how the musical notation, as a tool of description, strongly influences its object of description. Lindemann did not recognise this as an inadequacy of the tool, but rather as a "deficiency" of the reality to be described.

Knowledge Engineering and Elusive Answers

It is possible to draw some parallels between the collecting of folk music and knowledge engineering. The important task in both cases is the preservation of oral and unformalised knowledge by means of formal tools of description. While the ethnomusicologist uses musical notation as a tool for the description of music, the knowledge engineer uses various programming languages as tools for the description of professional experts; skill and knowledge.[10]

Knowledge engineers commonly complain of vague and elusive answers from experts whose knowledge does not easily lend itself to precise description. Because their job is to make running programs, they will have to use tools of formalisation to confront the experts with the possible programming alternatives. The experts will be "guided to a choice of their own" as to which version of their knowledge they consider to be the right one.

Once the knowledge is embedded in an expert system we may encounter the same kind of problems as beset the old *langeleik* player. The computerised form of the knowledge may be incompatible with a pre-computer way of thinking. The knowledge that "sounds false" will slowly be forgotten or actively suppressed. As is the case with notation and the piano, expert systems and knowledge acquisition tools may set the standard for all knowledge, not merely what is subject to computerisation.

The Tape Recorder – A Perfect Tool of Description?

With the above-mentioned problems in mind, it should be obvious that tape recorders have some great advantages for the preservation of music when compared with written musical notation. For instance, taped music renders all the subtleties of traditional scales that are eliminated in the abstraction of written music. But the problem of preserving the knowledge of music-making is by no means eliminated by this technique.

Norwegian folk musicians have always placed great value on a correct transmission of the tunes in their tradition. The registration of folk music by means of music textbooks and, to an even greater extent, by means of cassette tape recorders has contributed to the idea that a correct transmission from one generation to the next means detailed copying of the old forms. But music as a living aesthetic expression is not something that it is possible to copy in every detail. It must always be to some extent re-created at each single performance, and its success as music will never solely depend on the accurate transmission of every tone. The detailed and truthful rendering of a single musical performance does not show how intonation and improvisation are related to changing public and performance situations.

In a certain sense, learning orally transmitted music from tape will preserve the tradition in a better way than learning from simplified and formalised written music. But the descriptive (and prescriptive) power of a tape recording is so great that an exact copy will leave even less room than the written notes for giving the music a personal flavour. What has happened in some extreme cases among Norwegian folk musicians is that fanatic guardians of the tradition detect and arrest any deviation from well-known taped forms. Their corrections are particularly effective when these guardians act as the judges in the annual contest of traditional fiddlers.

This kind of traditionalism has been criticised of late. A growing number of young Norwegian folk musicians argue that the very idea of a detailed registration and copying of music as sound structure is incompatible with the intention of preserving music as a living tradition of music making. Improvisation, change and spontaneous response to each unique audience have always been important in folk music. The mastering of these aspects is the result of second-order learning, above the morphology (first-order) of a single tune

(Bateson 1973, pp 250–280). These aspects cannot be fully described with the actual tools of musical notation or registration. Perhaps they never will. This is knowledge that is rooted at a very complex interpersonal level.

Improvisation, intervals outside the standardised scale and other charac- teristic traits of Norwegian folk music not captured by musical notation have been gradually disappearing since the beginning of this century. There have been two basically opposing strategies to counteract this development. The scientific folkloristic strategy is to refine and improve the tools of description to avoid losing information in the act of description. The other, more paradoxical, strategy followed by some young folk musicians has been to delete information from written tunes that are considered too detailed. In this way, the written music once more increases its dependence on an oral learning context; the score as description becomes so coarse-grained that it is worthless as a prescription unless the musician considers the performance situation and the oral tradition. Learning the tunes directly from old performers with a minimal use of any descriptions or recordings is considered by some fiddlers to be the only real way of perpetuating the tradition. In their opinion, the concept of tradition should not be attached directly to the music at a describable morphological level, but to the traditional conditions for learning and performance.

This story has relevance for the current situation where previously human- dependent knowledge becomes externally available through knowledge based systems. Many expert systems are made and marketed with the idea of making expert knowledge more cheaply available to students. This is achieved as computers decrease the dependence on human experts as an expensive oral learning context. Explicitly or implicitly, it is assumed that this is a way of preserving knowledge traditions currently maintained by living experts. But it is an open question what kind of maintenance the computers actually enhance, since computer based descriptions can never capture more than some aspects of the total knowledge. And it is an equally open question whether more refined tools of description will make the situation better.

The Norwegian folk musicians realised that it was not the "bad" descriptions that were the most threatening to the living tradition, but the "good" ones. A good description generally means a context-free description, which means that the folk musicians as a social group (the context) lose control over their musical tradition.

Gregorian Chants and the Reconstruction of Authenticity

At the Benedictine Abbey of St Pierre at Solesmes in France, monks have been working for more than a hundred years on the restoration of the old Gregorian chants. Their situation is in many respects similar to that of the young Norwegian fiddlers. In the opinion of the Solesmes monks, the old chants have been "killed" by too sophisticated and precise a system of notation. Their strategy is twofold: on the one hand they are re-editing facsimiles of the oldest Gregorian manuscripts, and on the other hand, they are developing an oral practice around these rudimentary manuscripts. A thousand years after the chants were written down by means of the first systems of musical notation, we see a systematic work of reconstruction of the lost qualities of pre-notational plainsong. The Medician edition of the chants (1614) was considered to be the most oppressive and standardising of all, and the monks of Solesmes have laboured to recover from this papal act of description several centuries after it was imposed. The music had become trapped in its own system of preservation.

In an earlier version of this chapter, the story of the Solesmes monks ended at about this point. However, I met a French musicologist, Marcel Perez, who made me reconsider my view of the project of Solesmes, where he himself had been a pupil. Perez was doing research on the role of improvisation within Gregorian chant, when he found new evidence that it was formerly in widespread use. Primarily it was an oral praxis, but early manuscripts contained many symbols indicating when the singer should elaborate or improvise and when he should follow the written music. The system of notation implied some kind of alternation, where the initiative and control moved back and forth between the singer's imagination and the prescriptions of the score. This was eliminated in later and more precise systems. But the skills of improvisation survived as an oral tradition within certain schools until the nineteenth century.

The monks of Solesmes dismissed this practice as unauthentic and insisted on the study of the earliest notation as the sole way to "true" Gregorian chant. Because the early notes contained less information, we could say that their strategy increased the music's dependence on an oral tradition. However, all their studies of the oldest and most "correct" manuscripts made them more obsessed with the notation than ever before. The result of this quest for authenticity was that the little that remained of the still living tradition of improvisation disappeared completely. Instead they founded and promoted an entirely new "oral tradition" based on the "oldest written tradition". As the justification for authenticity is based entirely on notation, there should be no surprise that the resulting music is rather rigid and without improvisation.

Externalisation and Progress

When humans make tools for describing human activities, they will always involve themselves in a co-evolutionary process. An improvement of the tools for description of a certain domain will, in general, also be the starting point for new design and prescription which will change the domain originally to be described.

Tools of description (language, semiotic systems) are one basis for externalisation of knowledge; the storage and processing of knowledge independently of the human mind. Since the dawn of civilisation, human knowledge has always been perpetuated and developed by an interplay between internalised and externalised representations of knowledge. Oral tradition is the typical case of internalised knowledge, while writing is the most widespread tool for externalisation. The balance between the two seems to be important for creativity and flexibility.

Looking at the history of culture, we see a general trend where tools of description become increasingly precise and comprehensive. This is generally considered a positive development. However, as demonstrated by the examples in this chapter, we also find cases where people judge precise descriptions negatively. The Norwegian fiddlers and, to a certain extent, the monks of Solesmes seem to perceive the issue of externalised versus internalised representation (or dependence on versus independence of an oral tradition) to be a matter of choice.

In my opinion, the tendency to think of precise descriptions as something inherently good, or at least, as an inevitable result of scientific progress in accordance with some kind of destiny or natural law, is too strong. With the advent of the computer, and in particular with the development of artificial intelligence, we should become increasingly conscious of our possibilities for choice in this domain. Many essentially oral knowledge traditions stand at the threshold of an era of description comparable with that of music in the Middle Ages, with the difference that the current tools of description are far more refined and powerful.

Computer technology has made possible dynamic descriptions of processes through simulation. The range of possible tools of description will widen as science makes further progress in the understanding and description of fundamental properties of communication, perception and reasoning. The descriptive power of the computer may well be reducing the role of human language itself from the principal tool of description to the principal object of description. Principles of advanced computation have already become the meta-knowledge and meta- language for many domains.

Most critiques of artificial intelligence have concentrated on the limitations of computers. Typically, one of the best-known books criticising artificial intelligence is entitled *What Computers Can't Do* (Dreyfus 1979). I think it is time to realise that we are caught in a situation where the threat is twofold (and where the possibilities are also twofold). If the computer's power of description is too poor, then we lose subtleties and details. If the tool of description is too "good", however, we may lose orally-based improvisation and flexibility, and that will be more serious in the long run.

Flexibility and improvisation are not merely aesthetic concerns. Every knowledge tradition needs living sources for its renewal. History can teach us how the long-term processes shaping culture are the expression of a balance between two regimes; one characterised by notation, explicit knowledge, fixation and standardisation; the other by oral tradition, tacit knowledge, openness and improvisation. Our choice is of course not between one side and the other, but a viable balance between the two.

Some Final Remarks on the Externalisation of Language and the Evolution of Culture

The ambition of the theory of externalisation is to be able to conceptualise seemingly independent historical processes within a common framework. The evolution of musical notation, writing, computer programming and many other processes have something in common that the concept of externalisation can help us to grasp. We could even say that the concept of externalisation helps us to externalise the phenomenon of externalisation.

In a sense, human language is a premise underlying all of the other forms of externalisation. But personally I think that it is more fruitful to look at what we usually call language as just one kind of externalisation, although a fundamental one. The history of language then becomes an aspect of the general history of externalisation.

If we look at the three main periods in this perspective, the second step, writing, externalised the ephemeral structure of the first step, speech. That prepared the ground for an unprecedented accumulation of knowledge. But it also had an important influence on spoken language itself.

The languages of illiterate people generally have no concepts for the characterisation of linguistic entities like "verb", "noun", "grammar" etc. Some tribes don't even have a concept corresponding to our word "language". Language is something they use, not something they talk about. The externalised quality of writing made it possible to inspect and analyse sentences in ways which were inaccessible to oral cultures (Goody 1977). In a most important sense, it was writing that made language as a conceptual entity emerge from speech. But traditional writing was only able to externalise the end-product of our linguistic activity, namely the structure of speech (i.e. fixed sequences of sounds and words). By means of computers, we are able to make an externalisation of the linguistic processes producing speech, e.g. simple syntax and semantics. This externalisation creates new possibilities for reflection upon the phenomenon of language, as well as providing new conditions for linguistic practice. To program a computer is to be able to think and express ideas in programming languages. Thus it is reasonable to say that computer programming (and to some extent every use of computers) is a kind of linguistic activity. To a greater extent than ever before, language has become a question of conscious choice: we can evaluate the properties of one language against another. Through programming, and particularly through the construction of programming languages, language has become an object of construction and invention.

We may compare this process of externalisation with the case of musical notation. In the first phase of externalisation, the development of a tool of description is used to describe a domain existing independently of the new tool: notation of chants in oral tradition; computer simulation of natural language. In the second phase of externalisation, we see a co-evolution of the tool of description and the domain to be described. Spoken language has already been heavily influenced by externalisation through writing. And it is beyond doubt that computer simulated language will influence our way of speaking as well as writing. In the way that writing was the premise for the appearance of grammar and logic, we now see the contours of a future where informatics and cognitive science take the lead in making a framework for the way we think and express ourselves.

If one accepts my theory of externalisation, then the idea of artificial intelligence could be understood as a first phase in a process of externalisation; a phase where computers are used to describe and simulate processes of our pre-computer ("natural") intelligence. But very soon, and probably already, our own intelligence will enter into a kind of co-evolutionary process with its externalised computer simulation. In the second phase, all comparison between artificial and natural intelligence is difficult, just as it is very difficult today to study genuinely oral cultures.

Making or changing a natural language depends on the agreement and adjustments of the members of a linguistic community. In fact, constructing a natural language is identical to the construction of a linguistic community. With computers, it is possible to settle a kind of linguistic convention by means of a few key strokes. Language engineering has become a possibility. The conventions established between the programmer and his or her computer can quickly be spread through software distribution and indirectly have consequences for large human language communities.

Language has always been more than a tool for conversation or inter-human messages. Language is a way of organising complexity through comprehension and design. Language has never been a purely "inner" activity, either of an individual or of several communicating individuals. Language is linked to our material projections onto the world. It is a way of living in the world. We try to make our world intelligibly through making it readable. In fact, we transform our environment more and more according to our linguistic version of the world, so that most of our life becomes a reading of our own texts. Computers and telematics are pushing the evolution of culture a great step forward in just this direction.

The dominant rhetoric of development and progress is obsessed with the idea of technical inventions as solutions to problems. One aim of this chapter has been to argue the need to look at computers in general, and artificial intelligence in particular, not so much as devices that solve our current problems in a faster or more "intelligent" way, but rather as a technology that will transform our problems in the way that musical notation transformed music. In the same vein, it makes only very limited sense to say that the function of writing has been to solve the "problem" of memory in illiterate cultures. Illiterate cultures are unaware that any such "problem" exists, just as we may be unaware of the future "problems" that the computers of tomorrow are going to "solve" for us. I want to make it more difficult to compare stages in the evolution of culture in a normative sense. Too many people think that they know what progress is on behalf of others.

Social Science in the Information Society

Current research in social science in the sub-field of information technology and society is largely deficient of theories and concepts for understanding what is happening at a general level. The majority of social scientists working with computers receive their research grants from industry or technically oriented research councils. This "social science research" often takes the form of assistance to engineers engaged in designing more "human" computer systems. It is high time that large international research efforts were dedicated to the basic understanding of what is happening to human culture in the face of new information technologies.

It has become commonplace to talk about the information society. It is tacitly assumed that to understand the "information society" is to understand the role of advanced information technology in society. But all societies throughout time have been information societies. Computers and other information technologies have just forced us to realise this in a new way. To understand our present information society we need to re-write our cultural history from an information technology point of view. This chapter can of course do no more than to scratch the surface of such an endeavour.

Acknowledgement. The list would be too long if I were to acknowledge all those who have contributed to the ideas laid out above, so I shall confine myself to mentioning those who have read the manuscript and whose comments have been incorporated into the current version, namely Jeanne Banberger (MIT), Tamar Bermann (AFI, Oslo), Robbins Burling (University of Michigan), Tellef Kvifte and Viggo Vestel (University of Oslo). Thank you!

Notes

1 *Naissance de l'Ecriture. Cuneiformes et Hieroglyphes.* Editions de la Reunion des Musees Nationaux, Paris, 1982

2 Dag Wiese Schartum "Offentlig forvaltning i en ny teknologisk virkelighet", Projektbeskrivelse, Institutt for rettsinformatik, Univ. i Oslo, 1986 (in Norwegian)

3 My knowledge of early notation is based partly on reading and partly on my experience as a musician in Kalenda Maya, an ensemble performing medieval and renaissance music. Endless debates about the interpretation of old manuscripts have been particularly helpful.

4 Rudimentary and archaic forms of musical notation existed in ancient Egypt, Greece and Rome. This notation had, as far as we know, only very limited practical significance. Within these civilisations, music remained an orally transmitted knowledge.

5 The typical case of co-evolution in biology is a development where each of two or more species continually adapts itself to the possibilities and limitations created by the others. They constitute mutual environments for evolution, and the result is often some kind of symbiosis (Bateson 1979). It is of course questionable whether semiotic systems like music and notation can be regarded as evolving units in this strictly biological sense. Without investigating this (in my opinion) interesting question further, we can take the idea of co-evolution as a metaphor.

6 Contemporary electronic music is not considered in this context.

7 The Egyptian sacred hieroglphs remained stable for more than 3,000 years after a short period of evolution.

8 A little exercise in semiotics: note that the alphabet here is used to represent something quite different from the phonemes of spoken language. The alphabet as a semiotic system for the description of phonemes is not the set of contrasting elements (the characters) in itself, but a set of elementary contrasts in one domain (signs on paper) coupled with a set of contrasts in some other domain (spoken sounds, musical sounds etc.).

9 It is important to realise the difference between the tempered scale as an acoustic phenomenon and as a phenomenon of human aesthetics. There are no "false notes" in the physical realm of acoustics, but through culturally specific socialisation, we may learn to perceive and judge a certain set of tone intervals as correct. This is forced on us in the case of Western music because the tempered scale is physically embedded in many sound-producing instruments (e.g. the piano).

10 In fact, the knowledge engineer will usually not use a programming language directly, but rather a set of description tools called "systems

description languages" of "knowledge acquisition tools". As the end product in any case shall be a program in some programming language, all these other languages will have to approach the same overall logic as the final programming language.

References and Further Reading

Bateson G (1973) The logical categories of learning and communication. In: Bateson G (ed) Steps to an ecology of mind. Paladin Press, London, pp 250–280

Bateson G (1979) Mind and nature. EP Dutton, London

Bolter JD (1984) Turing's man. University of Carolina Press, Chapel Hill, South Carolina

Cattin G (1984) Music of the Middle Ages, vol I. Cambridge University Press, Cambridge

Dal E (1956) Nordisk folkeviseforskning siden 1800. Schultz, Copenhagen (in Danish)

Dreyfus H (1979). What computers can't do. Harper & Row, New York

Geertz C (1973) The interpretation of cultures. Basic Books, New York

Goody J (1977) The domestication of the savage mind. Cambridge University Press, Cambridge

Hindley G (ed) (1971) The Larousse encyclopaedia of music. Hamlyn, London

Holbaek-Hansen E, Handlykken P, Nygaard K (1975) Systems description and the delta language. Norwegian Computing Centre Publication no. 523, Oslo

Kvifte T (1981) On variability, ambiguity and formal structure in the Harding fiddle music. In: Studia instrumentorum musicae popularis, vol VII. Musikhistoriska museet, Stockholm

Kvifte T (1989) Instruments and the electronic age: Towards a terminology for a unified description of playing technique. Solum, Oslo

Naissance de l'Ecriture. Cuneiformes et Hieroglyphes (1982) Catalogue d'exposition. Editions de la Reunion des Musees Nationaux, Paris (ISBN 2–7118–0201–9)

Parrish C (1959) The notation of mediaeval music. Norton Press, New York

Schartum DW (1986) Offentlig forvaltning i en ny tecknologisk virkelighet. Prosjektbeskrivelse, Norwegian Centre for Computers and Law, University of Oslo (in Norwegian)

Sinding-Larsen H (1983) Fra fest til forestilling. Magister thesis, Department of Social Anthropology, University of Oslo (in Norwegian)

Sinding-Larsen H (1985) Le rite et le jeu – deux modes d'experience dans la fete. In: Le carnaval, la fete et la communication. Actes des premieres rencontres internationales, Nice, 1984. Editions Serre/UNESCO, Nice

Sinding-Larsen H (1987) Information technology and the management of knowledge. AI & Society 1(2)

Sinding-Larsen H (ed) (1988) Artificial intelligence and language: Old questions in a new key. Complex 7/88. Tano a/s, Oslo (ISBN 82–518–2550–4)

Stravinsky I (1947) The rite of spring. Boosey & Hawkes, London

Winograd T, Flores F (1985) Understanding computers and cognition. Ablex, Norwood, NJ

Chapter 8

Cognitive Science and the Computer Metaphor[1]

John R. Searle

"Cognitive science" is not the name of any well-defined research project but rather a whole family of overlapping research areas, including work in what would traditionally be thought of as psychology, artificial intelligence (AI), linguistics, anthropology, philosophy and even neurophysiology. Nonetheless, within this vast stew of different research aims and methods, there was until fairly recently a prevailing core idea of cognitive science. To put it very crudely, the idea was that the mind functions like a digital computer. Mental states are computational states and mental processes are computational processes. Many hardcore cognitive scientists still insist that the "computer metaphor" is not a metaphor at all, that the brain is literally a digital computer and the mind is simply a computer program (see, for example, Pylyshyn 1984). For this reason, many researchers see work in AI as absolutely essential to the cognitive science enterprise. So in this chapter, when I talk about the prospects for cognitive science, I am going to be talking about the prospects for a research programme based on the artificial intelligence, computational model of the mind.[2]

I have elsewhere distinguished between a stronger and a weaker version of this approach (Searle 1980). According to strong AI, the mind is just a computer program and consequently any system whatever that was appropriately programmed, regardless of its physical composition, would literally have a mind in the same sense that you and I do. Strong AI, I think, is rather easily refutable. I have refuted it elsewhere, and I won't repeat that refutation here (see Searle 1980, 1984 for details). Weak AI I define as the view that the computer is a useful tool for the study of mind. Stated so vaguely, I believe that one could hardly object to weak AI; but there are stronger and weaker versions within weak AI, and it is a stronger version that I wish to consider here.

It is sometimes argued that though the instantiation of a computer program might not be sufficient for having mental states, it is nonetheless necessary for having them (cf Fodor 1981). According to this view, whatever else mental states might be, they must at least have a formal or syntactical level of description, and mental processes operate over the syntactical or formal structure of mental states. So construed, mental states are computational states and mental processes are computational processes, even though there may be something more to mental states than just their computational features. Since this view is so widely held (often implicitly) in cognitive science, let us call it simply "cognitivism".

I believe strong AI is demonstrably false. But what about cognitivism? I don't have a refutation of cognitivism in the way that I do believe I have one for strong AI. Nonetheless, cognitivism does seem to me very implausible as a research programme in studying the mind. I believe that the best way to expose its implausibility is to examine the weaknesses of the reasons that people have for supposing that it's true. Why do people suppose that we can learn about the mind by studying the digital computer and designing computer programs to simulate cognitive achievements in ways that they would not hope to learn about the mind by studying other machinery, such as steam engines or sewing machines? And why do people suppose that the computer is specially relevant as a model for understanding the human mind in a way that it is not specially relevant to understanding evolution or the behaviour of the solar system or the pattern of rainstorms in Northern California?

What exactly is the appeal of the computational metaphor? Well, I have been able to discover at least six reasons why my colleagues in the cognitive sciences are attracted by cognitivism. And in this chapter, I will simply state these six reasons and criticise each of them. The reasons are given in descending order, since each reason tends to depend on the reasons preceding, but it also, if valid, lends further support to those earlier reasons. So here goes:

1. We do not know how the brain works, and the computer analogy seems the best theory (what else could the brain be if it is not a digital computer?)

Since we do not know how the brain works, it has, throughout history, always been tempting to try to understand the brain by comparing it with the latest technology. In my childhood, we were always told that the brain functioned like a telephone switchboard. The brain, in short, was a cross-bar system (what else could it be?). I was fascinated to find that Sherrington compared the brain to a telegraph system. Freud frequently uses electromagnetic and hydraulic analogies in discussing the brain. Leibniz compared the functioning of the brain to the functioning of a mill; and I am even told that certain Greek thinkers thought the brain functioned like a catapult. This reason is of course seldom, if ever, stated explicitly; and I believe it functions more or less unconsciously. Nonetheless, I think it is a fairly serious reason, since if we had a perfect science of the brain, in strictly neurobiological terms, no one would find it necessary to invoke a computer metaphor.

2. We can actually get machines to exhibit behaviour which, if we found it in humans, we would regard as intelligent. And this is surely proof of intelligence.

This I believe is the most potent reason of all. It is the great unfulfilled promise of artificial intelligence. Suppose, for example, we could actually program a computer so that it would engage in linguistic behaviour that was indistinguishable from that of a human being. Suppose we could get natural language understanding programs that could pass the Turing test. And I mean *really* pass the Turing test, not just fool a few bewildered employees seeking psychiatric solace or perform a few tricks with imaginary blocks or summarise the odd story in the New York Times. If we could actually get a good natural language understanding program, the achievement, I believe, would be so prodigious that a lot of the critics of AI would probably be cowed into submission.

But they would be mistaken to be so cowed. The situation we are in, if you combine reasons 1 and 2, is something like the following. Imagine that clocks grew on trees. Imagine that they were immensely useful, but that nobody knew how they worked. Imagine furthermore that any attempt to analyse the structure of the clock invariably tended to destroy the clock. Now suppose that in this situation a group of researchers said, "Well, we will understand how clocks work if we build a machine that is functionally the equivalent of the clock; that has input and output relations that are indistinguishable from clocks." So let's suppose these researchers design an hourglass. And then they say, "At last we understand clocks. They are really hourglasses." Or perhaps, "If only we could get an hourglass that keeps as good time as a clock can keep, then we will at last understand clocks." And we can imagine sceptics worrying whether hourglasses really are clocks and pointing out that we still did not have alarm hourglasses, etc. In this little parable, if you substitute "brain" for "clock", "body" for "trees", "digital computer programs" for "hourglasses", and the notion of cognitive competence for keeping time, you will have something like the present situation in cognitive science. The fact that two different systems can produce similar output behaviours, given similar inputs, is by itself insufficient evidence that they function on the same internal principles. If it were adequate evidence, we would have very strong evidence that gasoline engines and electrical engines functioned on the same internal principles.

There is an answer to this objection, however, that leads to the third reason. But before considering it, I want to digress a bit and ask why has AI research been so slow and so disappointing in producing programs that could pass the Turing test. Why do we not have good natural language understanding programs for example, and why are even the best "expert systems" confined to very restricted "microworlds"?

I believe that in large part the problems derive from the difficulties of doing a simulation of what I call "the background" (Searle 1983, Chap. 5) in the operation of human cognition. If one examines the early Schank programs for understanding stories, one finds that the program is capable of answering simple questions about the story, e.g. "Did the man who went into the restaurant eat the hamburger?" The machine will answer "yes" or "no" depending on the details of the story; and this is (correctly) regarded as something of an achievement because it did not say explicitly in the story whether or not the man actually ate the hamburger that he ordered. But in the original versions of these programs, if you then ask the machine, "And did the man eat the hamburger through his mouth or through his ear?", the machine would answer, "I don't know, it didn't say in the story." I am told that the answer to that question has now been put into the program. But the difficulty is that there is still an indefinite number of other such background questions that the machine cannot answer. "Was the hamburger more that three thousand years old or less than three thousand years old?" "Was the hamburger petrified or still in organic form?" "Did the hamburger weigh more than ten tons or less than ten tons?" "Did the waitress, when she brought the hamburger, walk or fly?" "Was the left-hand side of the waitress's face symmetrical with the right-hand side?" For a human being, the answer to these questions is so obvious that the very posing of the question would be likely to arouse puzzlement. Even if one programmed the answers to all of these questions in the machine, there would still be an indefinite range of other such questions.

This problem emerges in various AI writings as the difficulty of programming "common sense", and it is made to appear as a question of complexity and magnitude. But the evidence suggests that the difficulty is an "in principle" difficulty. The difficulty cannot be stated very simply. The common-sense background that enables us to understand does not consist in a set of beliefs or propositions of some other kind. Since all that can be programmed into the machine are "representations", then unless the background consists of representations, it cannot, as background, be programmed. And the evidence suggests that the background does not consist in representations, but rather, it consists in a set of abilities, stances, non-representational attitudes and general know-how. The non-representational, non-intentionalistic background forms the precondition of intentionality, but it is not itself intentional. (And this argument, or something like it, I take it, was one of the main theses of Dreyfus 1972).

However, let's assume for the sake of argument that there will be progress in simulating human cognitive capacities. Then the first two reasons for cognitivism can be supported by a third:

3. We know something about how both computational and human systems function because we know that they are both information processing systems that operate according to rules.

This claim answers the objection that cognitivism is just a variant form of behaviourism. It is one of the main theoretical motivations for the cognitivist view. In its most general form it goes something like this: Human beings think. Thinking is information processing. Information processing is symbol manipulation according to rules. But computers do information processing by way of symbol manipulation according to rules. Therefore the best way to study human thinking (or cognition) is to study computational rule-governed symbol manipulation (for an example of this argument, see Cummins 1983).

In order to assess this argument, we need to investigate the sense in which human beings can be said to do information processing and the sense in which they follow rules. And then we need to compare these senses to the ways in which computers do information processing and follow rules.

Let's start with the notion of rule following. We are told that human beings follow rules and that computers follow rules. But I want to argue that there is a crucial difference. In the case of human beings, whenever we follow a rule we are being guided by the actual content of the meaning of the rule. In the case of human rule following, meanings cause behaviour. Now, of course, they don't cause the behaviour all by themselves, but they certainly play a causal role in the production of the behaviour. For example, consider the rule: drive on the left-hand side of the road in Great Britain. Whenever I go to Britain I have to remind myself of this rule. How does it work? To say that I am obeying the rule is to say that the meaning of that rule, that is, its semantic content, plays a causal role in the production of what I actually do. Notice that there are lots of other rules that would describe what's happening, but they are not the rules I happen to be following. So, for example, assuming that I am on a two-lane road and that the steering wheel is located on the right-hand side of the car, then you could say that my behaviour is in accord with the rule: drive in such a way that the steering wheel is nearest to the centre line of the road. That is, in fact, a correct description of my behaviour. But that's not the rule that I follow in Britain. The rule that I follow is: drive on the left-hand side of the road.

I want this point to be completely clear, so let me give you another example. When my children went to the Oakland Driving School, they were taught a rule for parking cars. The rule was: when backing into a parking space on your right, manoeuvrur car towards the kerb with the steering wheel in the extreme right position until your front wheels are even with the rear wheels of the car in front; then turn the steering wheel all the way to the extreme left position. Now notice that if they are following this rule, then its meaning must play a causal role in the production of their behaviour. I was interested to learn this rule because it is not a rule that I follow. In fact, I don't follow a rule at all when I park a car. I just look at the kerb and try to get as close to the kerb as I can without bashing into the cars in front or behind. But notice, it might turn out that my behaviour viewed from outside, viewed externally, is identical with the behaviour of the person who is following the rule. Still, it would not be true to say of me that I was following the rule. The fact that the behaviour is in accord with the rule is not to say that the rule is being followed. In order that the rule be followed, the meaning of the rule has to play a causal role in the behaviour.

Now the moral of this discussion for cognitivism can be put very simply. *In the sense in which human beings follow rules* (and incidentally human beings follow rules a whole lot less than cognitivists claim they do), *computers don't follow rules at all. They only act in accord with certain formal procedures.* The program of the computer determines the various steps that the machinery will go through; it determines how one state will be transformed into a subsequent state. And we can speak metaphorically as if this were a matter of following rules, but in the literal sense in which human beings follow rules, computers do not follow rules at all, they only act as if they were following rules. We can speak metaphorically of any system as if it were following rules, the solar system for example. The metaphor only becomes harmful if it is confused with the literal sense. It is OK to use psychological metaphor to explain the computer. The confusion comes when you take the metaphor literally and use the metaphorical computer sense of rule following to try to explain the psychological sense of rule following, on which the metaphor was based in the first place.

So we have two sense of rule following, a literal and a metaphorical. And it is very easy to confuse the two. Now I want to apply these lessons to the notion of information processing. I believe that the notion of information processing embodies a similar massive confusion. The idea is that since I process information when I think, and since my calculating machine processes information when it takes something as input, transforms it and produces information as output, then there must be some unitary sense in which we are both processing information. But that seems to me obviously false. The sense in which I do information processing when I think is the sense in which I am consciously or unconsciously engaged in certain mental processes. But in that sense of information processing, the calculator does not do information processing since it does not have any mental processes at all. It simply mimics or simulates the formal features of mental processes I have. That is, even if the steps that the calculator goes through are formally the same as the steps that I go through, it would not follow that the machine does anything at all like what I do, for the very simple reason that the calculator has no mental phenomena. If I am doing my income tax and I add $600 to $300 the calculator doesn't know that the numeral "600" stands for six hundred dollars, or that the numeral "300" stands for three hundred dollars and that the plus sign stands for the operation of addition. And that's for the very simple reason that it doesn't know anything. Indeed, that is the reason why we have calculators. They can do calculations faster and more accurately than we can without having to go through any mental effort to do it. In the sense in which we have to go through information processing, they don't.

We need, then, to make a distinction between two senses of the notion of information processing, or at least, two radically different kinds of information processing. The first kind, which I will call "psychological information processing", involves mental states. To put it at its crudest, when people perform mental operations, they actually think, and thinking characteristically involves processing information of one kind or another. But there is another sense of information processing in which there are no mental states at all. In these cases, there are processes which are as if there were some mental information processing going on. Let us call these second kinds of information processing "as if" forms. It is perfectly harmless to use both of these two kinds of mental ascriptions provided we do not confuse them. However, what we find in cognitivism is a persistent confusion of the two.

Now once we see this distinction clearly, we can see one of the most profound weaknesses in the cognitivist argument. From the fact that I do information processing when I think and the fact that the computer also does information processing – even information processing which may simulate the formal features of my thinking – it simply doesn't follow that there is anything psychologically relevant about the computer program. In order to show psychological relevance, there would have to be some independent argument that the "as if" computational information processing is psychologically relevant. The notion of information processing is being used to mask this confusion because one expression is being used to cover two quite distinct phenomena. In short, the confusion we found in the notion of rule following has an exact parallel in the notion of information processing.

However, there is a deeper and more subtle confusion involved in the notion of information processing. Notice that in the "as if" sense of information processing, any system whatever can be described as if it were doing information processing, and indeed, we might even use it for gathering information. So, it isn't just a matter of using calculators and computers. Consider, for example, water running downhill. We can describe the water as if it were doing information processing, and we might even use the water to get information. We might use it, for example, to get information about the line of least resistance in the contours of the hill. But it doesn't follow from that there is anything of psychological relevance about water running downhill. There is no psychology to the action of gravity on water, even though in ordinary "as if" usage, the system is an information processing system.

We can apply the lessons of this point to the study of the brain. It is an obvious fact that the brain has a level of real psychological information processes. To repeat, people actually think, and the thinking goes on in their brains.

Furthermore, there are all sorts of things going on in the brain at the neurophysiological level that actually cause our thought processes. But many people suppose that in addition to these two levels, the level of naive psychology and the level of neurophysiology, there must be some additional level of computational information processing. Now why do they suppose that? I believe that it is partly because they confuse the psychologically real level of information processing with the possibility of giving "as if" information processing descriptions of the processes going on in the brain. If you talk about water running downhill, everyone can see that it is psychologically irrelevant, but it is harder to see that exactly the same point applies to the brain.

What is psychologically relevant about the brain are the facts that it contains psychological processes and that it has a neurophysiology that causes and realises these processes. But the fact that we can describe other processes in the brain from an "as if" information processing point of view, by itself provides no evidence that these are psychologically real or even psychologically relevant. Once we are talking about the inside of the brain, it's harder to see the confusion, but it's exactly the same confusion as the confusion of supposing that because water running downhill does "as if" information processing, that there is some hidden psychology in water running downhill.

There is an additional difficulty with the notion of the formal computer program level of brain operation. The computer program consists in a set of purely formal processes; qua formal processes these have no interpretation or meaning at all. Any interpretation has to be added from outside the system of formal processes. The consequence of this fact is that even if you designed a program of an "as if" sort about how the brain worked, there would be nothing specifically cognitive about this program. It could be given an interpretation as a series of dance steps or as a pattern of buying and selling or just as atractive uninterpreted pattern. To put this point more precisely in the terms that we introduced above in our discussion of rule following, if you abandon the common-sense notion of a rule, but still insist that what you are getting at is the rules according to which the brain operates, you pay two kinds of prices. First, since the rule is formal, since it has no content, it is subject to any interpretation at all, it has no special mental relevance. And secondly, you then cannot distinguish between the role of the rule in human behaviour which really motivates the behaviour and the role of such "rules" in hurricanes, fires, digestion etc. which play no motivational or causal role at all. In the sense that it is appropriate to talk about a formal level of information processing that goes on in the brain, it is equally appropriate to talk about that level of description in any formally specifiable system whatever. But this level has no specifically explanatory power for the mental phenomena in the brain because this formal level contains no mental content.

The fourth assumption behind the cognitivist research programme is seldom stated explicitly. It functions, I believe, more like a guiding methodological principle than an explicit hypothesis. But it is an old assumption, going back perhaps as far as Plato and certainly as far as Leibniz. It is the assumption that:

4. Meaningful human behaviour must be the product of an internal theory.

Consider for example our ability to learn a language or our ability to recognise faces. In both cases, it seems to me, we have at present good reason for supposing that these abilities are innate to the human species and are due to innate structures in the brain. However, most current research is not content to accept the idea that what we should investigate is the sheer physical mechanism that does the job. Rather, most research is based on the assumption that there must be some set of rules or some set of unconscious information processing that we go through in learning a language or in recognising faces.

One finds this assumption in many areas and not just in cognitive psychology. So for example, Chomsky's search for a universal grammar is based on the assumption that if there are certain features common to all languages and if these features are constrained by common features of the human brain, then there must be an entire complex set of rules of universal grammar in the brain. But a much simpler hypothesis would be that the physiological structure of the brain constrains possible grammars without the intervention of an intermediate level of rules or theories. Not only is this hypothesis simpler, but also the very existence of universal features of language constrained by the innate features of the brain suggests that the neurophysiological level of description is enough. You don't need to suppose that there are any rules on top of the neurophysiological structures.

A couple of analogies will, I hope, make this clear. It is a simple fact about human vision that we can't see infrared or ultraviolet. Now is that because we have a universal rule of visual grammar that says: if an object is infrared or ultraviolet, don't see it? No, it is obviously because our visual apparatus simply is not sensitive to these two ends of the spectrum. Of course, we could describe ourselves "as if" we were following a rule of visual grammar, but all the same, we are not. Or to take another example, if we tried to do a theoretical analysis of the human ability to stay in balance while walking, it might look as if there were some more or less complex mental processes going on; as if taking in cues of various kinds we solved a series of differential equations (unconsciously, of course) and these enabled us to walk without falling over. But we actually know that this sort of mental theory is not necessary to account for the achievement of walking without falling over. In fact, it is done in a very large part by fluids in the inner ear that simply do no calculating at all. If you spin around long enough so as to upset the fluids, you are likely to fall over. Now I want to suggest that a great deal of our cognitive achievements may well be like that. The brain just does them. We have no good reason for supposing that in addition to the level of our mental states and the level of our neurophysiology there is some unconscious calculating going on.

Consider face recognition. We all recognise the faces of our friends, relatives and acquaintances quite effortlessly; and indeed we now have evidence that certain portions of the brain are specialised for face recognition. How does it work? Well, suppose we were going to design a computer that could recognise faces as we do. It would carry out quite a computational task, involving a lot of calculation of geometrical and topographical features. But is there any evidence that the way we do it involves calculating and computing? Notice that when we step in wet sand and make a footprint, neither our feet nor the sand does any computing. But if we were going to design a program that would calculate the topology of a footprint from information about differential pressures on the sand, it would be a fairly complex computational task. The fact that a computational simulation of a natural phenomenon involves complex information processing does not show that the phenomenon itself involves such processing. And it may be that facial recognition is as simple and as automatic as making footprints in the sand.

Indeed, if we pursue the computer analogy consistently, we find that there are a great many things going on in the computer that are not computational processes either. For example, in some calculators, if you ask, "how does the calculator multiply seven times three?", the answer is "it adds three to itself six times". But if you then ask, "how does it add three to itself?" there isn't any computational answer to that; it is just done in the hardware. So the answer to the question is, "it just does it". And I want to suggest that for a great many absolutely fundamental abilities, such as our ability to see or our ability to learn a language, there may not be any theoretical mental level underlying those abilities; the brain just does them. We are neurophysiologically so constructed that the assault of photons on our photoreceptor cells enables us to see and we are neurophysiologically so constructed that the stimulation of hearing other people talk and interacting with them will enable us to learn a language.

Now I am not saying that rules play no role in our behaviour. On the contrary, rules of language or rules of games, for example, seem to play a crucial role in the relevant behaviour. But I am saying that it is a tricky question to decide which parts of behaviour are rule-governed and which are not. And we can't just assume that all meaningful behaviour is underlain by some system of rules.

The first four reasons for cognitivism are supported by a fifth:

5. We actually have solid empirical evidence that the brain works on computational principles.

The evidence that I have seen presented for this thesis is of two kinds. First, there are reaction time experiments and, second, there is linguistic evidence, usually from generative grammar.

The most commonly adduced evidence for the existence of a computational level in the brain is in the discovery of formal rules of language, particularly rules of syntax and phonology. The idea is that since we have discovered the rules of grammar, and since these rules of grammar are purely formal, and since the computer rules are similarly formal, what we have in fact discovered (or are discovering) is (at least part of) the computer program on which our linguistic abilities are based.

I believe that there is a simple and rather obvious fallacy in this argument. Because the rules of grammar are about formal matters, for example, syntax and phonology, it does not follow that the rules are formal in the computational sense of being entirely constituted by their formal structure without any reference to their semantic content. On the contrary, the formal syntactical rules of grammar are full of semantic content; they just happen to be about syntax. To illustrate this point, consider an example. It is a rule of French pronunciation that if a word ends in a consonant, that consonant is not pronounced if the next word begins with a consonant, but is pronounced if the next word begins with a vowel. Thus, in the plural noun phrase "beaux arts", one pronounces the final consonant of the adjective. But in the plural noun phrase "beaux garçons", one does not pronounce that consonant. Indeed, the plural "beaux garçons" is pronounced in the same way as the singular "beau garçon", though they are spelt differently. Assuming this is a rule of French pronunciation, it seems reasonable to conclude that native French speakers obey it unconsciously. But notice that in the specification of the rule, I presented you with a semantic content, that is to say, with a set of meanings. It just so happened that the words that I used refer to elements which can be specified without reference to their meanings, namely elements such as "words", "consonants", "vowels" and so on.

The moral of this is quite simple. Assume for sake of argument that people actually follow rules of grammar when they speak. If we take the notion of following a rule quite literally, then there is no evidence from the fact that people follow rules of grammar when they speak that therefore they are functioning like computers. The rules of grammar that they follow have a semantic content which plays a causal role in the production of their behaviour. The "rules" of computation are not rules at all, but formal procedures that the machine goes through.

6. The computer metaphor provides an easy solution to the mind–body problem, and unless the computational analogy is correct, we have no solution to the mind–body problem.

Many partisans of cognitivism, especially if they are philosophically inclined, welcome the computer metaphor because they feel it provides the only plausible solution to the mind–body problem: we understand the relation of the computer software to the computer hardware. There is nothing mysterious about the relation of the program to the system that implements it. Now, if the mind is to the brain as the program is to the hardware, then we have similarly an easy solution to the mind–body problem. But without this solution, it appears to be a mystery how mental states could actually cause anything physical or how cognition could be anything other than epiphenomenal.

In some authors such as Pylyshyn or Fodor, this version of the mind–body problem is used explicitly as an argument for cognitivism. The argument goes as follows: semantic content cannot function causally. As Pylyshyn (1984, p 39) writes:

the semantics of representations cannot literally cause a system to behave in the way it does; only the material form of the representation is causally efficacious.

But how can there be a parallel between the semantic content and the behaviour? Pylyshyn answers:

Only one non-question-begging answer to this dilemma has ever been proposed: that what the brain is doing is exactly what computers do when they compute numerical functions; namely, their behaviour is caused by the physically instantiated properties of classes of sub-states that correspond to symbolic codes.

In other words, semantics can only function causally if it is physically realised in a formal syntax, but then that is exactly what a computer is.

Paradoxically, this "solution" to the mind–body problem accepts the worst assumption of the dualism that it seeks to supplant. It assumes that the mind is something formal or abstract or non-material and not part of the ordinary physical–biological world that we all live in. If one assumes, as I believe one should, that mental processes are just as much a part of our biological natural history as digestion, growth or the secretion of bile, then there is no mind–body problem to start with. Mental processes stand to neurophysiological processes as higher level features of a system composed of micro-elements stand to the behaviour of the lower level elements. The higher level features are both caused by the behaviour of the micro-elements and realised in the system that consists of those micro-elements. These relations are quite familiar to us from the rest of nature, and there is no reason why the biology of cognition should not be treated as a set of natural processes like any others.

The tacit assumption, in short, behind the cognitivist solution of the mind–body problem is that of all biological processes, one and only one should be regarded as not in the realm of biochemistry, and that one is cognition. I believe the correct solution to the mind–body problem requires us to reject the Cartesian assumption that minds are not part of the physical world like everything else, and to treat mental phenomena – whether consciousness, intentionality or what have you – as natural processes in the physical world.

Notes

1 This paper was previously published in Göranzon B, Florin M (eds) *Artificial intelligence, culture and language: On education and work* (Artificial Intelligence and Society series) Springer-Verlag, 1990, pp 22–34. Some of the ideas in this chapter appear in a much shorter and preliminary form in Chap. 3 of *Minds, brains and science* (Searle 1984).

2 The original draft of this chapter was written before the recent popularity of Parallel Distributed Processing (PDP). These so-called "neural nets" or "new connectionist" models attempt to model cognition not at the level of information processing or intentionality but at something like the neuronal level. I say "something like" because the partisans of this approach are for the most part careful to point out that they are not modelling actual neural nets exactly, but rather they are simulating certain features of the behaviour of neurons and leaving out other features. I am more sympathetic to this approach to artificial intelligence than I am to the traditional information processing approach, but I also believe that it has difficulties of its own. I will not be discussing the strength and weaknesses of PDP here. This chapter will be devoted entirely to traditional artificial intelligence.

References

Cummins R (1983) The nature of psychological explanation. MIT Press, Cambridge, Mass

Dreyfus HL (1979) What computers can't do, 2nd edn. Harper & Row, New York

Fodor JA (1981) Methodological solipsism as a research strategy in psychology. In: Fodor JA, Representations: Philosophical essays on the foundations of cognitive science. MIT Press, Cambridge Mass

Pylyshyn ZW (1984) Computation and cognition: Towards a foundation for cognitive science. MIT Press, Cambridge Mass

Searle JR (1980) Minds, brains and programs. Behavioral and Brain Sciences 3:417–457

Searle JR (1983) Intentionality. An essay in the philosophy of mind. Cambridge University Press, Cambridge

Searle JR (1984) Minds, brains and science. Harvard University Press, Cambridge, Mass

Chapter 9

Intelligent Behaviour in Machines

Luigi Stringa

Introduction

With the publication in 1950 of Alan Turing's paper "Computing machinery and intelligence", the old question "can machines think?" acquired a new meaning, which soon proved to have a strong impact on the scientific community (Turing 1950). Operating methods for attacking the problem in a scientific way were finally made available. And both scientists and philosophers began to work on the positive assumption that "machines can think!"

Today, almost forty years after Turing's article, the question still lacks a satisfactory answer and in fact there is not even unanimous agreement about such basic terms as "think" and "intelligence". Indeed, if we applied Turing's test to any machine now available, it would not pass, and so would not be a "thinking" machine in the sense intended by Turing. Whereas on the other hand, one frequently-accepted definition of "intelligent behaviour" is so broad that one could even consider a pocket calculator to be intelligent!

For these reasons, I shall try in this chapter to take a look (though certainly not an exhaustive one) at some different approaches to the question of what constitutes intelligent behaviour. My point of departure will be the model of intelligence arrived at, after centuries of gestation, through first order formal logic. On this basis, I shall examine two opposing approaches to intelligence that I will call "global" and "sectorial". I shall conclude by highlighting the necessity for an integrated approach – even at the operational level – that allows the creation of systems with "common sense". The laws of deductive reasoning have long been considered the highest expression of intelligence, with common sense playing the role of poor country cousin. In my opinion, however, forty years of empirical research have revealed quite the opposite. The time has come to re-evaluate the importance of common sense, for this, I shall argue, is the true hallmark of intelligent behaviour.

The "Mechanical" Model of Intelligent Machines

Descartes' dictum "cogito ergo sum" is perhaps the best example of how thought, or intelligence, has traditionally been considered man's most important attribute; that which determines his identity (Descartes 1637). Man's characteristic organ is, for Descartes, the soul:

that distinct part of the body whose nature ... consists solely in thought

And this in turn implies that since machines and animals do not have a soul, they cannot think. There is for Descartes, however, no essential difference between machines, animals and the human body. Such a conception naturally stems from the models of machines with which Descartes was confronted in his own time: the automata that proliferated in seventeenth- century Europe. It is precisely through contemplation of such models that Descartes believed himself to have found the two factors which would prevent machines from showing intelligent behaviour:

1. Machines lack semantic capability (speech "is the only sign and the sole sure proof of thought hidden and enclosed within the body")
2. Machines are necessarily specialised – as opposed to universal – systems (and since it is only in combination that the careful ordering of parts can generate details of actions, it follows that "it is practically impossible that there could be in a machine, enough parts to make it react, in all the occurrences of life, in the same manner in which reason makes us react")

The first argument gradually lost its force, and evolving scientific practice has long since disproved it. But the second argument is still a challenge – in practice if not in principle – for daily research work in artificial intelligence (AI) laboratories.

In fact, long before ENIAC, UNIVAC and the rest, there were people who were convinced that symbolic-logic machines were possible. Without going all the way back in time to Lullo's *Ars magna*, consider Leibniz's faith in the possibility of conceiving a "calculus ratiocinator" capable of being implemented on machines: a calculus which would one day permit two opposing parties to resolve any intellectual dispute with a simple "Calculemus!" (Leibniz 1966). Or consider Boole's research programme: "the mathematics that we must build is the mathematics of the human intellect" (Boole 1847). And again, consider Torres y Quevedo, who, at the dawn of the present century, guaranteed that "automata can do many things that are commonly classified as thought" (Torres y Quevedo 1915). One can certainly not deny that there has been a certain tendency in western thought to believe in the possibility of mechanising human intellect, or at least some aspects of it. And to a certain extent one can even think of it as a winning tendency, since Von Neumann's "universal machine" can be regarded as a realisation of Leibniz's "calculus" and Boole's "laws of thought".

Despite all of this, one still gets the feeling that something has gone wrong: that something strange has happened. Sure, here we are, working on and discussing thinking machines and their intelligent behaviour (remember Turing's prophecy!). But there is an element of paradox in the situation. As soon as it is discovered that relays and transistors can reproduce the "laws of thought", these same "laws" are no longer considered to be at the heart of intelligence. As soon as some "mental function" is programmed, as D.R. Hofstadter observes, "people soon cease to consider it as an essential ingredient of "real thinking" (Hofstadter 1979).

What emerges once again is the dominant Cartesian position: "machine" is synonymous with "stupidity", and the difference between Man and machine is therefore insurmountable. Indeed, it is curious that even such big manufacturers as IBM have sought to increase the usage of computers by emphasising the slogan that "machines do only what they are told to". The fact that they have sought to calm public fears in this way is a sign that, subconsciously at least, people do not exclude the possibility that machines with "electronic brains" might truly act on their own in intelligent ways. After all, the presumption that man has a monopoly over intelligence is grounded in a sort of psychological self-protection on the part of the human species.

Beyond these motives, however, I want to underline two others: an old-fashioned conception of machines, and a simplistic vision of logic. The first point might sound obvious, but I think one should make it clear once and for all. The time has come for popular opinion to throw off obsolete ideas about machines: what Minsky calls "precomputerian" ideas (Minsky 1963). The term "machine" must be relieved of many historic connotations that have no reason to exist today. For example, past machines characteristically had no freedom, whilst today we have very widely integrated systems: complex systems that can show complex behaviours which were impossible for precomputerian machines.

As to the second point, it is often argued that another reason why machines cannot equal human intelligence is that they would be limited to using only the deductive methods of formal logic (otherwise, as J.R. Lucas puts it (Lucas 1961), "the system will have ceased to be a formal logical system and the machine will barely qualify for the title of a model of the mind").

However, the belief that a machine can only be a brute-force deductive computer derives from a confusion between physical and logical levels, from the assumption that there is only one level of existence for symbols and abstractions. Instead we now know how central the distinction between levels is to AI, and we need only look at recent research on meta-level organised architectures to see this.

Again, it is time to abandon obsolete ideas and naive beliefs that prevent people from accepting what is really happening today, namely that complex intelligent machines are actually being constructed.

Universally Intelligent Machines and Intelligent Fragmentation

Let's go back to Descartes' second point. (Even if these machines were able to do things as well as or perhaps even better than us, they would inevitably make mistakes in other things, thereby revealing that they were not acting on the basis of knowledge but according to the arrangement of their parts.) Thus, even though many expert systems exist today, they are not held to be truly intelligent: for they are mere "on/off" systems, which "know" how to carry out a few tasks very well, but don't know how to do anything else.

By contrast, three centuries after Descartes, Turing argued that the universal machine which is not bound to perform just a few things in a stupidly perfect way, is not merely conceivable but even capable of being built: "we don't need to have an infinity of different machines that perform different tasks. One is enough".

These two trends, specialisation and universality, are in fact two recurring foci for debate about intelligent machines (if not intelligence *tout court*), and it is therefore to be expected that both positions should be represented even in the brief history of AI.

As far as Turing is concerned, we all know that he was the first to list the different areas in which AI researchers would be involved for twenty years. Even so, he was most interested in the global aspect of intelligence. And when he proposed his anthropomorphic–behaviouristic test, he set a truly severe standard. It is true that "partial Turing tests" have been passed since the beginnings of AI (the comment of ex-chess champion R.W. Nealy after being beaten by Arthur Samuel's program covers them all: "As far as the final is concerned, I haven't had a similar confrontation with a human being since 1954, when I lost my last game"). But Turing's test is incomparably more severe than a test for a particular domain. Not only does it assume that the examiner is willing to put the machine into difficulty, but it also requires that the machine should be willing to dissemble and to try to entrap the questioner. (Turing says: "It is A's object in the game to try to cause C to make the wrong identification".) And this in turn requires that the machine:

Be knowledgeable about human behaviour in its entirety as well as its subtleties, so that it may make assumptions
Be knowledgeable about the behaviour usually expected from a machine, in order to avoid it

In short, what the test asks is nothing less than self-awareness from the machine (and even more than that, since it must also simulate the self-awareness of the human). Not an easy task! One might legitimately wonder whether in future humans would be able to pass a machine-made test analogous to Turing's!

Together with Turing's test, language development such as the General Problem Solver (GPS) is the other reference in the mainstream of research concerned with the laws and universal characteristics of intelligence (or at least, the relatively universal, if we want to take into account Meltzer's criticisms of Turing's test). Whilst a machine capable of passing Turing's test is still a long way off (and there won't even be any serious candidates for many years yet), the GPS program developed by Newell, Shaw and Simon has started an empirical enquiry into the overall characteristics of intelligence (Ernst and Newell 1969). The basic assumption is that intelligence is global, and that it cannot be reduced to a simple technique, or alternatively that the procedures of intelligent reasoning must be employed for a wide spectrum of tasks: "for going to the drugstore as well as for resolving a mathematical puzzle", as Pamela McCorduck argues (McCorduck 1979). From this point of view, a machine that is able to beat the world's foremost chess champion but does not know how to do anything else is not intelligent (whereas it would be so considered according to the most widespread definition of AI).

The GPS program undoubtedly opened the way to the study of the "universal heuristics" found in the opening chapters of most current manuals of AI, but it was already clear to the pioneers that a machine could never attain what we call intelligent behaviour without using heuristics to curtail crude searching. The proof of the success of GPS is the way in which its techniques have been incorporated into so many subsequent AI programs. But the limits of GPS research are well known, and have been highlighted by John McCarthy's attempt to build the "Advice Taker", a universal counsellor endowed with common sense which, however, never saw the light of day. The time was just not ripe, and AI research into natural language was in its infancy.

Consequently, the reaction to the "general purpose" ambitions of the first decade of AI was not long in coming, and it came with some force. Following on the heels of the generation of "generalists" came a whole new generation of "specialists", and the advent of large robotics programmes in the 1960s clearly demonstrated that the general principles of AI were not enough, and that practical intelligence needed a rich complement of specific knowledge. The difference, of course, is far from minor. Once again, it turns on what one understands by "intelligent behaviour" (machine or non-machine) and therefore on the basic goals of AI. For example, a machine such as MACSYMA would never be considered intelligent by a generalist like Minsky ("that is not AI", he maintains, and in this regard I tend to agree with him); but it certainly is an intelligent machine according to Joel Moses, inventor of MACSYMA and standard-bearer of the new paradigm, the primacy of its capability with respect to general methods (Moses 1971).

The dispute is not just terminological. Consider the definition of AI which is often given (and not only in derivative texts): "AI is that part of computer science that is concerned with intelligent systems, that is, systems that show behaviour that would be considered intelligent if encountered in a human being". This definition is in the spirit of Turing's test for at least two mutually correlated reasons:

1. It does not delineate but confronts
2. It is anthropocentric

All the same, however, this may be interpreted in less stringent terms than Turing's test: it may define a variety of intelligent behaviours; a variety of different, fragmented types of intelligence. For example, knowing how to calculate integrals is considered intelligent in humans (as students taking their first courses in numerical analysis know very well!), and this could be enough to validate the claim that even MACSYMA is an intelligent system, albeit only in respect of a specific behaviour.

The fact is that the above definition, apart from presupposing a notion of natural intelligence which is anything but obvious, contents itself with local achievements. In contrast to Turing's test, it is enumerative, and not holistic, leading to the classification of types of intelligence relative to this or that behaviour. (It is interesting to note how such a model finds a precise counterpart in psychological works such as *The Nature of Human Intelligence*, where J.P. Guilford and his colleagues expound a model of intelligence based on one hundred and twenty discrete abilities, modelled on a $6 \times 5 \times 4$ grid! (Guilford 1967))

I believe that the fragmented model of intelligence that this expresses at the theoretical level corresponds, at the operational level to a certain practice of AI whereby development goes hand in hand with fragmentation. And in the same spirit, though without embracing any global psychological model (such as that described by L.G. Humphreys under the symptomatic title "The Construct of General Intelligence"), I shall maintain that the mosaic of intelligence can only be reconstructed by a methodology of AI research which integrates the various approaches and techniques.

Towards an Integrated Approach

In this connection, an important role is played by what I call the "paradox of rules and common sense". It was believed for a long time that the laws of deductive thought represented the pinnacles of intelligence, whilst "good common sense" was at a lower level. In particular, AI research initially proceeded from the conviction that the construction of formidable logic machines (theorem provers, unbeatable chess players etc.) would take us straight to the heart of intelligence.

It hasn't turned out that way at all. That which seemed to be the summit (the rigour of logic) has been reached first, and that which seemed unimportant (common sense) has proved to be the most difficult thing to program: and has come to be seen as a very ambitious goal indeed. Those things that are truly difficult to reproduce are exactly the activities that seem most obvious to us because they are implanted in us by evolution or acquired through learning.

According to Douglas Hofstadter, this is indeed the core paradox in AI: it requires bridging "the seemingly unbridgeable gulf between the formal and informal, the animate and the inanimate, the flexible and the inflexible". The paradox disappears, however, if one assumes the existence of many symbolic levels rather than just one. Common sense comes easily for complex machines, like the human brain, endowed with multiple intertwined levels, whilst rigorous logic is a struggle ("the flexibility of intelligence comes from the enormous number of different rules and levels of rules", observes Hofstadter); whereas in systems which are not rich in levels, such as the first computers, the position is reversed, and logical algorithms are more easily realised than "common sense algorithms".

I believe that this new paradigm requires the integration of levels: an integrated approach to the definition of intelligence.

From the philosophical point of view, this probably implies moving from behaviourist definitions to definitions given in terms of knowledge representation, or, more precisely, an integration of the two. As McCarthy observed "a computer program capable of acting intelligently in the world must have a general representation of the world in terms of which its inputs are interpreted". In particular, "the first task is to define even a naive common sense view of the world precisely enough to program a computer to act accordingly".

From a more practical point of view, the nature of current research problems is itself bringing about the breakdown of the narrow "sectorial" perspective. It should no longer happen, to borrow a metaphor from McCarthy, that a researcher will believe that he can see a forest when he is looking at a single tree; that he identifies a particular problem with the entire field of research. This way of proceeding has meant that various points of departure have usually led to different approaches to the same problem: not a bad thing in itself unless the approaches are not co-ordinated or integrated. Consider, for example, knowledge representation studies, conducted using very different criteria depending on whether the researchers have operated in the area of expert systems development, image recognition or natural language understanding. Or consider robotics. It's true that twenty years ago it was robotics that led the way in overcoming the generalist approach to AI. But it is also true that today robotics can only progress through the study of means of representation and inference that are fundamentally the same for all solutions to various problems of knowledge manipulation (just think of the implications of the need for a homogeneous representation of data arriving through different types of sensor, such as touch and vision).

In short, we can say that AI systems have very often grown in a disorganised fashion, gradually accumulating solutions obtained at the level of sub-problems, but without a unifying project. Today we feel the need for an overall plan that is something more than the simple aggregation of different lines of research: a project that, using top-down methods, will lead to the integration of different research lines, bringing them to flow together into a single stream.

An examination of the principal lines of research in AI highlights a certain number of crucial problems which are common to all areas. For example, the low capacity for correctly treating semantic information limits the efficiency of vision systems, speech understanding, natural language processing, etc. Furthermore, the semantic schemes used in these areas are very different from each other and are often incompatible.

Analogous considerations lead us to identify the lack of efficient models of the world as one of the gaps that must be filled in order to obtain significant results. Also in this regard we feel the need for a unique world model, which must necessarily be knowledge-based, and therefore not specialised for vision, speech recognition or whatever. Even the descriptive techniques for knowledge, which are often rather poor, have normally been developed in an autonomous and, above all, uncoordinated way by researchers in different disciplines. And integration between techniques exclusive to AI and the technologies of conventional computer science is pretty rare.

More generally, what is lacking is a really *systematic approach* to the problems of AI. This lack cannot be minimised. For, as I have been arguing, intelligent behaviour can only be obtained through the integrated combination of different types of knowledge on one hand and interaction with a single model of the world on the other.

We are therefore facing the need to develop a global approach to AI which derives from a unified project, divided into the principal lines of research mentioned above, but directed towards a single objective. Such a project must be planned to allow the co-ordination of all the results obtained along the way in different areas, so that systems can be realised which are capable of showing progressively intelligent behaviour (in the sense mentioned previously).

This obviously necessitates the development of "sub-systems" capable of interpreting information coming from different types of sensors (optical, acoustical etc.), not only to produce coherent reactions to the environment, but also to enrich the global experience of the system, so that it interacts as dynamically as possible with the knowledge base as well as with the world model. For example, the inference algorithms that will need to be developed must operate in an analogous manner irrespective of the source of the information structure.

A concrete example of this approach is the research programme in the AI Division at IRST, Trento, where the problems of AI are being faced in the climate of a single project: "The Artificial Intelligence Project".

The eventual goal of this project is the construction of a robot capable of interpreting orders and of executing them, asking for any additional information that might be necessary for this purpose. With this specific goal in mind, a great amount of work is being done in every field of AI research. For example:

Interfaces: a starting point, since we can only begin to interact with our machines by having them see, hear and understand what they see and hear. This still calls for a great deal of research on machine vision, voice recognition, elaboration of natural languages (spoken, written, iconic, gestural and whatever else we use to communicate apart from the artificial "languages" we keep inventing to avoid the problem) and so on.

Models of cognitive processes: mathematical models of learning, reasoning, making deductive or inductive inferences, treating semantic information etc. All of this is quite important if the robot, initially rather "backward", is to be able to acquire higher and higher levels of intelligence on the basis of experience. And in this regard there is no doubt that one should also investigate the mechanisms of natural intelligence, since artificial and natural intelligence must eventually interface.

Expert systems: sure, the world is already full of such entities; programs developed from time to time for specific industrial applications. But they all speak funny languages, and interaction with them is hard (to say the least!).

Finally, quite a bit of research is going on into the necessary software and hardware instruments, so as to allow better solutions to cognitive problems and easier approaches to data processing. (I use the word "instruments" here in a slightly polemical fashion, as there is still a certain tendency to identify such tools with AI itself. In fact, most work traditionally classified as AI research has been devoted to these aspects. But no matter how we interpret the standard definition of AI reported above, we cannot reduce it simply to "computer power".)

Four main areas of research, then, but four areas which must be seen as facets of the same project – the construction of an intelligent machine: "intelligent" in the sense that it satisfies the definition (and, hopefully, passes the Turing test), but does so in an intelligent way, as it were: a machine whose intelligence can grow and develop by integrating different fields of knowledge.

Otherwise, we are going to get stuck with the sorts of silly "robots" that are now beginning to come into our lives: robots that can perhaps recognise images very well but don't know why on earth wheels are round and not square. I'm sure that if that is what artificial intelligence is all about, then I prefer natural stupidity.

References

Boole G (1847) The mathematical analysis of logic, being an essay toward a calculus of deductive reasoning. Macmillan, Barclay & Macmillan, Cambridge; and George Bell, London

Descartes R (1637) Discours de la méthode.

Ernst G, Newell A (1969) GPS: A case study in generality and problem solving. Academic Press, New York

Guilford JP (1967) The nature of human intelligence. McGraw- Hill, New York

Hofstadter DR (1979) Gödel, Escher, Bach: Eternal Golden Braid. Basic Books, New York

Leibniz GW (1666) Dissertatio de arte combinatoria

Lucas JR (1961) Minds, machines, and Gödel. Philosophy 36:112–127

McCorduck P (1979) Machines who think. Freeman, San Francisco

Minsky M (1963) Steps towards artificial intelligence. In: Feigenbaum EA, Feldman J (eds) Computers and thought. McGraw- Hill, New York

Moses J (1971) Symbolic integration – the stormy decade. Communications of the ACM 14(August)

Torres y Quevedo (1915) Essays sur l'automatique

Turing A (1950) Computing machinery and intelligence. Mind 59:433–460

Chapter 10

Conclusions: The Dissymmetry of Mind and the Role of the Artificial

Massimo Negrotti

The aim of this book is not merely criticism of artificial intelligence (AI) by indication of its limits in reproducing the human mind as a whole, nor that of indicating the "right" way for the advancement of this technology. Rather, it intends to present different epistemological perspectives on problems raised by AI, both from a technical and from a cultural point of view.

My hope is that from this account of the nature, limits of AI, and its developments, one may get an introductory idea of what could be conceived as the *artificial* dimension of our environment and culture as well as of its role in setting up a symbiosis with man. The debate on AI gives us a better possibility to define human intelligence as *different* from machine intelligence. This is a first step towards the definition of both kinds of intelligence, i.e. the natural and the artificial.

If we assume that intelligence is, generally speaking, a quality which allows systems to survive by solving problems, then its definition cannot be the same in all cases, since the range of problems that systems should solve varies greatly with sensitivity to the environment and the rates of its fluctuations.

Presumably, human intelligence is the best known example of a kind of *general* intelligence developed under the constraint of very complex sensitivity and of a complex and changing environment. However, the bio-cultural evolution which has challenged and, at the same time, induced this capacity by selection is, perhaps, only one alternative among many.

Technological evolution, which man has intentionally advanced, is an instance of a different way of assigning intelligence to non-human systems. Though almost all species are able to build up simple "machines" by means of biologically controlled processes in order to survive, only man is concerned with the building of the intelligent machine by creating what Simon has called the *sciences of the artificial* (Simon 1969). In so doing we have discovered that, on the one hand, the intelligence we can transfer to the machine is a *subset* isolated from our own (we can design intelligent machines but no machine can design a man); on the other, we begin to understand that the transferred intelligence can be driven by man towards levels of performance that are virtually or actually impossible for the human being.

Human intelligence is so deeply linked to the whole nature of man that only by isolating it from the whole human system can we get from it the highest levels and the widest range of performance. The introduction of the *non-perturbed intelligence* concept clearly defines the kind of mental isolated subset which conventional symbolic AI is transferring to the machine. Table 10.1 helps us to clarify this point through the taxonomy of the methodological stages available to the human mind.

Table 10.1. A model of the methodological stages of the human mind. The undetermined stage is a sort of "clearing station" starting from which an internal or external input can be answered by bio-cultural stereotyed solutions or be processed by the rational stage.

Methodological stages	Processing types	Typical activities	AI types
Rational	Sequential	Theoretical reasoning, problem solving	Symbolic
Undetermined	Randomly mixed?	Intuition, problem finding, common-sense reasoning	... the real challenge
Non-rational	Parallel	Reaction, recognition, pattern-matching	Connectionist

The two mainstreams of research in AI, namely the symbolic approach and the connectionist one, as we have seen, appear to correspond not only to two precise cultural traditions but also to two real modes of operation of our mind, i.e. to two methodological extremes. But as a provisional model, it seems to be appropriate to set up a three-stage model to describe our mental activity.

The lowest stage corresponds to what is commonly known as a massive parallel pattern-matching activity, often unconscious, reactive and, probably, strongly dominated by the physiology of our brain and its capacity to induce mental behaviour.

The highest stage, conversely, corresponds to a rational, frequently sequential, conscious way of dealing with concepts, ideas, formal reasoning and so on. In a word, the latter is the ideal "site" of *non-perturbed intelligence*, while the former is the "site" of the complete immersion of the mind in the real world, through the functions of the brain.

The middle stage is, in my opinion, the most crucial in defining human mental activity and, at the same time, the most powerful in clarifying AI achievements and limits (see Fig. 10.1). It accounts for those kinds of activity which are waiting, so to speak, to be processed by the highest or lowest stages. An external or internal stimulus, for instance, can start alternatively a rational or a reactive process. In the same way, a doubt, or a curiosity, can initiate a reasoning process or a purely instinctive one. Intuition belongs to the high level of this stage. An intuitive idea can be neglected or taken into account; it can start a well-reasoned process and critical thinking or it can fire some kind of low level response aimed at avoiding fatigue or risk. Ordinary reasoning, for instance, very often adopts criteria which assign, I suppose for thought economy reasons and by cultural experience, to extra-logical principles (such as the authority of the source) the role of warranting explanations (Draper 1988).

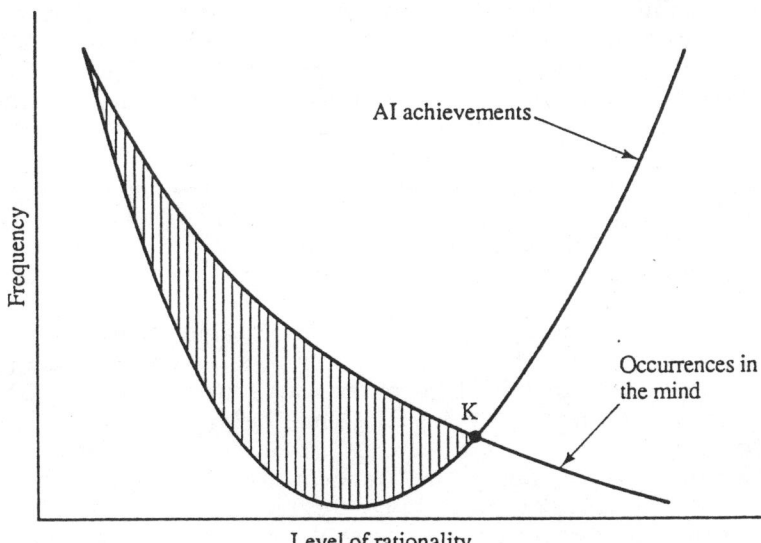

Fig. 10.1. The dissymmetry of mental processes and the least considered and most challenging area for AI research. The crossing point K indicates the threshold beyond which mental processes become rational and explicit enought to be formalised and transferred to a machine.

The logic of so-called common sense also belongs to this stage, since it seems to be equally guided by a low level of *knowing* rationality and by a high level of methodology of thinking oriented to a pure *recognising* activity. By the way, the proposed model applies also to the memory processes, which may be classified by a taxonomy ranging from the biological to the most symbolic and intentional level.

Probably, our daily life consists of a frequent shift from the highest to the lowest stages and vice versa, generally starting from the middle. On a cultural level, we can exemplify this process by the interesting practice, followed by many composers, of drawing from popular songs the inspiration for building complex and learned music, while for others the original themes continue to act on a low level of psychological involvement.

We lack reliable knowledge of what happens at the middle stage and, particularly, of the process of switching between rational and non-rational stages.

What kind of principle governs the switching activity? Why do we often let our behaviour be controlled by the non-rational stage even when facing a great variety of activities, yet in contrast, our highest level of attention (not a purely physiological one) can suddenly focus on an apparently trivial issue upon which our mind starts to work? What amount of importance have past experience or random control factors in this process? At the middle stage, are processes sequential or parallel? Or do they, perhaps, overlap at a presumably very high frequency waiting for a "clearing" decision?

Such a series of questions is plainly crucial not only to our better understanding of central mental activities but also to the potential for advancement of a kind of AI pursuing the reproduction of the human mind rather than the setting up of a *really artificial* intelligence. The idea of a continuously shifting activity has already been theorised by some researchers in order to explain our capacity to adapt ourselves mentally to different situations. So, for instance, "we should indeed realize that, as complex information processing systems, most of us change from one representational model to another even more easily and more frequently than we change clothes" (De Mey 1990).

The activity we are introducing refers not to a representational or *content* oriented shifting, but to the corresponding *methodological* processes which act by assigning predominance to one or another of the outlined stages.

What should be clear, in my opinion, is that, despite the apparent symmetry between the highest and the lowest stages of the model, we are dealing with a strong *non-symmetric* reality. In other words, the probability that an input to the mind may be processed by the lowest stage is higher than the probability that it may be assigned to the highest stage. By the way, some sub-part of the lowest stage works even during our sleeping time while the highest stage needs all our consciousness.

Furthermore, owing to our nature, we are inclined to *recognise* much more than to *know*, or to act by means of repertoires rather than by means of efforts oriented to the discovery of new responses. Almost always, we prefer to follow a comforting and cheap high probability/low information strategy rather than a risky and expensive low probability/high information one. Rational activity, including science and technology, is, from this point of view, a recent conquest of western civilisation, while eastern tradition appears to have preserved in some measure a holistic way of dealing with the world.

The model introduced here does not claim to be a detailed description of the dynamics implied by our mental processes. Rather, it accounts for the vacancy in the methodological possibilities available to our mental activity. The dissymmetry discussed above indicates, from this point of view, that we need particular aid in our rational activity rather than in non-rational processes. While the former are accomplished by man through expensive efforts aimed at isolating his mind from the perturbations of the real internal and external world, the latter can be performed by means of well-practised models of biological, psychological and cultural behaviour.

Though connectionist and neural net AI seems to be able to reproduce some kinds of non-rational and self organising processes, the complete reproduction of the complexity of this stage as performed by man would require the same evolutionary procedures and the same amount of information adopted by biological systems in their development. Conversely, symbolic AI refers to a kind of mental activity which *per se* is not biologically constrained, and which, from many points of view, could be defined as *pre-artificial*. Indeed, rationality is a non-universal cultural disposition aimed at building up theories, models, rules, i.e. different kinds of machines, by *artificially* separating aspects of the world that are, in fact, deeply connected in a whole reality. The concept and the execution of the *machine* is concrete evidence of this disposition, and symbolic

AI offers to the human need for survival in the new technical or artificial environment the potentially right and coherent device.

As rightly stated by Fetzer, "AI can proceed ... by embracing a more modest and rationally warranted conception of its boundaries. The representation of knowledge, the development of expert systems, the simulation and modelling of natural and behavioral phenomena, the rapid processing of vast quantities of data, information, and knowledge are destined to assume a major role in shaping the future of our species" (Fetzer 1990).

In fact, from a certain point of view, the artificial is also an extension of our natural abilities, especially of those that are the more difficult and expensive and less reliable in our nature.

Perhaps the connectionist devices will be helpful in terms of direct interface with the real world in the same manner as the non-rational stage of the human mind assigns to man the right methodology for interacting with the environment by drawing from it information allowing a self-preserving regulatory behaviour. But as for its nature, rational thought is sequential and symbolically oriented and we cannot wait for a sudden and autonomous rising of this capacity from a neural net. Rational thought, in this sense, isn't a program but surely matches many characteristics of the logic of a program. A given rational process doesn't come *from* a computer- like programming activity of the mind, but, provided it is formally expressible, it can be transferred *to* the machine by means of an unusual way of thinking named "program", as the simulation and expert systems traditions demonstrate.

Once we have transferred to the machine some part of our rationality, we can explore more deeply its power to derive more knowledge from our premises or data, than we ourselves can.

As this book has shown from different points of view, the most difficult aim of AI is that of modelling and then of reproducing what I have defined as the middle stage of the human mind methodology. As far as daily behaviour is concerned, we can look at the middle stage as a very complex mix of mental devices which filter every internal or external input, deciding whether or not it should be processed at the rational stage. While the extremes of the model (the rational and the non-rational stages) have already begun to be investigated with some success, this complex and *sui generis* decision making process has not yet been modelled.

Presumably it concentrates on biological, psychological and cultural problems, but I think that at least some need for economy drives this process. Indeed, we feel that the non-rational stage always has a solution to offer to problems arising during our life (ranging from stand-by or trial-and-error strategies to stereotype and pseudo-rational responses) while the same is not true of the rational stage, for it needs time, knowledge, concentration; and is often bound by formal rules, thus increasing the probability of error or failure.

Herein lies the reason why the problem finding activity, i.e. the true root of creativity,[1] is much rarer than the problem solving one. At the middle stage, the human mind, both on the individual and cultural level, has inherent potential to *look* at reality's problematic nature, but only occasionally does it see the latter as interesting or urgent. Admitting the interest or the urgency of a problem implies, particularly if it appears to be something new, a disposition to work rationally in order to characterise and solve it, and this procedure isn't always an easy one for the human mind. More frequently the non-rational stage prevails since it is less expensive. After all, the human biological structure is not at all interested in the *problematic nature* of reality but only in current problems relating to survival. Adopting a cybernetic terminology, we can say that the problem finding activity is regulated by a de-stabilising positive feedback, while the biological activity is controlled by negative feedback loops. In this sense, on the one hand, rationality can be seen as a sort of pathology of our culture, and AI as its homeopathic drug. On the other, rationality can be conceived as a unique way to exceed the pure self- conservation level. If so, AI could be a key technology in supporting the challenging adventure of human reason by amplifying its chances of success.

Note

1 As I have maintained in my contribution to this book, the creativity process always begins by means of the discovery of an original problem. It is possible, of course, to speak of a resolutive creativity defined as the ability to solve a problem by means of original ways of following given procedures of even by inventing new procedures, rules or heuristics. Nevertheless, my opinion is that only the critical ability to find problems to which the established views, theories or paradigms don't apply, describes the very starting point of creative thinking. This doesn't imply that creative behaviour should produce revolutions: in fact, the novelty which should be present in creative activity (at the problem or at the solution level) has no *sine qua non* dimensional condition. For an interesting discussion of this point, see Bailin (1988).

References

Bailin S (1988) Achieving extraordinary ends: An essay on creativity. Kluwer, Dordrecht
De Mey M (1990) The cognitive paradigm. Reidel, Dordrecht
Draper SW (1988) What's going on in everyday explanation? In: Antaki C (ed) Analysing everyday explanation. Sage, London, pp 20–21
Fetzer JH (1990) Artificial intelligence: Its scope and limits. Kluwer, Dordrecht
Simon HA (1969) The sciences of the artificial. MIT Press, Cambridge, MA

Appendix A: One Hundred Definitions of AI

Massimo Negrotti

The following is a list of 100 definitions of AI collected in our first survey of AI people, during the 8th IJCAI held in Karlsruhe in 1983. The AI researchers and designers interviewed came from many countries, and particularly from the USA, Canada, Great Britain, West Germany, France, Italy, Austria, Switzerland, Holland, Sweden, Belgium, and Denmark. Notice the extreme variety of definitions, ranging from the technologically oriented to the pure-research oriented; from the intellectually committed to the comical.

Ability of machines to adequately function in human culture
Ability of machines to do something which looks like an intelligent behaviour
AI gives reasonable answers to ill-stated problems based on inaccurate knowledge
AI is always beyond human intelligence
AI is getting more out of a computer then the designer could predict
AI is that which machines cannot do – once a problem is solved it isn't AI
AI is the attempt to map human intelligence on to computer software
Applied epistemology
Art of making computers think and learn
Attempting to build theories that help to build machines that mimic behaviour that humans call intelligent
Attempting to compete with a human being without feeling
Attempting to find useful solutions to problems which we do not know how to solve
Attempting to pass a sophisticated version of the Turing test
Attempting to reinvent human abilities on a different technological basis
Attempting to represent human thought processes
Attempting to reproduce aspects of human intelligence in machines
Attempting to simulate human thought processes on alternate hardware
Attempting to understand and reproduce man's intellectual processes
Attempting to understand the processes of consciousness

Attempting to write programs that exhibit intelligence in their results and their methodological criteria

Attempting to explain human behaviour from a design stance

Behaviour which if observed in a human would be ascribed as intelligent

Building computer programs which behave intelligently

Building understandable programs that can be improved "externally"

Cognitive mechanics

Computational modelling of cognitive processes

Computational study of learning, reasoning, problem solving and understanding

Computer simulation of human behaviour in order to produce useful and if possible illuminating programs

Computer simulation of intelligent processes (often human)

Constructing theories and models of cognitive processes and implementing them in experimental systems

Construction of finite processes which duplicate or mimic human behaviour

Construction of machines which behave in a way people describe as intelligent

Creating a theory of intelligence *in abstracto* – regardless of carrying agent

Creation of systems which look intelligent to human beings

Cybernetics with a program

Decisions and work with incomplete information

Developing models of intelligent processes

Development of a theory of mental processes as implementable procedures

Development of formal models of human behaviour

Development of judgemental heuristics

Doing with computers things requiring intelligence in humans

Enabling an automaton to perceive process and manipulate complex data

Engineering of conscious behaviour

Ensemble of decisions and actions which permits a system to survive

Exploring what cannot be algorithmically understood now in human affect reasoning

Extension of human capabilities in the area of knowledge processing and problem solving

Formal and operationalised model building

Formal models of complex and context-sensitive information processing

Formalisation of intelligent behaviour

Getting computers to act as if they are doing intelligent things

How to accomplish tasks by exactly defined processes which humans call intelligent

Information sculpture. Left-overs other computers systems can't handle

Intelligence comparable to human for task

Learn how people think and how to do it better using computers as tools

Learned or developed behaviour

Make a computer simulate intelligent human behaviour

Make programs behave in an intelligent way using knowledge

Making computers more usable

Making machines behave in a way functionally equivalent to humans in specific domains

Making machines from the models for our own minds

Management of knowledge with computers

Mechanical epistemology?

Model the mind brain

No matter how "intelligent" AI programs become, they will never be better (in a moral sense) than the people who use them

Performance of tasks previously considered as exclusive to human intelligence

Produce artificial machines who acts or behave as humans

Producing a formal theory of cognition

Production of models that perform tasks normally said to require intellect and/ or a complex neural system

Programming machines to do complex tasks using mind as model if necessary

Reasoning machine learning

Sagacity

Science aimed at producing systems that perform tasks as a human applied epistemology

Science of intelligence

Science of trying to build automata which behave intelligently

Select a good strategy for performing a task while creating new ones when needed

Simulation by computer of intellectual tasks considered typical of human intelligence

Simulation of human behaviour by a machine

Simulation of human intelligence

Simulation of mental processes

Simulation of problem solving processes in humans

Simulation of purposeful behaviour

Simulation of the functions of mind

Solving the riddle of human with satisfactory methods

Strengthen human intelligence by computers

Study of apparently or actually intelligent behaviour in machines

Study of control of understanding

Study of general principles underlying mental processes

Study of how humans (and animals) actually do the amazing range of activities that we perform: in particular intelligent activities. The building of mechanisms that exhibit aspects of human behaviour; usually intelligent

Study of intelligence by building and analysing computer programs

Successful problem solving on "difficult" tasks

Symbolic processing

To get machines to perform complex tasks which require intelligence from people

Techniques which make the computer act as a human being

The step just beyond where AI research has gotten to today (cynical!)

Theory of entities behaving in a given environment achieving goals

There is no adequate description

To get a handle on mentality

To me it is the study of the nature of intelligence independent of (human) hardware

Trying to achieve a closer match between computers and human thought behaviour

Trying to make computers do things that people can do better

Appendix B: An Attempt at Getting a Basis for a Rational Definition of the Artificial

Massimo Negrotti

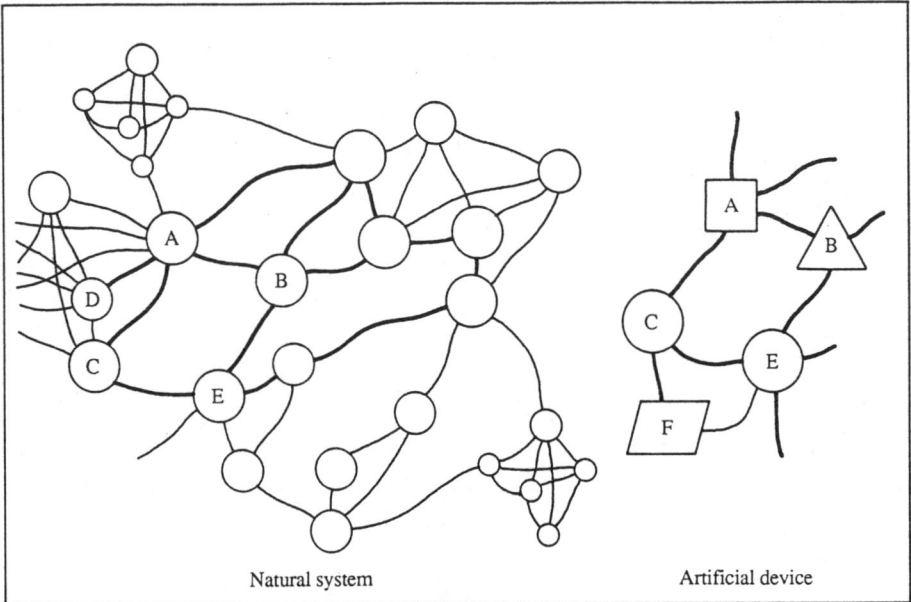

Fig. B.1. The *artificial* as an extraction of a sub-system from a natural system in order to reproduce some functions of it. Note:
The number of homologous components is reduced.
  The homologous components are structurally different.
  New components may appear (such as *F*).
  Some kinds of internal or external relations are lost, and others may be added.
  New types of internal and external relations may appear.

Some basic statements:

1. An artificial device is a machine which reproduces some essential functions of a sub-system of a natural system.
2. In the artificial sub-system the number of homologous components is reduced.
3. In the artificial sub-system the homologous components are structurally different.
4. In the artificial sub-system new components may appear.
5. In the artificial sub-system new types of internal and external relations may appear.
6. In the artificial sub-system, some kinds of internal or external relations are lost, and others may be added.
7. Every artificial device is a machine, but not all machines are to be conceived as *artificial* devices.

8. The performances of an artificial device usually show a different spectrum (sometimes wider and sometimes narrower) compared to the one shown by the correspondent natural sub-system.

9. The research and the development of enhancements of the artificial device consist in the deepening of its own artificial characteristics as such and, usually, this moves the new generations of the device further and further from the natural sub-system.

10. The artificial device will be accepted as a good reproduction of the natural system if, and only if, its functioning allows a good reproduction of the main and *essential* features and performances of the natural sub- system.

Subject Index

Printing: Druckerei Zechner, Speyer
Binding: Buchbinderei Schäffer, Grünstadt